Dreamlife
of Families

"Healthy families dream together. This is the essential good sense of *The Dreamlife of Families,* which carefully amasses evidence that family members dream of each other and *for* each other and may have shared adventures in deeper realities accessible in dreaming. He helps us recognize the vital function of 'crisis telepathy,' in which we receive alerts about emergency situations that prepare us to handle them and sometimes to contain them. Bynum grounds his study of family dreams in an understanding of the vital role of dreaming in human evolution. He gives us the science of the dreaming brain while recognizing that the brain is within the mind. He encourages us to expand our understanding and practice to aspire to the continuity of consciousness called Yoga Nidra in the East. I recommend this wise and heartening book."

ROBERT MOSS, AUTHOR OF *CONSCIOUS DREAMING*
AND *THE SECRET HISTORY OF DREAMING*

"*The Dreamlife of Families* presents a novel approach to working with dream-based family interrelatedness. Drawing on a broad range of ancient beliefs, the book emphasizes African traditions especially, which are less known to modern psychology than those of ancient Greece or China. Bynum writes with a level of scholarly sophistication such that dream psychologists, family therapists, and other clinicians will learn much from the book. However, it's also clear and entertaining and will engage families who want to utilize this approach to dreams to enrich their relationship."

DEIRDRE BARRETT, PH.D., PSYCHOLOGIST ON THE FACULTY OF
HARVARD MEDICAL SCHOOL'S BEHAVIORAL MEDICINE PROGRAM AND
AUTHOR OF *THE COMMITTEE OF SLEEP*

"An effective case that nocturnal dreams can be interpersonal communications between family members. The numerous examples that Bynum provides make for fascinating reading while providing a convincing argument. I recommend it for anyone interested in dreams or the deeper levels of their own psyche."

WILLIAM M. BOYLIN, PH.D., SUPERVISING PSYCHOLOGIST AT
THE CONNECTICUT VALLEY HOSPITAL IN
MIDDLETOWN, CONNECTICUT

"A beautiful and visionary book. Bynum explores the world that lives between private and public space—the unconscious of the family. He shows us how this understanding can be applied to healing and therapy. Fascinating read for the professional and lay reader."

LYNN HOFFMAN, ACSW, AUTHOR OF
FOUNDATIONS OF FAMILY THERAPY

"This book guides us to true connectedness in the family. A must-read for the serious family worker or member."

JAYNE GACKENBACH, PH.D., COAUTHOR OF
CONTROL YOUR DREAMS

The Dreamlife of Families

The Psychospiritual Connection

Edward Bruce Bynum, Ph.D., ABPP

Inner Traditions
Rochester, Vermont • Toronto, Canada

Inner Traditions
One Park Street
Rochester, Vermont 05767
www.InnerTraditions.com

Text stock is SFI certified

Originally published in 1993 by Haworth Press under the title *Families and the Interpretation of Dreams: Awakening the Intimate Web*
Special edition published in 2003 by Paraview Special Editions

Library of Congress Cataloging-in-Publication Data
Names: Bynum, Edward Bruce, 1948– author.
Title: The dreamlife of families : the psychospiritual connection / Edward Bruce Bynum, Ph.D, ABPP.
Other titles: Families and the interpretation of dreams
Description: Rochester, VT : Inner Traditions, 2017. | Previously published under title: Families and the interpretation of dreams : awakening the intimate web. New York : Paraview Special Editions, c2003. | Includes bibliographical references and index.
Identifiers: LCCN 2016053495 (print) | LCCN 2017009552 (e-book) | ISBN 9781620556320 (pbk.) | ISBN 9781620556337 (e-book)
Subjects: LCSH: Families in dreams. | Families—Psychological aspects. | Telepathy.
Classification: LCC BF1099.F34 B96 2017 (print) | LCC BF1099.F34 (e-book) | DDC 154.6/3—dc23
LC record available at https://lccn.loc.gov/2016053495

Printed and bound in the United States by Lake Book Manufacturing, Inc. The text stock is SFI certified. The Sustainable Forestry Initiative® program promotes sustainable forest management.

10 9 8 7 6 5 4 3 2 1

Text design by Virginia Scott Bowman and layout by Debbie Glogover
This book was typeset in Garamond Premier Pro with ITC Avant Garde Gothic Std, Helvetica Neue LT Std, Gill Sans MT Pro, and ITC Legacy Sans Std for display fonts

To send correspondence to the author of this book, mail a first-class letter to the author c/o Inner Traditions • Bear & Company, One Park Street, Rochester, VT 05767, and we will forward the communication. The author's website is **www.obeliskfoundation.com.**

For my sons,
Elijah Jordan and Ezra Sage;
may they also dream themselves
into Light.

Contents

Does Your Family Need a Catalyst?

Dare you push yourself into the family dream as part of the family's life? Dare you read research series and clinical data that might at first seem to be above your own head and even appear to disorganize the way you think of the family organism itself? This brilliant clinical investigator shares both the cross-cultural and the mythical sophistication of an old professional student. His thinking is clear, his writing is explicit and detailed, and his area of expertise is immense and global. We know about the family web. We are each flies captured in that web, the strands of several or maybe even many generations.

As Bynum presents the current data from the dream laboratories in a long series of dream stories, one begins to glimpse an expanded field of dream experience. The exploration of the shadows of life from many cultures and many families expands our view of family forces and the body's intimate reverberations from this organism's coordinated dreaming. Dreams can be healing factors as well as diagnostic signals to the body of the individuals and to the family itself. His Family Dreams Research Protocol has resulted in many fascinating expansions of dreamlife. In addition to his presentation of clinical data and his healing assessment protocol one also sees the powerful stimulus and force arising from his creative theory constructs. To integrate dreams, culture, science, family dynamics, mythology, and psychoanalysis is really mind-boggling. I loved having my mind boggled. I think you will too.

CARL A. WHITAKER, M.D.

DR. CARL A. WHITAKER (1912–1995) was a physician and psychotherapist and a pioneer in the field of family therapy. Many of his theories are presented in the seminal work *The Family Crucible,* which he wrote with Dr. Augustus Napier (New York: Harper and Row, 1978).

The Labyrinth of Dreams

We are such stuff as dreams are made on, and our little life is rounded with a sleep.

WILLIAM SHAKESPEARE, *THE TEMPEST*

Who of us has not had a profound experience in our dreaming life that had some deep intuitive connection to our waking life? Who of us has not had a dream of a lover or a relative or a friend that expressed precisely the nature, the depth, and the tone of our relationship to them? Who of us does not feel, at least while dreaming, that dreams are an authentic voice in our deep sleep life? This book is about individual or intrapsychic dreams and also about family dreams or family-related dreams. It is about how such dreams affect our minds and bodies in both health and illness. It is also about those occasional dreams of members of the same family that express an uncanny intimacy or that share common themes, patterns, or images. Sometimes there is even apparently direct communication of information in dreams between family members. The ancients had many names for it. Today it is understood to be one of several forms of paranormal or anomalous communication known as

1

extrasensory perception (ESP) or telepathy. Other forms in this family of unusual phenomena are clairvoyance, the awareness of a previously unknown physical environment by anomalous means; precognition, the similar awareness of a future event; and psychokinesis (PK), the alteration or movement of physical objects or processes by anomalous means. They are collectively referred to as psi or paranormal phenomena.

Sigmund Freud himself was always ambivalent about this area of investigation. At one point the founder of psychoanalysis confessed that

> it is an uncontestable fact that our sleep creates favorable conditions for telepathy. . . . Telepathy may be the original archaic method by which individuals understood one another, and which has been pushed into the background in the course of phylogenetic evolutionary development by the better method of communication by means of signs apprehended by the sense organs. But such older methods may have persisted in the background, and may still manifest themselves under certain conditions.

Then in another instance he completely rejected the whole idea:

> You know that by telepathy we mean the alleged fact that an event which occurs at a specific time comes more or less simultaneously into the consciousness of a person who is spatially distant, without any of the known methods of communication coming into play. The tacit assumption is that this event occurs to a person in whom the receiver of the message has some strong emotional interest. . . . I need not emphasize to you the improbability of such processes, and anyway there are good reasons for rejecting the majority of such reports.[2]

And then again at other times Freud admitted, "it is probable that the study of . . . (psi) will result in the admission that some of these phenomena are real . . . my personal attitude toward such materials remains one of reluctance and ambivalence."[3] It was a major disagreement with Jung. In a letter to Carrington, which he later forgot he ever wrote, Freud states that if he had his life to live over again he would devote it to psychic research. Despite his constantly changing and ambivalent views on telepathic communication, Freud would be the last to say that family matters, family-motivated feelings, and family relationships had little or no influence on the dream content of our lives while we are awake and while we dream and sleep. Indeed, by reflecting on our own dreams over the years, most of us cannot fail to see the numerous cameo shots, short dramatic scenes, and at other times long, involved, highly emotional, convoluted, and bizarre ways family faces, themes, and events surface in our dreamlife.

Thus, this book is primarily grounded in what all of us have roots in: some form of family life and a nightly dream cycle. It is written for those individuals interested in seeing how their own lives are reflected in their own dreams and in the dreams of others. These realms of intimate relationships and personal experience comprise a vast area of our dreamlife and our waking life, both in illness and in health.

Finally, this book is about the ways in which our deepest emotional and family patterns, patterns capable of reflecting across several generations, and our most intimate feelings and motivations, are reflected in the inner chambers of one another's dreams. Yes we dream *about* each other and sometimes perhaps *for* each other. To that end this book will cover the history of dream interpretation, both contemporary and ancient, from today's theories to those of Joseph and Daniel in the Bible and on back to the pharaohs of the first Pyramid Texts of the old kingdom around 3200–2100 BCE. We will see that the ancient Kemetic pharaohs and the seers of Israel had a good deal in common with you and me. Freud and Carl Jung were very aware of these influences. Over the centuries this great arch of interest and research has generated a number of theories about dreams and how they reflect our deepest preoccupations. These preoccupations almost always to some degree concern our family, our struggles in the world both psychological and somatic, and our relationships to the divine or the Absolute.

This classical view of dream theory, along with the European theories about dreaming and the theories promulgated by the Chinese, the Indian yogis, and the even older Kemetic mystery schools of the upper Nile, will all be explored and shown to be the roots of the clinical interpretation of dreams today. This will of necessity send an engulfing loop of interest around the presently more controversial areas of psychological experience and healing (e.g., anomalous or paranormal cognition, including precognition, PK, telepathy, and clairvoyance). We will also touch upon philosophy and mythology. In this book a good deal of emphasis will be placed on how we can (1) recognize dreams in which these elements play a part and understand their impact on our emotions and our decision-making processes, (2) learn from one another's dreams about ourselves and our still-evolving culture, (3) grow from such dreams in a psychological, somatic, and even psychospiritual sense, (4) expand ourselves and explore our uniqueness as it unfolds within us, and (5) understand how such dreams may, in some sense, reflect a common cultural worldview, which in later chapters will be referred to as "personalism." I will be drawing on the combined research of a number of scholars in several areas, as well as on case materials of the Family Dreams Research Project, an ongoing study of family dreams and their connection to family relationships and family process (see appendix A). This is a unique focus in both its content and the fact that it is the largest collection and presentation of family dreams to date.

Eventually the family dream will be presented as a shared field, a kind of shared hologram where each significant other in the family is partially reflected or implicated and enfolded into each other member's dreams. These dreams themselves will all be outlined and will come to be seen as one of the many dynamic and specifically transpersonal aspects of our lives. Family dreams offer a potential for healing that is often ignored by both medicine and clinical psychology. I hope to provide clear evidence that both illness and health are reflected in dreams and that dreaming has an active role in the healing process of the family. More specifically I will present research that supports the following notions: (1) metaphors of illness often appear in our dreams prior to somatic symptoms, (2) metaphors of death often appear in our dreams and especially in our family dreams either coincident with or prior to a family death (i.e., precognition and/or "crisis telepathy,") and that there are specific dynamics involved that can be observed in the psyche and soma or at the psychophysical level, (3) dreams and family dreams in particular can be directly supportive of the healing process, both at the somatic and psychological level, and (4) this field is not new to humanity but stretches back to the days of antiquity.

The chapters are outlined and presented in a progressive manner from a general overview, through historical and cross-cultural perspectives, to laboratory and experiential work. Both intrapsychic or individualistic ordinary dreams are presented and contrasted with more unusual or anomalous dreams. Examples are used throughout the book to flesh out the reality of these experiences. In part 2, "Family Dreams and Healing," more attention is focused on specific dream styles as they reflect familial patterns and life events. The chapter on adult children of alcoholics (ACOA) reflects a certain emotional and thematic constellation, as does the dream series and examples presented in the chapter on the era of pregnancy in the family. Why and how dreams are used in a therapeutic context naturally follows from this. The final section unfolds into the further reaches of dreamwork in the self and family and its implications for the reaches of human consciousness and intuition.

At different times you may notice a certain correlation between family dream motifs and levels of consciousness encountered in meditative disciplines, philosophy, and your own life circumstances. Specifically speaking you may note a relationship between the psychological issues of violence, survival, and fear in the dreams of ACOA family dreams and base level, or what are termed "root chakra," preoccupations found in yogic philosophical and meditative traditions. Furthermore, you may see the relationship between "heart-opening" emotions, empathic linkages, and what are called "anahata chakra" themes mixed with issues of pregnancy. While this undercurrent is not overtly emphasized, it is implicit throughout each chapter. No one dream, dream style, or person ever exhibits a pure reflection of any level of consciousness. The vast variability in this flux is part of the adventure of this study.

We will come to see that a working understanding of the dynamic unconscious was not, as generally believed, the original discovery of eighteenth and nineteenth century Europe.[4] Indeed it has its clinical and observational roots in the ancient Kemetic Egyptian idea of the Amenta and the primeval waters of Nun and even bears an affinity to the old West African philosophical lineage of the Ayanmo concept.[5] Each worldview and culture has unfolded a different philosophy and method of dream interpretation. However, in each one, the family, the unconscious, and the deeply personal dimension are unequivocally acknowledged. We hope to bring those three connections into sharper focus here.

Finally, the exploration of family dreams and the family relationships reflected in these dreams can be seen as a chosen "path" of loving discipline from the past into the future. A deeper understanding of our family dream dynamics is not only a way of growing individually but is also a means of recognizing our primordial connection with nameless ancestors ages ago and our progeny yet to be born in the distant future. Implicitly they too are a living part of us. We share waking life; we share dreaming life. The function of self-knowledge on both levels is to help the individual truly awaken to that nameless reality that is beyond waking, dreaming, and deep sleep.

PART ONE

The Nocturnal Emissary

Discovery commences with the awareness of anomaly, i.e., with the recognition that nature has somehow violated the paradigm-induced expectations that govern normal science. It then continues with a more or less extended exploration of the area of anomaly. And it closes only when the paradigm theory has been adjusted so that the anomalous has become the expected.

T. S. KUHN,
THE STRUCTURE OF SCIENTIFIC REVOLUTIONS

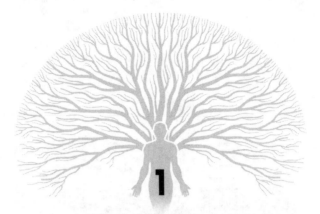

The Inner Landscape
of Dreams

Dreams are the royal road to the unconscious.

S. FREUD

This Self has four states of consciousness. . . . Taijasa is the second (state), the dreaming state in which, with his senses turned inward, he (the dreamer) enacts the impression of past deeds and present desires.

RAMA, *ENLIGHTENMENT WITHOUT GOD*

THE INTIMATE WEB
OF FAMILY AND SELF

The following is a powerful, very real, and yet rather common nightly occurrence. As is the case here, and will be with all the dreams presented throughout the book, the language and punctuation remains as it was reported by the dreamer, except in the rare case where it might cause confusion for the reader.

My mother, Dorothy K., was living in a small, barely furnished flat in an old rundown apartment block, right up from a steep flight of stairs. She was very sick and I visited her each day after work. This particular day I came and had a great shock, as all I found in her bed was a skeleton. I was so overcome with grief and guilt because I was blind to her true condition. Nothing was said by Mom in this dream, as with the following dreams, except for one. Although I was visiting her each day in this dream I felt agitated that it was taking up too much of my time, but when facing that skeleton in bed I felt low and very selfish and insensitive. I had really been selfish and in some way was punishing myself for the way that I thought.

Also, notice the tragic and the family themes played out in this dream:

Seventeen years ago my older brother, age 27, died in a plane crash. Ever since then I have had many encounters with him in dreams. In these dreams it is as though he's been gone on a long trip, and we usually discuss what I am doing in my life. One dream involved the presence of the whole family. We were all gathered to welcome him back. In this dream he had aged and we were discussing a career that he might undertake in his return home.

These are individual dreams. Now note a series of concurrent family dreams (bold added):

*My dream: I have **a little cut on the ankle of my right foot**. It bleeds a lot, and I put pressure on it to stop the bleeding. Some famous man is there with his girlfriend.*

*My son Gregg's dream (he is twelve): I'm at the beach swimming in the water. The water was high and went way up on the beach. **Something grabbed my foot and it was a horseshoe crab on my big toe on my right foot.** It let go and crawled to the end of the beach and **shed its shell** and went back into the water, and as soon as that happened a bunch of* *horseshoe crabs came and* **dropped their shells too.** *We started helping them up to the beach (me, Lucia, and Mom).*

Lucia's dream (age 8): We are at the point of rocks that goes into the lake. High waves are coming over the land at the point. When one wave came over **I stepped on a stone, and there was a white mussel shell in the water.** *I wanted to get it but I didn't.*

This last series of family dreams was submitted by a professor who teaches and works on dreams in her clinical setting. Notice the repeating foot and water motifs. This same professor submitted another dream that she felt reflected a shared family unconscious. She indicated that she had this dream some time ago, wrote it down, then found that its impact stayed with her.

I dreamed of a futuristic scene on the moon. There was a colony of earth people living under a plastic bubble dome into which an earth-type atmosphere could be pumped. It was so expensive to maintain this atmosphere that the cars and vehicles had to be parked outside of the dome, conserving space for the oxygen-breathing people. When I woke up I couldn't make sense of this dream in the usual way so I told it to my husband. He was amazed and showed me the page in a science fiction book which he had been reading, which had the exact description of a moon colony.

All of these were very powerful and yet very normal dreams. As you are reading this book, I will ask you to simply note the powerful effect or emotion of the dreams and how the perceived meaning or the idea of the dream can seem to be influenced profoundly by our emotions and relationships in waking life. Note the powerful motivations and how space and time are often changed around in the dream. You might even notice some of the somatic, or felt, senses that are changed in the dream and how the dream stays with you for a while long after its actual experience in the mind. These are dreams we all have. They are the evidence of our consciousness in a sleeping state. You may have already noticed that when we do not reflect upon our dreams while they are occurring, we usually cannot tell the difference between the dream state and the waking state. Yet in one state, the waking one, we generally feel that our experience is somehow ultimately more real or true than when we are dreaming. Now let's go a little further and explore some of the more unusual types of dreams.

The following is a dream in which the family in some configuration is involved and yet all the emotions we talked about earlier are also deeply implicated.

I awake sobbing in the arms of a peasant girl or some other lonely figure who has a slightly damaged face. She lives at a "home" for the disadvantaged, more like a prison. I am a disembodied spirit walking through the aisles, leading them in songs. Their dress is late 1930s and I am Polish. I am describing the experience of my death (recorded on a small graph with a sound level gauge) and also my subsequent fatherhood (also recorded on this gauge) several months later to this Polish girl. It is tragic and sad.

I am in the room because of an experiment with death which I entered into with my sister Ann. We have an Indian instructor who promises that we will enter deep meditation for three hours to three days and experience the death process. We began this procedure by changing places with the guru, and she and I sit together on a park bench in Park Slope, Brooklyn. Many things occur as we enter the "death state" with several other initiates on a park bench nearby.

I'm unsure how Ann is experiencing it, but I experienced the ability to fly in an astral body and to enter deeply into the consciousness of living persons. At one point there are several potentially dangerous entities. There is a man swinging a stick coming toward us. I tell Ann not to worry, that there may be some problems but that she should sit tight and not worry. But that statement scares her and her whole body jumps up in a fright. I go confidently up to the dangerous man, throw a big stick at him and he retreats like I expected, he only looked scary.

Then I drift up to a window and enter a brothel of some sort, looking for someone to have sex with. They can't see me but can feel my presence. I enter into the consciousness of a young woman, saying, "feel my love for you." Face to face. She becomes ecstatic and emotionally charged, happiness and sadness are felt, expressed, and released. It is as if I am a catalyst for spiritual healing in my disembodied state. Other disembodied spirits are sharing their healing experiences with me. One experience happened to someone as the result of saying one word in Japanese and bowing deeply. It's all very exciting, healing, and emotional, but there is some difficulty to overcome. It is also subconscious spiritual sharing, soul to soul, spirit to spirit.

I woke long enough to record the dream and fell back to sleep. At about 7 a.m. the phone rang. It was Ann. On an impulse, I asked if she had a scary dream that night. She had dreamt that an evil female presence was after her. She called because she missed me and wanted me to visit her and during her morning meditation around 5 a.m. she had powerfully felt my presence with her. I had been thinking of visiting her the coming weekend to talk over family matters with her. We had both been thinking of one another before going to sleep.

The person who submitted this dream had his own interpretation of it. He said that he felt the dream had such a healing effect because he had been feeling estranged from his sister Ann. She lived in relative seclusion at a religious retreat. Her religious beliefs led her to view dreams and dreamwork as simply another aspect of what is referred to in Eastern philosophy as "maya," or illusion. With this dream, the dreamer felt that he had communicated deeply in the unconscious world, then followed it up in the waking world. Both experiences were of a sharing, transformative nature. Loving ties were reestablished, and he reports having a good visit with her the following weekend during which they made an effort to renew their love and strengthen the family bond between them.

Here is another powerful and unusual type of family-related dream:

I relate the following story, which I was personally a witness to. In the summer of 1970 I was still living home with my mother in Fort Wayne, Indiana. My oldest brother, Bill, was then in college at Indiana University at Bloomington. I was on one night awakened suddenly just past 2 a.m. by my mother shouting my name and shaking me in the dark. "What's wrong? I heard you call me. Are you hurt? What happened?" After assuring her that I was fine and had been soundly asleep before her intrusion, she asked me if I had been dreaming, had I had a nightmare and called out. No, I told her. I was aware of nothing until she woke me. She seemed confused and then told me what had happened. She too had been soundly asleep, dreaming about something she could not recall. What she was acutely aware of, though, was that she was awakened from her dream by what she thought was my voice, shouting, "Mom, Mom, I'm hurt. Help me, Mom." That is what sent her running to my room. One of her children was hurt and needed her.

We both returned to sleep, she, as she said the next day, a little uneasily. The voice in her sleep had been so strikingly real. I might point out that to this day my mother confuses my voice with that of my brothers. The next morning we received a call. Bill was in the hospital in Bloomington. He had been doing some late night caving the night before and somewhere around 2 o'clock he had been starting his rope ascent of a pit known as Glory Hole. One of the other cavers, careless of a basic rule, that is to say, never go near the edge of a pit during ascent, did just that and dislodged a rock roughly the size of a softball. Bill was only 3 or 4 meters up the rope when he heard a warning, "rock!" He tucked his head in too late. The rock fell the 4 or 5 meters to its mark, splitting the back of his helmet and seriously fracturing his skull. As he hung limp on the rope, he told me later, the last thing he remembered as he lost consciousness was trying desperately to call out: he was thinking about our mother, trying to call "Mom."

The two dream series above show how intimately the family dynamics are implicated in both normal dreams and somewhat more unusual dreams. The last two dreams, while somewhat unusual, are nevertheless normal, just much more statistically rare.

By and large the latter category of unusual dreams are those that are termed either "crisis telepathy," "clairvoyant," or "precognitive" dreams. Crisis telepathy is the simultaneous awareness of another person's mental processes, usually in a crisis or life-threatening situation, by anomalous means. Clairvoyance is a similar awareness, but of the physical environment primarily, and precognition is the awareness of an event in time that has supposedly not yet transpired. These are all different modes of communication in the psi or paranormal mode. They are quite common. Dreams of information communicated back and forth, especially those occurring around a crisis situation, have specific dynamics that are by this time well attested to in the clinical literature by a large number of professionals and researchers. They are also very powerful. The term "crisis telepathy" itself stems from nineteenth-century psychical research when "crisis apparitions" were catalogued and submitted to scientific observation. Technically the apparition had to "appear" to the observer within twelve hours before or after the actual event.[1] The term was also used by Montague Ullman and Stanley Krippner to describe anomalous information received in dream states.[2]

Note the dynamics of the following dreams. They involve a crisis and may be termed "crisis telepathy," but there is no overt indication that one person attempted to deliberately contact another person as occurs in the classical crisis telepathy dream. In this sense the dreams have elements of clairvoyance in them because a physical environment previously unknown to one of the persons emerges in the situation and becomes known in an anomalous fashion.

On July 3, 1975, my stepfather was mugged and killed behind a tavern. It was about 1 a.m. when he stopped in the parking lot to go to the bathroom. Someone shot him in the back of the head.

That night I happened to be sleeping on the living room floor (I was almost eleven years old). My Mom was in the same room sewing me a *shirt. At about 1 a.m. (the same time he was killed) I got up and started walking. My Mom asked what I was doing and I replied, "I'm going to the bathroom." She told me to go lie down, which I did. I then walked outside to go to the bathroom the same time my stepfather stopped in the parking lot to do the same thing before he was shot. The most shocking part was that when I woke up the next morning I knew that he was dead before anyone told me.*

Here is a similar family dream:

Let me begin by saying that I am not prone to nightmares, and that the dream I had was the only dream or nightmare which ever concerned my brother Doug.

The setting of the dream looked like London in the 1700s. It was a city with soot-covered buildings. I was walking down a sidewalk when I came upon a barred window of a building. The window was below sidewalk level, set into a recessed area. The window had bars only, no glass. All of a sudden my younger brother Doug appeared at the bars. He was filthy and malnourished. His face and hair were dirty and there were big dark circles under his eyes. I felt in the dream that he was in a prison. He looked so badly off that it seemed to me he was near death. I can remember in my dream feeling that I couldn't bear seeing him like that. He then thrust his arm out through the bars and extended it towards me, beseeching my help. He opened his mouth wide to scream, but he was so weak that only a squealing hiss came out. As he screamed one of his rotted teeth fell out of his gums onto his tongue. At this point I woke up, and I remember gasping for breath. I was extremely upset by the dream and couldn't go back to sleep for quite a while. The memory of that dream upset me for days, and thirteen years later I still remember it vividly.

At the time of this dream I was living in St. Petersburg, Florida. My brother Doug was in Falmouth, Massachusetts, living with my mother. About a week after my dream my mother called me up and told me that

Doug almost died. He had fallen asleep, drunk, in a snowdrift and lay there the night. A little girl saw him the next morning and he was taken to the hospital. He had a body temperature of 74 degrees and he was given last rites by the priest. Only a miracle caused him to survive.

My mother did not tell me about Doug's accident until many days after it happened, when she was sure he was going to survive. As soon as she called with the news I thought of that terrible dream I had. I cannot be sure that the dream and Doug's accident occurred on the same night, but the two were very close if not the exact same night.

This is another example of a critical or life-threatening situation that manifests itself in the form of a crisis telepathy dream. Again, while there is no overt indication that one person deliberately attempted to contact another person, these individuals did communicate around a crisis situation. A clairvoyant dimension to these dreams is not obvious, but since they may have occurred prior to the actual event, they may have been precognitive. All we know for certain is that information about a significant other's emotional, psychological, and critical physical condition was communicated by anomalous means. What is unusual about this type of dream is that it seems to occur with greater frequency during wartime than in other times. Perhaps you or someone you know has had a similar dream. Notice the dynamics, motivations, and imagery that occur in the following dreams:

Dear Dr. Bynum,

After reading the article about you in Omni *magazine, describing the dream a mother had in relation to her soldier son, I was vividly reminded of an episode involving my own brother and mother that took place in 1970 while my brother was serving as a Green Beret in Vietnam. It seems that my mother had a disturbing dream that her mother (at the time dead for ten years) was directing my brother safely through a field of land mines. The dream shook her up enough so that she dwelled on it for several days, keeping it to herself. Then, I guess, unable to contain herself, she told the rest of the family about this dream. My father and I shrugged it off and tried to alleviate my mother's fears.*

Several weeks later we received a letter from my brother describing a dream that he felt had saved his life. He described a dream in which my grandmother was sitting cross-legged on a tank rumbling through a mine field. My brother was walking behind the tank while my grandmother laughingly pointed to the safe areas of the field. A few days later he was point man for the day. He recalled the dream, and visualizing the directions, he made it through the mine field unharmed.

My mother, a great believer in ESP, felt that she had somehow picked up on my brother's thoughts or vice versa. She regarded this as proof positive that her bizarre dreams were not the working of an overactive imagination. This was not her first ESP experience.

Still skeptical, my father and I teased her and insisted that it was just a coincidence. Then we watched in bewilderment as this strong tomboyish woman who rarely cried dissolved into tears over our doubt in her credibility and sanity. I've never forgotten how hard she cried and always wondered if perhaps she was really afflicted with this ability.

So far we have touched upon ordinary or common family dreams, unusual dreams, and dreams that involve some sort of psi or telepathy. In future chapters we will elaborate on these types of dreams, especially the family of psi-related dreams. What is clear already, however, is that dreams touch us both on an individual level and on our family dreaming level. The dynamics of this are not totally understood, but we have made progress toward identifying some patterns that repeat themselves across many dreams, both usual and unusual. As dream researcher and clinician Montague Ullman, M.D., says, "normally when we are dreaming, we tap into some kind of informational black hole that generally has to do with us; but sometimes, for reasons we don't understand, we get into that black hole deeper than we thought, and touch on somebody or something else."[3]

So what are these deep, archaic emotions and feelings? What are these primordial images and patterns and relationships that seem to be embedded in our dreamlife? What are dreams actually and where do they come from? What are dreams composed of and what emotional language do they speak?

MODERN DREAM INTERPRETATION

Dreamwork and dream interpretation are as old as humanity, but dreaming itself is older than humankind. Rapid eye movement, or REM, which is associated with the experience of dreaming, is found in mammals other than humans, but the inner world of these other mammals is not overtly perceptible to us. So we will stick with human beings and their motivations, images, and feelings.

Dreams occur when we are sleeping, and we are not conscious in the usual sense. They occur when we are unconscious. The exception to this general rule is the "lucid dream," whereby through accident, discipline, or serendipity we become aware that we are dreaming while the actual dreaming continues. We will have more to say about these extraordinary dreams in chapter 10, since a great deal here depends upon our definition of "conscious."

Dreams, given their power, dynamic impact, and expansive process of reflecting the mind at different levels, were seen by Sigmund Freud as the royal road to the unconscious. Freud used dreams as one way to map the terrain of the individual unconscious. Freud also outlined five other kinds of evidence to support the notion of an active, dynamic unconscious aspect of the mind itself that had a powerful effect on the waking state. While much of this is technical and of little relevance to certain areas of study, it is quite important here, for it points to the fact that the mind in sleep can be a restless, dynamic, and highly energetic domain of reality.

As evidence of a dynamic unconscious Freud cited: (1) different forms of amnesia and what are commonly referred to as split personalities, (2) dream interpretation in the process of the dream world, which is our focal point here, (3) slips of the tongue, motivated forgetting, and other aspects of the ubiquitous cycle of psychopathology in everyday life, (4) symptom formation on both a psychological and a somatic level, and (5) the process of resistance, transference, and countertransference in actual psychoanalytic treatment. These transference or countertransference figures and dynamics are from our childhood and as such family figures loomed large in and over effect, images, and motivations. This notion is implicit in Freud's work. The unconscious mind is always active on some level, and our personal dreams reflect this operation. But exactly what do dreams and dreamwork do?

Freud believed that dreams were a reaction of the mind to external and internal stimuli that acted upon the organism in sleep. At the end of his monumental work, *The Interpretation of Dreams,* Freud cites the dream of a French nurse. In this dream the nurse fused or integrated the sound of her sleeping and then eventually crying child with that of her own internal imagery. She integrated external information with internal stimuli.

Freud also believed that since the unconscious is the dynamic source of hidden desires, and the conscious mind can censor these desires, then the remembered dream is really a compromise structure of the psyche whereby a forbidden wish or fear is disguised and only then allowed to emerge into the overt or manifest level of the dream. In other words, the deepest level of the dream holds a secret or latent or unmanifest wish or desire for the sleeping person. This is of course termed "wish fulfillment." It is believed that the elaborate symbols of our dreams are the disguise of the fears and desires hidden below the surface of our conscious minds. This fluid or deeper primary process state of affairs allows a single element of the manifest dream to represent many other areas or latent dream thoughts. Freud's interpretive method involved "free association" to dream content and other techniques. Events or persons or images, however, can also be displaced or recombined in a variety of ways reflecting a high degree of novelty and creativity. This is beyond merely recombining old, already-seen situations. It is a creative synthesis, an imaginative and emotional tapestry of our inner land-scape.[4] Thus a family member and their emotional dynamism can be represented by a symbol or image or even a recurrent scenario in one's life.

By no means did Freud corner the market on dream interpretation. He did admit, however, based on the evidence he had, that dreams can move beyond the individual and have the capacity to touch or express a broader context of humanity:

> There probably exists in the mental life of the individual not only what he has experienced himself, but also what he brought with him at birth, fragments of phylogenetic origin and archaic heritage. . . . The archaic heritage of mankind includes not only dispositions, but also ideational contents, memory traces of experiences of former generations.[5]

Yet even though Freud accepted this idea implicitly, passively, he did not develop it far. It is to Jung that we must turn for the full development of this idea that dreams reach beyond that of the narrow personal or intrapsychic meaning and dynamics. For Jung the dream was a little hidden door to the confines and the recesses of our inner individual and collective life.

> The dream is a little hidden door in the inner and most secret recesses of the soul, opening into that cosmic night which was psyche long before there was any ego consciousness, and which will remain psyche no matter how far our ego consciousness may extend. For all ego consciousness is isolated; it separates and discriminates, knows only particulars, and sees only what can be related to the ego. Its essence is limitation, though we reach to the farthest nebulae among the stars. All consciousness separates; but in dreams we put on likeness of that more universal, truer, more eternal man dwelling in the darkness of primordial night. There he is still the whole, the

whole is in him, indistinguishable from pure nature and bearer of all egohood. It is from these all uniting depths that the dream arises be it ever so childish, grotesque and immoral. So flower-like in its candor and veracity that it makes us blush for the deceitfulness of our lives.[6]

Thus, Jung saw how the dream can reflect not only the individual truths about ourselves but also the truths of our relationships with significant others and with the divine or the Absolute and the transpersonal states associated with that knowledge. His method involved "active imagination" and associations to the dream's content.

While Freud and Jung may have disagreed on many crucial matters, there were several subjects in relationship to dreams in which they were very much in agreement. Both Freud and Jung agreed that dreams tell us about our innermost intrapsychic and personal fears, avoidances, and desires. Dreams tell us much about our repeated patterns of interaction with significant others in our lives. Both also agreed that dreams inform us of what our deeper reactions, identifications, perceptions, and beliefs—be they good or bad—are about these significant people in our lives. This is both literally and metaphorically true. Therefore, themes of power, passion, sex, guilt, betrayal, honor, rejection, violence, fear, helplessness, beauty, rage, and so on fill the nightly vortex of dreams. They both agreed that sometimes these dreams even reveal our forgotten, hidden, and atrophied capacities as human beings.

We do not know exactly what percentage of our monthly dream experiences involve the appearance of family members and family-related themes. This obviously varies from person to person based on our individual psychologies, the content of our lives and experiences, and our emotional interest in family matters. What we do know, however, is that this percentage is very high in almost all of us. Dream researcher Louisa E. Rhine tabulated these dreams involving family members in some fashion, and her research indicated that they comprise approximately 40 percent of our dreamlife.[7]

It is no wonder then that normal and unusual dreams about our family members should populate our consciousness. Family members appear in our intrapsychic or personal dreams in terms of actual images, personalities, and symbolic acts and events more often than we can really remember. The family is deeply implicated in our conscious and unconscious development. It should be remembered that we generally grow up in families. We first learn about symbols, signs, and consensual or shared meaning and imagery in the family context. Early identity is largely a family affair. There is both conscious and unconscious learning over many, many years, sometimes over generations. In a very real sense each family member is deeply interwoven in our intimate psychological functioning. Each is enfolded and reflected in the other. The fragments of past dreamers are the living tissue of our present lives and all are unfolding toward some new extended identity in the future. This system of shared meaning, shared feeling, and shared emotion is generally termed the "family unconscious" level of the psyche. It is a dimension of our psychological function that lies in a space between the individual or individuated intrapsychic unconscious illuminated by Freud and the shared collective unconscious illuminated by Jung. Both Freud and Jung characterize the unconscious as a determined system. However, the family unconscious lies somewhere between their theories and is capable of being modified by those who participate in its common or shared field. The work of dreams in the family unconscious has been explored by many researchers.[8] There are divergences and commonalities in theory, but the clinical observations are highly similar.

Dreams and dream interpretation are as old as humanity, but the life of the dream is etched in the mammalian unfoldment of evolution itself. So we now ask, what are our deepest roots, what have been our earliest intuitions and technologies for working with and learning from these intimate, pervasive, and ancient nocturnal visitors?

2

The Ancient Way

This civilization, called Egyptian in our own period, developed for a long time in its early cradle; then it slowly descended the Nile valley to spread out around the Mediterranean basin. This cycle of civilization, the longest in our history, presumably lasted 10,000 years. This is a reasonable compromise between the long chronology (based on data provided by Egyptian priests, Herodotus and Manetho who place the beginning at 17,000 B.C.) and the short chronology of the moderns—for the latter are obliged to admit that by 4245 B.C. the Egyptians had already invented the calendar which necessarily requires the passage of thousands of years.

C. A. DIOP,
THE AFRICAN ORIGIN OF CIVILIZATION

THE AFRICAN CRADLE

Long before Rome and the Appian Way, long before Zoroaster and the domed cities of Persia, long before Meroë and the ancient cities of the upper Nile, and long before China and Israel, our species was fascinated by the theater of its dreams. We can only speculate on the relationship and beliefs that antediluvian humans had about their dreams, their waking life, and the world around them. Were the drawings on cave walls an expression not only of their plans, ceremonies, and religious and mystical beliefs, but also of their dreamlife? Did they project their nightmares and nightly terrors on the walls? Did they wonder if all the other animals of the night forest also dream?

From all we have been able to gather so far, the ancient earth religions dealt extensively with dreams. Witchcraft, sorcery, and demonization all were within the accepted worldview of humanity at that time, as was the intuition of light and intelligence, of birth and death, and even of form and substance itself. The collective dreams of ancient peoples were expressed and lived through their myths. All the possibilities and beings that populate the human mind had ready access to expression in the inner dreamlife and the outward reality of early humankind.

In ancient times, the boundaries of what was real and what was not real were very different from those we know today. We now teach our children to differentiate between dreams and reality with the aid of adult rationality. It seems evident that in earlier times no such emphasis was placed on this somewhat arbitrary boundary distinction in the sea of consciousness. This is especially important when it comes to issues concerning the boundary of the beginning of life or the intuition about the termination of life. The living and the dead appeared in our ancestors' dreams just as they do in ours. In the minds of early humans, however, it was not always clear when a person was really alive and when a person was really dead. As you might imagine, this had definite consequences for human society.

The Indo-German tribes often kept their dead family members with them long after they had died, sometimes for over a month. They ate with them, sat them up, and essentially took care of them, maintaining the belief that on some level, these dead family members still lived. No doubt they also dreamed of them. The question arises as to whether early people believed, on the basis of their dreams, that they and their family members had souls that survived death. This belief is not difficult to comprehend, since phenomenologically the dead are *emotionally present* in both waking life and dreams. Even today, data on the dreams of older persons indicates that dream symbols prepare the subject for the approach of impending death. This should not surprise us, since death is a natural occurrence that every embodied consciousness must experience. However, as Jung showed, the deeper recesses of our psyche pay very little attention to the quick end of embodied life and continue to function as though the deceased person was an active member in our lives by way of their behavior, conversations, and appearances in our dreams. This, of course, includes the dreamer. The unconscious, in other words, seems to believe in a continuous life.[1]

Dream interpretation really took hold in the early civilizations. From evidence we have today it appears clear that the earliest human civilizations, the Afro-Asiatic civilizations, began somewhere in the upper Nile region of East Africa, perhaps eight to twelve thousand years ago.[2] The civilizing influence then spread across Africa and the Middle East and then into Europe, India, China, and Japan. It carried with it humanity's earliest unconscious humanoid experiences in a collective record. Given that humanity initially evolved and spent its formative years on the African continent, the deepest and oldest aspect of man's collective consciousness is firmly rooted in what we would term the "African unconscious."[3] It is more than an interesting biological coincidence that the early prehuman type, *Australopithecus africanus,* began in the same area where the first human civilizations are generally known to have arisen.

We are historically aware of the prophetic dreams of an expanding empire by the pharaoh Thutmose III around 1470 BCE. He had one of them carved in a stone pillar, or stela, and placed before the ancient and mysterious Sphinx. Prophetic dreams stand out more than others since they have an aura of predicting the future, and in this sense they expand the mind beyond the narrowing confines of waking causality and give man a feeling of control over his anxiety about the future. Prophetic dreams in the Bible are well known. We remember the prophetic dreams of Joseph in the Bible as told to another pharaoh. One was the story of the seven lean cows and the seven fat cows. Joseph's interpretation of his dream to the pharaoh was that there would be seven lean years and seven bountiful years of harvest for Egypt. Apparently this prophetic dream came true. Today many clinical psychologists and some experimental physicists as well as a large number of psychiatrists have come to accept the existence of prophetic dreams. These are often worked with in the clinical hour.[4]

Dream interpretation (oneiromancy) as a written skill was first outlined and cataloged in terms of symbols and their meaning in Europe by the Greek scholar Artemidorus of Daldis in the second century CE. He quoted from earlier Kemetic Egyptian and Sumerian sources. Apparently he did not want numerous copies of his book to be circulated for fear of too many people coming into the dream interpretation business. From what we can tell, this early dream interpreter was quite successful in his craft, both professionally and financially. He interpreted more than 3,000 dreams in five surviving volumes of work and came to represent the classical tradition in the prophetic interpretation of dreams. His books were even republished 1,300 years later in 1518 under the title of *Oneirocritica* and then later in English in 1606. No doubt he was in touch with the heartbeat of the culture and society of the time and was thus, like any healer, able in his interpretations to mirror the intuitions of his clients to an uncanny degree. He came to do so by stressing the individualistic dimension of the dream and the particular context or life circumstance of the dreamer.

CROSS-CULTURAL AND TRANSCULTURAL MODES OF DREAMING

Individual, family, and divine or spiritual dreams are rooted in every culture, every society. When they emerged has long been forgotten, but their expressions are active and vital even today. The Native Americans are well known for their method of seeking a spiritual guide in their "vision quests." Here a spirit embodied as an animal or other being emerges after long preparation to help guide and initiate the neophyte into the mysteries of the spiritual process. The Plains Indians, during their adolescence, were sent out to seek such a vision or dream that would embody a protective spirit that could shield them from malevolent forces throughout their waking and dreaming lives.[5] Others, especially the Mohave Native Americans, believed that essentially "all special abilities or funds of knowledge were to be had by dreaming and by dreaming alone."[6] This is a remarkable belief and one reflecting a highly articulated metaphysical system implying a tacit knowledge of unconscious forces. It is similar to the Yuman tribe's belief that every prosperous person's creative work and accomplishments had been literally dreamed into reality. This includes information received in an anomalous fashion, special skills and talents they had, and the gift of giving birth to the future by having children.[7]

Sometimes the relationship between dreams and other unconscious psychological processes was even more explicit among the Native Americans. An example is the belief held by the Iroquois that a wish in a dream must be acted out in some way, by oneself or others, in the waking state. If, for example, an Iroquois had a dream about giving a great feast, such a banquet had to be given either by them or another person soon.[8] This in a sense is a form of dreaming *for* someone else. This secret wish, called "ondinok," was a hidden wish of the soul and bears a certain affinity to Freud's concept of the dream process as largely wish fulfillment. The Native Americans of the plains, eastern woodlands, lower Colorado River, central California, and the northwest coast all believed and acted on the basis of their belief in guardian spirits who could and frequently would speak, sing, grant wishes, and even dance with them in their dreams.[9] In this way, the dream's process was felt, heard, and identified with on a very intimate level and even acted out behaviorally in the waking state, often to enormous therapeutic benefit. This implies a highly *personalized* view or paradigm of the world process that, in addition to including some elements of classically archaic thought processes, also embraced a more interconnected and energetic conception of the universe.

Gestalt therapy and dreamwork is only one contemporary psychological school that has benefited immensely from these insights.[10] Instead of merely *reacting* to the dream, the dreamer is taught to take ownership of the dream, *approach* the beings, forces, and situations in the dream, and thereby change the dream's outcome. This has very powerful implications for events and "beings" that inhabit the dynamic world of the dream. Since many of these figures are actual or symbolic expressions of family members, this interaction with the dream can be viewed as a form of family therapy.

In Australia, this mode of family and individual "spiritual dreamwork" has evolved in a different direction. Here a methodology has developed that enables an individual to "travel" in the dream world to other places for particular purposes. The dream journey may be for the purpose of seeking spiritual guidance, it may be part of the hunting and tracking process of food acquisition, or it may be a search for a cure for an ailing family member. It may and often does have several motivations operating at once. This form of Aboriginal dreamtime has yet to be recognized in clinical circles for its powerful somatic and psychological healing possibilities.[11] However, it is a real phenomenon and an authentic, highly evolved psychological and psychophysical technology.

For the Australian Aborigines, the Dreaming, or Dreamtime, is conceptualized as the eternally present life principle that must *personally* be sustained and reinvigorated by human beings by way of sacred ritual and belief. The purpose of ritual and ceremony itself is to make a place in the waking world where the Dreamtime is dynamically active in their lives. This includes the *dynamically experienced presence* of ancestors and other family members. Here their family unconscious stretches out to enfold not only the living but also the mythic and powerful deceased. For these gentle and sensitive people who intuit that everything partakes of the eternal life principle, the Dreamtime is really an active historical principle that structures both time and space. It was created by the mythical ancestors at the dawn of memory and can be consciously entered into by sacred dreaming.[12]

In Africa, the importance of dreams, and family dreams in particular, also has a long cultural, clinical, and psychospiritual history. It is a given in many religious societies that family members, both living and deceased, and also the gods themselves, can and do communicate with the dreamer in the dream.[13] This belief greatly expands the personal matrix of experience, causality, and time flows since this extended family unconscious system enfolds not only the generation to be born and the currently living but also up to five generations of the departed.[14]

The recently departed ancestors are referred to as "the living dead" because they are thought to be in a state of personal immortality, and it is through them that the spirit world is believed to become personal. There are many cults devoted to this period of the living dead. After five generations in this Sasa—the period immediately following the termination of bodily life—they are said to disappear into the great Zamani, that vast time period beyond death when the soul slowly approaches God over the eons. There is thought to be much traffic from the Sasa into the Zamani. Implicitly there are waves in this sea of familial consciousness. The living dead in particular are thought to be deeply concerned with family affairs since they have just left this realm.

These beliefs, particularly in their West African expression, are still seen today in the cultural fabric of African-American life to some degree. The dream is infused with spirituality and an aesthetic sensibility and accompanies some forms of healing found in the early foundations of African medicine and healing.[15] It is believed that one's dreams and ancestors can and do directly affect the life of other people. Some disciplines and religions have extended this to the belief in the conscious influence upon another person's dream by a powerful person for either positive or negative motivations. This strong belief was prominent with the ancient Kemetic Egyptians and later found expression in the religion and cosmology of what may be some of their diasporic descendants called the "Yoruba" and other nations of West Africa. In these situations, as in modern family therapy, the question the clinician asks is not so much "*what* is the matter with you?" but rather "*who* is the matter with you?" This has spread to the New World and suffuses many of the religious beliefs of South America and the Caribbean (e.g., Santeria, Candomblé). Its most potent expression, however, is found in the psychospiritual dreamwork technology of what is termed "vodun," or "voodoo."[16] The Zambian shamans and dreamworkers have taken this in a slightly different direction. They believe they can correctly diagnose a patient's illness through powers and information enfolded in dreams. The genius of these traditions again has yet to reach the clinical insight of modern science. There are many more examples.

In China, dreamwork and dream interpretation were largely the province of traditional doctors, Taoists, and monks of different doctrines. As in Africa, the Chinese felt that while dreams were important and held or communicated vital information, they might originate from a negative or demonic source. The dream could be a wild dream (*yemeng*) or freak dream (*kuang-meng*) initiated by a demonic force intent on stealing the soul of the dreamer! Divination was and is a widespread practice in both China and Africa. The imperial court and emperor often sought the assistance of the skilled dream interpreter for unnerving or prophetic dreams. These often had political implications along with familial and other ramifications.[17]

The oldest known Chinese book on dreams is the *Meno Shy* from about 640 CE. Here the Chinese psychological system classified dreams of all kinds on the basis of their source, which then revealed both psychological and somatic changes occurring in the patient. Their interactive view held that while the dream was initiated internally by the patient's soul, external physical stimuli could also influence or be incorporated into the dream. Sleeping on a belt, for example, was believed to stimulate dreams about snakes.[18]

The Yellow Emperor's Classic of Internal Medicine was a widely used text in ancient China in which dreams were also used for diagnostic purposes. This book covered all areas of medical practice, from the vital internal organs and their imbalances to the sexual congress of women with demons and ghosts (i.e., the incubus). Demonic dream possession is a deeply rooted notion in most forms of early religion and is trans-cultural in expression. Many methods were used to "cure" the afflicted. After the arrival of the Buddha in China, the dream process was taken and used more as a metaphor to point out the ultimately illusory and "empty" nature of reality. Both of these traditions peacefully coexisted, as they coexist side by side today.

In the Middle East, dreamwork and dream incubation took still another direction, yet kept enough in common with the others to demonstrate some parallel developments. The ancient Assyrians developed a series of sacred prayers in order to elicit good dreams and ward off malevolent forces. In fact many of the Middle Eastern traditions were deeply preoccupied with the possibility of negative forces influencing one's life either by way of dreams, magic, or other methods. The most famous book in this tradition, the *Necronomicon,* was written by Abdul Alhazred in Damascus around the eighth century CE and was largely compiled from earlier writings and beliefs in this vein.[19] It is full of occultism, rituals, curses, and techniques to either invoke these forces or protect the practitioners and their families and loved ones from influences, both waking and dreaming.

The Muslims also developed ritual prayers that have a certain affinity to the dream incubation process, even though, unlike the Egyptians and Greeks, they did not require a special sleeping temple. The practice, called "istiqara," requires a highly crafted prayer to be repeated, almost mantra-like, just prior to going to sleep. The dreamers are highly motivated, both consciously and unconsciously, and thereby expect an answer or some response to their prayer or request.[20] In a certain sense, this metaphysical and psychological system held that the dream was a higher form of consciousness or reality than the waking state.

In India, the yogis also often hold the dream to be a higher level of reality than the waking state. The *Mandukya Upanishad* held that the dream world, while an expression of the dreamer, was also deeper and closer to the ultimate reality of the divine principle, or Atman. It has also found elaborated expression in certain forms of intense Tantric Buddhism that exist as a living discipline in China, India, and Tibet.

Japan has its own tradition of dream interpretation found in Japanese Buddhism and its ancient earth religion of Shinto. Like other indigenous early religions, it focuses on the worship of and devotion to deities of natural forces, the sun itself at times, and the cultural-religious leader of the society as an intermediary between man and God. The transpersonal nature of consciousness is implicit here and as such the dream is an open vehicle for influence of many types and on many levels, both inner and outer, as in the many other traditions previously mentioned.

THE ANCIENT METHOD ITSELF

It is clear that dream interpretation, religion, and healing were all in some permutation and to some degree part of the interconnected worldview of ancient humanity. Despite the diverse methods among the different peoples, much was held in common. One finds some variation of these combinations among the ancient Hebrews and certainly in the upper Nile Egyptian civilizations as they cross-fertilized continually over the years with perhaps an even more ancient civilization still shrouded in mystery. We find it in the works of the Syrians, the Indians, the Mesoamericans, the Chinese, the Japanese, the Muslims, and in all the ancient cultural and religious traditions. In all of these, a dream incubation process and practice was used. Persons would go into a dream incubation practice prescribed by their particular society or culture and would emotionally approach the dynamically emergent image in the dream with a number of requests. These requests or desires took the form of attempting to obtain advice and wisdom, the healing of psychological and physical diseases, the ability to see into the future, or, as you might expect, the ability to exercise power over others.

These people saw the living *personalized* embodiment of the archetypal healer in their dreams. Those seeking advice, wisdom, or healing developed their religious and healing practices even further, creating entire cultures and dream temples in the service of their dream healers. In the temples and libraries of ancient Egypt, called "Houses of Life," or "per ankh," and then later in Greece and Rome, pilgrims would come from hundreds of miles away, a great distance in those times, for dream incubation purification rites and healing. At one time there were more than four hundred such temples to the god Asclepius. They were in existence from 600 BCE to 500 CE. In fact, the medical caduceus, a symbol of a staff with two serpents entwined around it seven times, was taken from that period. It is even more interesting that the Asclepius symbol itself was taken from an earlier Egyptian civilization that the Greeks admired and then helped to transmit to the rest of Western civilization.[21] It has a very ancient and deep shared meaning.

The ancient Kemetic Egyptians, like the Babylonians, Assyrians, and others, were concerned with malevolent forces in dreams, but they were not as preoccupied with them. They were more deeply concerned with how to "clinically" elicit messages and information from the gods. The papyrus of Deral-Madineh from before 2000 BCE gives elaborate instructions on obtaining a specific healing dream message from a god. Serapis was the Egyptian god of dreams and his Houses of Life often served as both library and dream temple where the priests practiced their sacred art of dream incubation and later interpretation with the community of believers.

These same Egyptians had a highly evolved knowledge of anatomy and physiology due to their practice of mummification. But this science did not stop there. In the classical medical text dating prior to 3000 BCE called the "papyrus Ebers" after its discoverer George Ebers, who found it in a tomb in 1873 and placed it—ostensibly for safekeeping—in the Leipzig University Library, there are early references to dreams and hypnosis as a clinical practice.[22] From the thousands of written medical papyri, sadly only ten survive to this day, with the Ebers and the Edwin Smith surgical papyri being the most famous. Some have documented Egyptian knowledge of subtle endocrine system functions, emotional reactions, and cognitive states, which may actually be the real origin of biological psychiatry.[23]

Finally, it must be noted that all the findings above, along with other research, strongly suggest a complex awareness of psychology, biology, and deep subjective processes extensively mirrored in religious and cosmological beliefs. In other words, there is considerable support for the notion that, prior to 3000 BCE, the ancient Egyptians were conscious and aware of the influence and dynamics of the unconscious mind and its capacity to influence bodily processes.[24] This knowledge was written in the libraries and practiced clinically in the Kemetic Houses of Life millennia earlier than imagined by contemporary scientists. Their astronomical calendar, accurate to within days of our own, was already in use by 4245 BCE and was based on the 1,460 years of the sidereal calendar, the lapse of time that separates two heliacal risings of Sirius, the most luminous fixed star of the night sky located in the constellation of Canis Major.[25] This sophisticated range of clinical knowledge, along with all the attendant social and psychological influences or "demand characteristics" of the cultural milieu, created a powerful psycho-technology for these ancient healers and their long-distance, dream-swept patients.

Thus, when the dreamer finally, after miles and miles, came to a temple of healing, he would rest for some time and regain his strength. He would eat the special foods prescribed by the priest and the seers of the temple area. After the cleansing and the purification, after the soothing waters and the quieting of the mind, the healing process moved into its second phase. In one temple, after extensive washings and consultations with the priest, who could be male or female, the person with the affliction would go into a tomb-like structure. He would then lie in a bed above the temple's sanctuary floor. On the floor were often a number of colorful, dramatic-looking, but harmless snakes. The connection between the healing process and the coiling, perhaps even rising, snake and the energy serpent in the human spine called kundalini will be discussed later. There is, however, a deep primordial human intuition and organismic perception concerning energy and healing in the rising of two currents of serpentine energy through the body (see figure 1, page 36).

After the subject had been lying quietly on the healing table for a while, he would find a peaceful place within his mind and then enter into it more deeply, amplifying the feeling while often expressing a specific wish or prayer or expectation as he attempted to go to deep sleep or dream sleep with this notion held firmly in his mind. In this way the conscious mind would make contact with the unconscious depths. Sometimes outside the walls of this healing chamber the priest would chant a sacred song, and sometimes through a small opening in the wall the priest or priestess would direct a verbal message to the half-sleeping and, paradoxically, by this time highly aroused patient. The combination of a dark room with primordial figures moving on the floor, a long passageway, and the priests applying their healing procedures had enormous demand characteristics that influenced the body. They were able to unleash tremendous healing powers from the somatic and the psychological unconscious, which appear to be subtly enfolded into each other. Armed with a powerful image or metaphor, which was often a family or tribal deity, the power of the priest, and the awakened experience, along with the repetitive almost mantra-like message or *sankalpa*, the initiate would go into a healing sleep. The deep somatic and autonomic energies of the body could then do their work.

This again appears to be at least a functional awareness of the dynamic unconscious. While the ancient Egyptians specifically referred to the unconscious as Amenta and the primeval waters of Nun, other African peoples, particularly those in West Africa, have referred to similar, but not identical, processes they call the Ayanmo concept.[26] The latter is more intimately associated with the existential choices one makes in life even though on some level these choices are not fully known or conscious to the individual. The notions of fate and destiny enter the equation

Dormant

The medical caduceus and its seven
centers each associated with a specific
hormonal and endocrine function.
The current is in its dormant state.

The Egyptian ankh
or symbol of life and
the life current in its
potential state.

Awakened

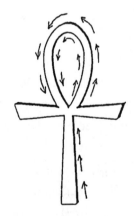

The yogic seven chakras each associated
with a plexus and a level of consciousness.
This is the symbol of the awakened
current moving to the brain.

The flow of the life
current awakened
and fulfilled in the
braincore.

Figure 1. Ancient Symbols of the Awakened and Dormant Life Current

along with spirituality and family dynamics, all of which are believed to have their expression in the dreamwork and its influence on the mind and body itself. These were common beliefs in the ancient world.

Hippocrates, a Greek physician living sometime between 460 and 370 BCE, believed that the sun, the moon, and the stars were representative of the dreamer's organic state. He had trained in Egypt in the library of the temple of Imhotep at Memphis where Galen was taught seven centuries later. He too believed that dreams can tell an illness before its overt expression in the body and that powerful images affect and heal the body. These beliefs manifest today in the growing discipline of psychoneuroimmunology. We use different symbols, different assumptions, and different categories of diagnosis, yet we are still attempting to experience and make vital contact with the deep unconscious of the patient, both psychologically and somatically. Hippocrates wrote:

> It is a sign of sickness if the (dream) star appears dim and moves either westwards or down into the earth or sea or upwards. Upward movement indicates fuxes (an abnormal discharge of fluid) in the head; movement into the sea, disease of the bowels; eastward movement, the growing of tumors in the flesh.[27]

These dreams in which physical expressions of illness appear in symbolic form are called "prodromic." Thus, in a sense there is a certain prophetic or precognitive process in these somatic situations. In some way or other we are always trying to see into the future. Some seven centuries later, in 200 CE, Galen was practicing essentially the same medicine in dreamwork as a physician in his practice.

One of the more powerful curing symbols was the integration of the feminine aspect of the self with the energies of healing in the ancient world. We are most familiar with the female oracle at Delphi. But female divination was in all of the ancient world, especially later in Rome and China and even earlier in Egypt. In some parts of the world, as we have seen, the belief in male or female divination still thrives and is formally practiced today in West Africa, in Southeast Asia, and in certain areas of the hills of Japan.

Who can forget how dreams have played out in early mythologies and family histories over the long march of humanity toward our current civilization? Oedipus the king, his dream, and his tragedy spread through psychoanalysis even today like a great current. The myth of Romulus and Remus may have begun in a mother's dream of twins. Myths are the shared dreams of a culture. Family dreams are family myths about ourselves and our intimate web. Indeed myths are another form of knowledge—valuable, dynamic, and real. Regardless of the chimerical quality of myths, every culture believes in them—even our own.

Dreams have not been confined to the nightly philosophy of life. Dreams and their reality have deeply influenced and invigorated the waking-state philosophies of humanity. It has quickened but at the same time made more subtle the dance with reality. The Chinese philosopher Chuang-tzu said: "I fell asleep and dreamed I was a butterfly. When I awoke, I wondered, was it Chuang-tzu dreaming he was a butterfly, or am I a butterfly dreaming it is Chuang-tzu?" Some have gone even farther in dreamwork. Milarepa, the Tibetan yogi poet, achieved spiritual liberation by his study, practice, and realization of dreams. There is an extensive and profound psychospiritual technology and methodology in the dream yoga of Tibetan lamas. It is a working methodology of consciously integrating the waking state and the dreaming state in order to move toward the state that enfolds and is consciously beyond both waking and dreaming. This technology has an enormous potential. It also has an uncanny resemblance to the theories of the subtle bodies, or sheaths of reality, in India, the five subtle bodies of ancient Egyptian philosophies, and, curiously enough, some levels of the Western "emotional body" or autonomic nervous system so often aroused and expressed in dreams. All have an enormous capacity for healing. Given this we might ask ourselves: How do all these currents move into the ocean of the self and family life? It is in that direction that we now turn.

3

The Web of Dreamlife in Family and Self

Where the West is said to favor materialism and the East, meaning largely India, is said to favor spiritualism, Africa combines the material and spiritual. Personalism invades the material as well as the spiritual . . . the trees and the mountains have always possessed essences. We do not have to make absolute distinctions between mind and matter, form and substance, ourselves and the world. The self is the center of the world, animating it and making it living and personal.

M. K. ASANTE, *AFROCENTRICITY*

A woman recalled the following family dream series about her family and herself. As an adult she still remembers these dreams that occurred at the ages of eight and twelve.

My Parents Drive Away

I am walking down a sidewalk on the fronthand side of the Main Street downtown in my childhood hometown. I watch my parents exit a building and cross the sidewalk in front of me. They get into our blue Plymouth station wagon and deliberately pull off and drive away. All the while they are looking straight at me. I start running after them yelling "stop" or "wait," but they continue to drive on. They're both very smug in the knowledge that I can't possibly catch up with them. I awake crying.

Driverless Car

There is something wrong with my bicycle so I get off it and began walking downhill on the right hand side of a narrow, paved road. Turning around, I see, up through the tree, our Plymouth station wagon coming down a curvy road. I wait for a ride as the car passes the trees and comes into view again. As it approaches me, it suddenly swings around to face the opposite direction. The door on the driver side is flung open. My parents are seated on the passenger's side on the front seat. My father beckons to me to climb in. I realize that he expects me to drive and that I don't know how. Children are supposed to obey their parents, but how can he ask me to do such a thing? I wake up in a panic.

This dreamer is obviously a very sophisticated dream recorder. She is aware of the autonomy-separation issues of family and self. She also has considerable observational skills and has grown enormously from a profound interpretation of her dreams in relationship to her family's dynamics and motifs. As she meditated on this dream, another one came to her soon after she recorded the above two. Her daughter Theresa also had a parallel or similar dream. When the same symbol appears in more than one person's dream it may reflect a family's unconscious synchronous symbology. In group or collective dreamwork such symbols have been observed to seemingly skip from dreamer to dreamer over time, almost as though a shared language had evolved between the dreamers. In this respect the process can be likened to a decoupage in art where many separate pieces of information and objects are laminated together into a new coherent pattern of communication.[1]

Alaska Driving

. . . the children and I are being driven north in a white station wagon (similar to my parents' when I was a teenager). I open the back right-hand door to look out with the intention to disembark while the station wagon is in motion. When I see a metal guardrail approaching, I quickly pull the door closed so that it won't impact.

Afterwards I reopen the door, while the car is still moving, and jump out with a child in my arms as if I'm going to "save" this child. I run up the hill into a parking lot with multisized buildings which seem to be under construction.

As I look back, I see (my children) Vic and Theresa walking along a median of grass and trees. They are stopped by a man who hassles them, but they are able to get past him and come along towards me.

After I awoke, I guess that "child" I was rescuing was the "child-self" who had experienced those nightmares in the earlier dreams. Before I had a chance to develop this line of thinking further, Theresa, my daughter, related her dream of that night at breakfast and I recorded it. Theresa was 9 years old, Vic was 13. I had never mentioned my dream to either of them.

Our Old Car

(Theresa M.). . . Vic, Dad, and I get into two cars, our old blue and white Mustang and Dad's blue Honda. Vic got into the Mustang and so did I, and Dad got into the Honda Accord. So Vic started driving the car and I was curious, how he was doing it, and why . . .

Then we took off. I suggested to Victor that we wait for Dad but he said "no" so we kept on going. Then I heard an engine start; it was Dad in the Honda. I said, "Vic, stop!" and he called "No."

Then finally we came up to a construction site; the building was almost done. There was a desert in front of it, like sand. I opened up the door, got out on the curb, and was running. Then he stopped and I closed the door.

Soon Dad came up, and he stopped and got out of the car. He scolded Vic for driving off without him, and he scolded me for getting out of the car while it was still going.

The mother who had the original two dreams was an observant dreamer and felt that the "hassle man" from her dream was her husband! It made sense to her in terms of what she felt her family dynamics at the time were (i.e., no major problems but a lot of minor hassles). She was gratified that neither Theresa nor she had experienced any nightmares. She felt that her own growth in controlling the vehicle of self was reflected in a steadily improving dream scenario. Perhaps, she reasoned, her own children were benefiting from that fact, too, in both the dreaming and waking states.

We see in the above family dream series that this is a normal and healthy family struggling with normal family issues. These dynamics in one form or another populate most of our dreamlife. There is the possibility of some psi process, particularly the ESP form, operating here but it is not strong or exact enough to be seen as clearly as in other psi dreams. It is, however, clearly a normal psychodynamic dream in a larger family-systems dream process or matrix. In many ways, given its shared imagery, affect, and motivations, it is a direct expression of the family unconscious.[2]

As we look at this dream, we see how powerful emotions and normal motivations are integrated in a dynamic and shared framework. Various relationships are revealed and these relationships in turn reveal normal stages of development in family themes. Obviously, social-cultural forces and family influences affect the dream's content, though not necessarily the dream's structure or function.[3] Gender and ethnic background are also factors that influence family styles and family therapy practices[4] and can certainly be expected to influence the content of family dreams. In your own dreams you have no doubt noticed issues of love, authority, power, religion, fear, and all of the other experiences that make up the enormous constellation of our lives.

Different levels of emotion and association and imagery are seen in all varieties of dreams, from the normal psychodynamic ones seen above to the more unusual and transpersonal ones that were mentioned earlier. In the Family Dreams Research Project (see appendix A), hundreds of family dreams have been catalogued according to the levels and degrees of feeling, association, and themes woven throughout.

Note this gentle family dream that first occurred on September 5, 1985, and the family events that followed later:

> *In the dream I was sitting in my Grandmother R.'s rocking chair. My husband (Gene T.) was standing outside greeting my parents Ralph and Dorothy R. who were coming to visit. I was smoking a cigarette and quickly tried to hide it before my parents came in and saw me with it. My parents came in, walked past me into another room out of my sight. My brother, Gary R., came into the room where I was and sat down across from me. He was carrying a painting of purple mountains.*

Here is the corollary waking-time experience of the dreamer:

Personal life experience,
Sunday, September 22, 1985

My husband and I were outside in the back of our house. (I was sitting on a chair on the patio. My husband was mowing the lawn.) My mother, father, and Grandmother R. came to visit and had come around the house to the back (we weren't expecting them). While my husband opened the gates for them, I quickly got rid of the cigarette I was smoking (they disapprove of my smoking). About an hour or two after they had gone home, my brother Gary R. and girlfriend Carol B. visited. The first thing my brother did when he came in the door was to comment on the picture I had hanging on my wall, which I bought a couple of days before. He said he and Carol had been looking for a picture like it with the same colors in it. The picture has purple mountains in it, which I really wasn't aware of when I bought it because the most prominent color in it is orange, and when I bought it I thought it would go well in my living room.

These are normal family dreams. The date of the first dream that this person had was September 5, 1985; the personal experience was September 22, 1985. Though there is a correspondence between the events in the dreams and the events in waking time, this dream would not necessarily classify as a psi dream. This is clearly just a normal systems-wide and psychodynamically informed dream. In other words, this is the kind of dream that makes up most of our dreaming life.

What follows is another dream submitted to the Family Dreams Research Project that is suffused with the normal emotional dynamics of love, authority, anger, fear, power, and intimacy that largely populate our collective dreamlife.

October 1, 1987

I dreamed that it was Halloween and that I was playing with small children on someone's front porch. It was a wooden porch at night. It might have been my brother, John, but I'm not sure. Then I was in some woods with these two guys and I was playing around with them. It was supposed to be a joke that I was going to tie them up and leave them in the woods tied to a large picket fence. I did this and left. I went back to the house in the city where we lived. In the kitchen of my old house in A. I was helping Henny (my mother in the dream) slice ham. She wanted the ham sliced thin and then told me to stop because she did not want to eat too much salt. (Now in my bedroom) I put on my blue jeans and looked out my bedroom window and in the rain I watched the house next door and noticed when the lights went off at the end of the house. I then saw John P. and his brother coming across our lawn to our house. John was holding a large black umbrella. I knew they were coming to try to find the two people I had tied up. Suddenly I was panic-stricken because I had not let them go and many years had passed, and I now knew it was too late to let them go and that they were probably dead. I hurried up to get to them before John and his brother did and then I woke up.

The woman who submitted this dream series submitted many others in which she was consciously aware of intense themes of family interaction. She also dreamed of the emotions and dynamics that are common in the normal family romance.*

July 1987

I dreamed that I was at a baking contest. I had made roast beef. My mother was there. The contest was conducted outside. There were several rows of entries, and I was searching for my own when I realized that I could not find it. I asked my mother if she would help me find my entry of roast beef and potatoes (I had watched a cooking show on TV the night before so I must have remembered the potatoes) but she said she would not help me. I felt very bad about this. I suddenly saw my father and went over to him and told him that I asked Mom to help me but she said she wouldn't. He was sympathetic as he was when I was a child.

Shortly after this dreamer's father had suffered a second heart attack, she had one dream of him going to the hospital and surviving and another dream of him not surviving and thus having to go back to the hospital. These are both very normal anxiety dreams. Now notice the next long dream for its intensity and the subtle interconnections between persons, relationships, and events. It was related by a dreamer who was a clinical psychologist and psychotherapist, and it concerns the practical dimension of practice that every clinician must deal with: fees for services.

> *Here is a story for your files. I think this one is a dandy. I had to tell it to you.*
>
> *Our thirtyish male tenant, Mark, who is obese by about 80 pounds, who drinks nightly at a local bar, and who rarely talks to us, told my wife that he wanted to lose his excess weight. She recommended that he talk to me about hypnosis. He did and I agreed to give him one free session.*

---

*"Family romance" refers to the normal libidinal triangular relationship that develops in a family's dynamics and is sometimes a source of competition or jealousy (e.g., father and daughter vs. mother, mother and son vs. father, etc.).

He entered trance readily at the appointed time and was generally a very good subject. He told me later that he walked around in a pleasant daze the rest of that morning. After the session he asked for more, and I told him that I would have to charge. He said that would be difficult but would I stop by his apartment some evening soon and give him a price. This was last Thursday (September 27, 1984).

Last Tuesday night I told him my fee. He said that was too much but that he would talk to his parents. They were willing to help out; particularly this father worried about Mark's weight. I asked how much he would contribute. He said that his parents could pay 100%. I asked him why not go fifty-fifty? He said that 50% of my fee was way too much for him; he'd spent that much at his local haunt last week, that he'd have to cut down on drinking to contribute. I worried about the effect of letting his parents pay 100% on him, maybe that would cause him some problems. He said that it was no problem; he borrows money from his parents all the time. I pressed. He said, "It doesn't bother me at all consciously.*" I repeated the word* consciously *back to him. He agreed he may think differently unconsciously.*

I said, "We really don't know what your unconscious problems are." Just then the phone rang. It was his mother, calling from Boston! He said he'd call her back.

I closed shortly after that, saying, "You don't know how your unconscious feels about letting your parents pay 100 percent, but it may come to you in a dream." I went home and went to bed.

I woke up the next morning after one of those dreams that you feel kinesthetically long after you awaken. In my dream, I was in a friend's or relative's apartment (not a real place I know). They were away, and I was charged with watching the place. That included a tropical fish tank. I noticed one or two of the fish were missing. I became alarmed, figuring the tank cover had come loose, allowing the fish to jump out. I was looking under the tank when something caught my peripheral vision: it seemed like it was a fish swimming away, on the other side of the room! I turned toward the tank again and something bumped my back. I turned around. Facing me was a fish in mid room, fins waving, staring at me. It had big eyes; it was fat! I suddenly realized that the fish tank was somewhat superfluous, since the entire room was underwater, and I was underwater with it. That was an uncanny realization which led to the kinesthesia which outlasted the dream. It was a warm and calming feeling.

I walked the dog, ate breakfast with the kids, and saw them off to school. I thought of the dream again while shaving. I suddenly felt it had a connection to Mark, my patient. I realized I had had the dream I told him he might have. Moreover, I realized the water meant engulfment and overinvolvement with the mother. Mark has no wife, constant girlfriend problems, obesity, and a drinking problem.

Elated at my discovery, for it meant that I'd know how to work with him, I went to the bedroom to tell my wife. She shushed me before I got a chance to tell her anything. She was listening to the Today Show news. There was a story about two cosmonauts who "drank their way to safety in space" in 1977. Seems their spaceship was flooded by floating water which spilled; it threatened their instruments and circuits. Their solution was to drink the water out of the air!! Dumbfounded I went back to shaving, still without discussing this at all with Dotty, my wife. I went to work till 9:00 p.m.

When I went to bed that night I found a Time magazine opened on the bed. The story looking up at me was: "The Most Powerful Bond of All: The Mother-Son Relationship Can Sometimes Exact a Heavy Price"!!

Well, there it is. Thursday, my patient was one of the best hypnotic subjects I ever had. No wonder, right? I could not help thinking of you and your discovery.

As you can see, this is the report of a highly skilled clinician who is aware of the technical aspects of a therapeutic process in the individual therapy arena. Particularly apparent were the dynamics of transference and countertransference as they interface with family dynamics. The practice of hypnosis will often intensify the transference relationship and, as Freud believed, sometimes increases the capacity for unusual forms of communication in therapy.

You may well be asking yourself what the difference is between a psi-mediated dream and a normal family or psychodynamic dream when the images, emotions, and events are sometimes very similar. In other words, what criteria may be used to distinguish between psi and non-psi dreams? Actually, there are no *absolute* criteria any more than there are absolute criteria regarding the dawn of life and consciousness prior to birth or the termination of life and individual consciousness. In these nebulous regions there is always room for honest people to disagree. This book is not about establishing the final truth on this matter but rather about suggesting to you some helpful guidelines and some particularly useful maps for navigating this terrain. In later chapters, a preponderance of normal dreams and then of psi dreams will be presented so that you can more easily see the trends, content, and styles that differentiate the two classifications. In this chapter, both are presented alternately because in reality a family and individual may experience both types of dreams alternately.

The following dream series falls between the extremes of an absolutely normal psychodynamic and family-systems-wide dream series and one that involves the more unusual forms of communication including psi.

In this family dream series, it is not clear whether the passage of time and concurrent shifting of memory has altered the perceptions of a woman who was very close to her sister, or whether it is unequivocally a psi-mediated dream. From what we can understand, it falls somewhere between these two possibilities. In any case, it is a dream about a shared family image or shared scenario, and in that sense, at least, it is significant.

When I was about 9 years old and my sister 6, we had the same dream. The same exact dream on the same exact night. In this dream, as well as I can remember it, we had a guest over for dinner and she wanted some ice cream. So our mother sent us to Baskin-Robbins to get some. When we got there it was empty so we went up some stairs in the back. The stairs lead to a laboratory, complete with "mad scientist" character and an assistant. They, I believe, wanted to run some bizarre experiments on us. Anyway, the doctor managed to get a handful of pills down my throat so that I was immobilized. Fortunately, my sister had found a way to escape. She got me and pushed me down a sort of laundry chute that led to the street, then followed behind me. When we got home my mother asked us what took us so long and why we didn't have any ice cream. We told her what happened, but she did not believe us (in the dream).

When I woke up I started to tell my sister about the dream when, in the middle, she took up the story and finished telling it exactly as it happened up to the ending. When I asked her how she knew, she told me that she had had the dream also. I hope this information can aid you in your research.

The following dream also falls into the gray area between psi and non-psi dreams:

One morning I was sleeping late in my apartment, far from my home and family. My dream was interspersed with the sound of my mother crying. As I awakened, I could still hear her crying. The sound continued, even after my eyes were opened. I called home long distance that afternoon and found that my mother had indeed been crying that morning about a personal problem.

Most of our dreams are of this nature; however, the same woman experienced the following dream, which is undeniably a family-related psi dream:

My husband and I were stationed overseas in Panama. He had gone away with the Air Force Band on a two-week tour in Venezuela. I went to bed early one night. As I dozed off, I saw a strange vision. A robed man was carrying a large cornucopia-shaped object that tapered into a long tube.

He said, "You can talk to your husband through this." And he held it apparently toward my face. Then I heard my husband's voice saying, "Oh, honey, . . . Oh . . ." He was in obvious distress. The next morning I was awakened by a telephone call. My husband had been injured in an accident the night before, at the same time that I had heard his voice. He would be arriving by air transport to the base that day.

As you can see, the same person can have dreams that are distinctly psi-mediated as well as dreams that cannot be so neatly classified. Most of our dreams, however, are systems-wide and psychodynamic dreams.

Notice the following extended dream in which the strong emotions and motivations of family, both positive and negative, emerge in the dreamscape:

Both my maternal grandfather and I have experienced bad dreams during stressful times in our lives. When my father died in October of 1983, I began to have recurring dreams in which a beautiful, superior man was bent on killing me. Usually a complicated game of chase would develop, but I never managed to elude him. In the end, I would collapse from exhaustion and give in. Also, he had sort of a hypnotic effect on me, dazzling and enervating. He would compliment me on my increasing skill, for giving him a good chase and so forth, before killing me, usually by strangulation. I had been in the Navy in Florida at the time, and my grandfather had lived in Texas. I had been fighting with the notion of suicide for several months, and I had been getting tired. Once in a crisis, I had telephoned my mother in Texas.

She said, "Strange thing, last night your grandfather had such a terrible dream about you that he refused to talk about it. He has been worried and upset all day." This had bothered him at the time.

Time passed. I survived. In November of 1986 I was sleeping in the bed across from my grandfather who was dying. For the first time in a long time I dreamed again about that man. I heard his footsteps outside the house and recognized them immediately. "I really don't have the time for this kind of nonsense," I thought. The next thing I knew, he had thrown a dead cat (strangled) through the door.

"How tacky," I thought. At that point, both I and my grandfather awoke.

"There is a dead cat on the floor," he announced and pointed to the exact spot where it had landed in the dream. Since the sound of breaking glass was still fresh in my ears, I actually looked to see for myself before reassuring him. "You were seeing my shoe," I explained, "and you mistook it for a cat." I handed him the shoe. He examined it very closely and tossed it to the floor almost with contempt, as if I had tried to deceive him.

"There is a dead cat in here somewhere." He said this with a dignified finality before lapsing again into sleep. I reasoned to myself that people approaching death had fewer boundaries perhaps and could walk into the dream lives of those near to them. Still, I had been unsettled by the whole thing. And by the reappearance of that man.

Another woman shared a personal conflict dream centered on a specific image with her sister. This type of sibling dream is quite common and goes something like this:

I was lying naked in a bathtub of comfortably warm water. Although I could see the room clearly, it was not familiar to my waking self. It was definitely me in the tub; I was not looking in at myself but rather viewing the dream from inside the tub. I looked down the length of my body. I was warm and very much at ease, but there was something new and wonderful. I had my very own penis. I felt aroused and it was erect. I reached down and held it and it felt very good.

I looked up and could see out the doorway into another room, which I believe was a bedroom. There was a man standing there watching me. I think he was either my husband or my lover. As I looked at him I thought: Go away, I don't need you anymore. He noticed the expression on my face, which expressed both anger and bitterness. The anger was not overwhelming; I felt apathy toward the man. I just wanted him to go away.

This dream occurred sometime at the first part of April. I had recently had surgery for cervical cancer. I have not been involved in a serious relationship since January. I had been dating a couple of men but they were not very positive relationships. One man I labeled as egocentric, the other as self-absorbed. I had been feeling frustrated both sexually and emotionally. The obvious interpretation from my own opinion was simply, "If I had one of those I wouldn't need a man." What makes the dream interesting to me is that upon braving the dream to one of my sisters with whom I have a close relationship, she confided that she had a similar dream. I have asked her to write the dream down . . . She said she simply dreamed that she had a penis and that it was a very good feeling, and that when she awoke she felt disappointed because it was only a dream. I told her my interpretation of my dream and she expressed her agreement.

My sister has never been involved in a long-term relationship and has difficulty with men who express any kind of devotion to her. When she is in the relationship in which she is in she has constant doubt of his affections [that they will] last much longer. I'm not sure what this means, but it seems to me that neither of us is happy with the other half of the species. Note: I am 32 years old and my sister is 30. I'm divorced after eight years of marriage and have been for six years. My sister has been divorced for ten years after a two-month marriage.

Again, a similarity of images appears in these dreams, though the dreams did not exactly occur at the same time. However, this same woman submitted the following dreams:

My three-year-old son and I had recently moved from our house where we had lived with his dad, my husband. We were now on our own. On this particular night, I dreamed that a fire had started in the woods behind our apartment and was slowly creeping across the grassy field toward our apartment. As it moved closer, I began to panic and thought, "I have to call someone but first I have to get Jason (my son) and then run across the street to call a neighbor." But I couldn't find Jason. Then I heard a scream and I awoke; it was Jason. I ran into his room and he was sitting up in his bed crying. When I asked him, he said he was dreaming that our apartment was on fire.

* * *

The following night I dreamed I was standing in a big old barn, like a tobacco barn. It had a dirt floor. Nothing was happening. I was just standing there, but I began feeling very uncomfortable. I was in the center all alone and I began to feel panic, when again I heard a scream which woke me. I went to Jason's room; he was sitting in his bed crying. I asked him, "What were you dreaming?"

(Jason): I was dreaming that I was in a big barn with some kids. We were sitting up on the boards (rafters probably) and a big wind came and lifted the barn off the ground. It was whirling faster and faster and there was no floor and I thought I was going to fall.

I believe these dreams stem from our insecurities relative to being alone and in a new environment. Who do you suppose was tuned into whose dreams?

* * *

I have a very strong aversion to spiders, no matter how minute. However, on this night I dreamed of a very large, disgustingly furry spider. The spider was just sitting still on the wall. I didn't like it but I was not frightened. When I woke the following morning I could not dismiss the image.

Saturday night I went to a house party with some close friends. I walked into the living room of this home, where I had never been before, and there on the wall was an art piece, metal work, of a giant spiderweb with my spider sitting right in the center of it.

Clearly, it is not always easy to classify a dream as either undeniably psi-mediated or psychodynamic. However, close attention to details and patterns will help determine which of these types a dream is more likely to be. The following dream is a more striking example of psi:

I awoke from this dream about 2 a.m. quite shaken and trying to decide what to do. There was no doubt I had to do something.

I had dreamed that I was walking in a wooded area and came up to an edge of a cliff. I looked straight down. At the bottom lay my mother. She was wedged between a great rock and a wall, which rose straight up to where I stood. This shock woke me. I sprang from the bed and felt very frightened. I went to the telephone and called. There was no answer at the home that my mother and father shared in upstate New York. There was no going back to sleep. I believed my mother was lying somewhere injured. At 6:30 a.m. I went into work and called my parents' house again. No answer. At 7 a.m. I called my sister. She said she'd spoken to both my parents the day before in the afternoon and everything was fine. She gave me the telephone number of a neighbor. This neighbor, upon my telephone request, went to my parents' house. He repeated to me that no one answered the door but that he could hear a steady knock, knocking, but in looking into the house through the windows he could see nothing. I called the New York State Police, who forced their way into the house. They found my father wedged between his bed and the wall. He had his walking stick in his hand but was only able to move so much as to knock it against the wall which he faced. My mother had gone to a nearby town and wasn't expected back for days. After examination at the hospital, in addition to his Parkinson's disease, my father may have suffered a mild stroke. Later while staying with him he told me that it must have happened around 2 a.m. when he usually gets up for coffee. I learned that he does get up for coffee about 2 a.m.

As you have read about these different family-related dreams, you may have begun to notice a shared field of emotions, images, and feelings that emerge through the recurrence of shared symbols over time. In many ways, especially in family thematic dreams, it is once again not so much a question of *what* is the matter with you or the situation, but rather *who* is the matter with you. It is a personalized universe of psychic and psychological needs and dynamics. This field or shared fabric of influence has been termed the "family unconscious." From this point of view, the notion of boundaries is radically different than it is in other understandings of the way the psyche operates. It is neither the "materialist" view of the psyche that has been prominent in European theories nor the completely "spiritualized" view prevalent in Eastern theories. It is a more "personalized" and implicitly African philosophically rooted intuition of the dream process.

This family unconscious has been explored by this author and in the European Swiss movement by Leopold Szondi.[5] The orientation of these two approaches is quite different in many ways, yet the clinical observations are strikingly similar.

The dream, it seems, is like a continuous tissue of images, emotions, and events woven around the psychospiritual or numinous skeleton of our primordial existence. In later chapters, we will examine in greater detail the dynamics behind both the individual or psychodynamic dreams and systems-related family unconscious dreams. We will also look at those family unconscious dreams that at times go beyond the usual and express the more transpersonal dimensions of our consciousness. Indeed consciousness itself, like matter and energy, appears to be fundamentally transtemporal and trans-spatial or nonlocal in nature. But before we go even deeper into the labyrinth and the subjective chamber of dreaming sleep, what do we really know objectively about occurrences in sleep? What goes on psychophysiologically and psychologically that can be correlated with other information about the body and mind? For answers to these questions, we turn to the contribution of the modern sleep laboratory.

Research on Dreams

The Contribution of the Laboratory

Change and modification are a most prominent characteristic of any developing, or well-developed, science. No law or theory is to be accepted as final or absolute. Even the best developed sciences have abandoned or at least modified certain of the most strongly established of principles. . . . All that can be asked is that our theory maintain its close relationship to observation.

M. H. MARX, "THE GENERAL NATURE OF
THEORY CONSTRUCTION"

The mystery does not get clearer by repeating the question, nor is it bought with going to amazing places.

RUMI,
OPEN SECRET

THE FIRST
LABORATORIES

Formal trance induction, which dates back to perhaps 10,000 to 15,000 years BCE in the Nile Valley Fayum area, was the first systematic method of studying the corridors of sleep. The valleys were rich with food production and cattle raising. These peoples worshipped the sun and lived in the open, very close to the cycles and tides of nature. This expressed itself not only in their religion but in the precision with which nature expressed itself in the yearly rising and falling of the Nile. They carved the Sphinx and raised the pyramids. Here under the sun, not in the ice-covered caves of northern Europe, civilization as we currently know it took root. Here, the first great temples, celestial observatories, and tombs were erected in humanity's search for meaning, the purpose of our existence, and literally our place in the cosmos. Modern archaeology's technology has revealed this as an undeniable fact.[1] Other great outcrops of early civilization such as Göbekli Tepe in Turkey seemed to be derivatives of this great human expansion. In 1871 Charles Darwin wrote in *The Descent of Man* that "it is more probable that our early progenitors lived on the African continent more than anywhere else."[2] It is the place of the birth of humanity as a species and also the birth of civilization as we know it in some form today. It is also the birthplace of science, medicine, and the great arts of humankind. For the first time man became aware that there were four states of human consciousness—waking, dreaming, deep sleep, and the transcendental state or turyia—embedded in him. For the first time, the waking and the dreaming states were scientifically explored by direct observation and then by the codified comparison and reporting of these observations. Initially, this information was the exclusive province of the priests, the seers, the poets, and the scribes. Many centuries would pass before the knowledge spread beyond secret or initiate societies into the realm of the wider public.

THE MODERN MAP OF
REM AND NON-REM

Freud and Jung were the early chroniclers, in the European tradition, of a clinical and introspective study of dreams and sleep. They were operating primarily from a clinical and theoretical position. Their findings were both penetrating and controversial and, from a certain perspective, ultimately complementary. However, it was not until 1953, with the work of Eugene Aserinsky and Nathaniel Kleitman,[3] that detailed and intimate studies of the sleep experience were performed in the laboratory. These laboratory studies gave us new maps of this unseen but seeing world. Their laboratory work was the first clearly replicable clinical work on dreaming that had a significant degree of physiological and psychological correlation to the ongoing dreaming experience. More recent research since then has focused on dream content and the stages of activity in the midst of various periods of the sleep cycle. These periods of the sleep cycle are measured by EEG brain wave patterns and other physiological monitors. For the first time, Aserinsky and Kleitman had clearly demonstrated that the dream phase of the sleep cycle is a very active state in which there is coordinated rapid eye movement, or REM. While we are sleeping, our eyes move back and forth in a manner seemingly correlated with our dream process just as they do in the waking state. In the dreaming state, the rest of the body does not respond to conscious direction; in a certain sense it is dissociated, or what is known as sleep paralysis. This, of course, is not true of the waking state.

In addition, Aserinsky and Kleitman's work lent some mixed support to Freud's earlier notions of dreams as the guardian of sleep. There is a general sense that dreams occur "down in" sleep, and so the idea of "depth" is associated with dreaming sleep. Deep dreaming was once thought to be equal to a deep sleep. However, this is not true. Deep sleep and dreaming are different conditions and stages in the sleep cycle. Other arguments on the depth of sleep are possible, however, if you do not equate the depth of sleep with EEG patterns but rather with how difficult it is to rouse the person from sleep or the degree of activity of psychophysical processes that are known to be active only in certain states of sleep.[4] The *intensity* of dream experience is a better way to express the idea of depth here than the notion of deep EEG patterns. Aserinsky and Kleitman found the dream experience to be a fluid mental state in which nonlogical events, ideas, and associations occurred. There is an uncritical acceptance of such events as real and true as they are happening and a corresponding emotional reaction to this fluid "reality." Freud had noted how images in the dreams can be condensed, distorted, and mixed with recent memories of the last two or three days—called "day residue"—and trace memories from long ago then manifested dynamically in thematic and emotional stories. The laboratory also showed that when a person was not dreaming in sleep, his or her eyes did not show rapid eye movement. In other words, nondream episodes were expressed by non-REM states.

Over the next two decades, more and more data emerged from the laboratory about the dream and the nondream phases of the sleep cycle. It was found that the dream cycle rhythmically supervened the sleep cycle roughly every ninety minutes, and that this cycle of dreaming increased from approximately five minutes in the beginning of the nightly dream cycle to anywhere from twenty-five to forty minutes in the latter part of the dream cycle, usually occurring in the later part of the morning (see figure 2 on page 60). One theory is that this dream cycle is triggered by a noncortical system, which is one of the lowest in the phylogenic scale, the pontine-limbic system. If so, on some subtle level perhaps the REM dream activity is actually occurring almost all the time, and it is only outshined in the brighter light of the waking state! After all, even in the waking state there is often a constant background of buzzing mental reverie and dreamlike imaginal activity in most of us.

Now at the onset of sleep, the observing ego or witness consciousness experiences an open, loose, flowing state that eventually gives up

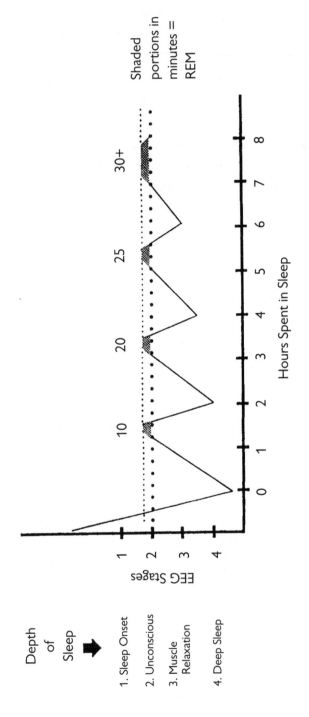

Depth
of
Sleep

1. Sleep Onset

2. Unconscious

3. Muscle
   Relaxation

4. Deep Sleep

Depth of Sleep =

EEG Stages

Hours Spent in Sleep

Shaded
portions in
minutes =
REM

1. General decrease in "awareness" of external stimuli and resistance to awakening
    when externally approached.

2. General decrease in Alpha EEG and increase in Theta, Delta EEG

Figure 2. REM-Dream Periods Averaged in Minutes

waking reality in a very prescribed sequence.[5] At first, the observing ego experiences itself as structuring and in control of internal and external mental stimuli. Then it goes through a destructuring process in which brief hallucinatory experiences occur, followed by a quick restructuring of imagery processes, almost in a defensive posture against the unfolding chaos. This occurs in a matter of minutes. As stated earlier, the mental and emotional content of the mind in sleep can be divided into two streams of consciousness and generally reflected by two types of eye movement, REM and non-REM. The REM cycle of one stream of consciousness is very active and is characterized by what is termed "primary process mentation," often of an extremely intense kind. It is rather thematic or story-like in its presentation of psychological material and carries with it varying degrees of emotional arousal. The non-REM mentation is characterized by a less fluid and more waking reality orientation. It is somewhat more logical than the primary process mode and came to be described by Freud as a kind of secondary elaboration process.

Dreaming actually can occur in some variation during all phases of the sleep cycle; these dreams are either remembered, forgotten, or repressed. There is some scattered evidence as we have suggested that dreaming may occur in non-REM sleep and that some brief REM periods may not be associated with dreaming.[6] However, in general the REM-dreaming association is quite strong for most of us. Typically, our morning dreams are remembered more than dreams occurring earlier in the sleep cycle.

A number of physiological correlates have been identified with our dreaming experience. Several of the more prominent ones are irregular heart rate, increased blood flow and blood pressure, increased respiration, sexual arousal in both men and women, coordinated rapid eye movement, sporadic activity of certain eye muscle groups accompanied by a motor paralysis or inhibition of the rest of the body, a low-voltage desynchronized cortical EEG pattern, and increased brain temperature in its metabolic state, all associated with the subjective recollection of dreams. As you can see, the autonomic nervous system becomes highly aroused. States of quiescence or relaxation or what we term a "cholinergic" state and an agitated or heightened state termed "adrenergic" occur very quickly, sometimes oscillating in the same person. This last fact is important in terms of our understanding of the dynamics enfolded in the psi process. The non-REM state, in contrast, is a more quiet state with a lower heart rate, respiration, and blood pressure. The brain's EEG pattern is a slowed and synchronized brain wave during the non-REM state.

The psychological events in the dream can be stimulated by external events but are generally the result of internal stimulation. Since the body is largely immobilized by the inhibition of motor neurons in the spinal cord and select regions of the brain stem, in all likelihood these internal signals to consciousness arise from the ponto-geniculo-occipital[7] (PGO) waves of the pontine brain stem. Dreaming is clearly a biologically stimulated process and not purely the result of repressed wishes and desires. All mammals have some REM and therefore probably some form of dream experience. Yes your dog probably dreams, sometimes maybe about you! However insofar as we know reptiles do not. Oddly enough the animal that sleeps the most is the Australian platypus, up to fourteen hours a day, while some marine mammals like dolphins, porpoises, whales, and even some birds sleep with one hemisphere at a time. Also, we must note in support of the biological activation-synthesis view of dream origin that certain regions of the brain are more stimulated during dreaming than other areas. In particular, the sensorimotor regions are quite active and manifest in subjective dream experience, while the senses of taste, smell, and actual physical pain are rarely so expressed. This does not in the least diminish the fact that dreams are *meaningful* and *symbolic* and may at times *transcend* waking-ego boundaries. "Information" patterns shared from one system to another are inherently such processes, because mind, meaning, and information are enfolded in curious ways. As energy-information-consciousness systems, they are by nature and definition on a deeper quantum mechanical level like energy itself, transtemporal and trans-spatial. This has implications for dream information sharing in human systems.

The biological impetus of dreaming, now established, relates to the biological *roots* of dreaming, not to the *meaning* of dreams. Origin is not teleology. Besides, the purely biological interpretation of dreams is predicated on the notion that the dreaming experience is a completely uncontrollable unconscious process. All this would be compromised or even radically altered should the dreamer suddenly transcend unconscious biology and become lucid or self-aware in the dream! This latter process of becoming self-aware or lucid in the dream is now also a laboratory-verified phenomenon.

Laboratory experiments have also taught us that sleep itself seems to be divided into four stages. The first stage—the sleep onset stage—which can be measured by a brain wave EEG, is what we described during our discussion of what happens when a person is just beginning to fall asleep.

The first level is not even really a stage of sleep but more what one would call a form of the waking state. It is usually described simply as drowsiness. Fluid imagery often emerges during this stage and is referred to as "hypnagogic" imagery. It is not, however, a form of hypnosis. The body temperature during this time is generally declining. One's eyes are closed and usually no longer moving. As drowsiness sets in, the usually irregular brain patterns become more synchronized into what is called "alpha." This alpha brain wave pattern usually engages us from 9 to 12 cycles per second and indicates a general state of relaxed wakefulness. However, once sleep onset really begins one moves further and further away from this condition. Then genuine stage one of sleep begins.

This new stage one begins with the brain going through some changes. If we were watching the EEG, we would note that the little written patterns on the EEG are smaller, indicating lower voltages. These squiggly lines change a great deal as they become more desynchronized and uneven. The person awakened at this state often experiences a floating sensation as the alpha rhythm gives way to a lower-voltage irregular pattern of the first stage of sleep. It would be relatively easy to awaken somebody at this stage.

The second classical stage of sleep reflects another shift in the field of experience. Stage two of sleep is a stage in which people are generally unconscious. If their eyes are held open, a technical procedure sometimes done in the sleep laboratory, the sleeping individuals do not perceive anything in the external world. External stimuli, while registered on the psychophysiological monitors, do not seem to disturb them. Their mental experience at this time is one of a vague floating sensation accompanied by a dreamlike quality to stimuli and events.

Stage three of classical sleep is when the brain enters yet another phase and reflects another shift in subjective experience. The muscles become very relaxed. The person breathes very evenly and the heart rate continues to slow down. Subjective experience is bland, sparse, and often themeless.

Finally, in the fourth stage of sleep, the person is most oblivious to any external stimuli. The muscles are extremely relaxed and the person rarely moves. This stage of "deep sleep" is dominated by the brain waves usually termed "delta." They are very slow, moving somewhere from .5 to 5 cycles per second. It is interesting to note that the intelligent mammals of the sea, the dolphins and whales, are often in this brain wave stage. However, for most humans, dreams do not occur in stage four, but curiously enough in the "higher" stages of sleep. You can see now why, as we mentioned earlier, the notions of depth in sleep, while correlated with the EEG pattern, are not absolute. Dreams obviously occur in sleep, but not in deep sleep. Yet if a dream is very intense and emotionally engaging, a person may be more difficult to arouse from the dream than if they were in a deeper stage of sleep.

About an hour and a half after sleep onset, the dreamer begins to move back up to the higher stages of sleep, into emergent stage one or REM sleep. This is the time in which dreams proliferate in the inner landscape. As a dream begins, many changes occur in the body. Breathing becomes irregular, and the heart rate becomes more variable. Interestingly enough, the same organs innervated by the autonomic nervous system are activated as they would be in a waking stage. People blush or become frightened, aroused, angry, elated, or depressed. Cognitive activity of all kinds is being mediated in this state. Thus, again, stages of extreme activation, termed "adrenergic" states, and extreme quiescence, termed "cholinergic" states, may occur very close together. This seems to be deeply related to the process of psi-mediated dreaming, as will be seen in the next few chapters.

During deep sleep without dreams, heart rate, respiration, and blood pressure are at their lowest. However, when REM occurs, heart rate, respiration, blood pressure, and other autonomic nervous system functions are extremely stimulated. After anywhere from five to twenty minutes of dream activity, called "dream mentation," we usually fall back into a lower stage or deeper level of sleep. This particular cycle occurs three to seven times a night, each time getting longer and longer toward morning. There is also correspondingly less time during the night spent in the deepest levels of sleep. Given that the autonomic nervous system and imagery are intensified during this stage, it is clear that this is a fertile area for research on the effects of imagery and metaphors on the autonomic nervous system and its role in the healing process. Indeed, there is some evidence to indicate that the immune system may be deeply implicated in some of these activities and holds out a potential for clinical treatment. These possibilities harken back to the older ways, the older systems of Delphi, Thebes, and of the lost, almost forgotten Meroë.

PATHWAYS OF THE UNCONSCIOUS: DREAMING, BIOCHEMISTRY, AND THE BRAIN

In ancient times, the dreaming self and its brain were ultimately a great and intimate mystery to humanity despite the knowledge teased from it by the hands of "science." This is no less true today. It has always been a passageway from one world to the next. J. Allan Hobson[8] and others have come to define the brain as a dream-state generator and have charted the downward and upward course of memory images of the brain system along with their subtle biochemical interactions. Apparently the pineal gland hormone called "melatonin" is released at night and acts directly on the dreaming system to increase and intensify the movement of sensory images from the brain stem itself to the cortex. This process moves us literally from the realm of the unconscious to the conscious. In balance with this, the pineal gland—known to be sensitive to light itself and identified in many meditative disciplines with the center of consciousness—releases the neurotransmitter "serotonin" during daylight. It is thought to increase the flow of memory images from the center of the conscious brain back to the unconscious memory storage.[9]

The role of the molecule "melanin" is crucial here. *Melanin absorbs light and energy.* It is located in crucial areas throughout the neurological system. One of these crucial areas, called the "locus coeruleus," is at the top of a long system of black neuromelanin, or melanin in the brain, that extends from this center and may project itself in a line all the way down the neuroembryological anlage (traces of the brain's earlier development in our mother's womb) that are still coiled deep in the brain from an earlier individual and collective or phylogenetic stage of development. Some believe that our collective unconscious memories and images move along this black neuromelanin nerve track from the unconscious brain stem up and through the locus coeruleus to consciousness itself in the higher brain centers.[10]

The eleventh pigmented nucleus of this neuromelanin nerve tract, a tract whose amount and degree of brain melanin steadily increases as one moves up the evolutionary scale, is located right below the locus coeruleus and is called the "substantia nigra," or black substance. It derives its name from the high concentration of this melanin, again a molecule exceedingly responsive to light.[11] Richard D. King, M.D., and others have pointed out that when there is a loss of melanin, afflicted patients develop Parkinson's disease, a disorder of motor movement and thought. It is treated by administering L-dopa, a chemical that produces melanin and compensates for the loss of melanin in the substantia nigra. King also points out that when an increase of melanin is provided, patients experience an increase in vivid dreams, hallucinations, illusions, and even confusional psychosis, which may reflect the intense flooding of consciousness by the upward flow of memory images of all kinds—personal, familial, and collective.

The usual medications employed to treat psychotic states are phenothiazines, which are believed to work by blocking dopamine. Hallucinogens and stimulants such as LSD, DMT, mescaline, and amphetamines all serve to increase melatonin, melanin, and dopamine. DMT (dimethyltryptamine) in particular is thought to be a natural hormone and neurotransmitter/neuromodulator that is implicated in dreaming. It is found naturally in the human body, including the pineal gland, and seems to reach its highest concentration in our bloodstream at about 3 a.m., right when our dreaming cycle is increasing. Tranquilizers, such as phenobarbital, decrease melatonin, melanin formation, and dopamine. Finally, King has noted that melatonin, the hormone that increases melanin when given to normal people, will increase feelings of tranquility and enhance dream states in persons able to translate unconscious memory images into consciousness.

For King and others, the locus coeruleus is quite literally the brain's doorway to the collective unconscious. It is a critical brain center which, when appropriately stimulated, will initiate REM sleep and the flow of dream images of a personal, familial, and collective nature.

It is no wonder that so many images of the collective unconscious have both highly personalized and universal dynamics that play out in our dreams. Sometimes they may be derivatives of some actual historical event in our shared memory that rises to our attention when stimulated by critical moments in our personal history. An excellent candidate for this is the Black Madonna.

Many writers and clinicians have recently drawn our attention to the large emergence or reemergence of powerful archetypal feminine symbols arising in our dreams.[12] In particular, the archetypal figure of the Black Madonna holds a great deal of meaning for us on a collective and personalized level. She was a common image in ancient Kemetic Egypt. The Egyptian goddess Isis was black, as were many goddesses. At one time the cultic influence of Isis in some form stretched from Ethiopia and Dravidian southern India, through the Middle East and the northern Mediterranean. She preceded Christianity by thousands of years and reflected the matriarchal essence and origin of religion and civilization.[13] A variation of her was worshipped in ancient Europe when Europe was a matriarchal, goddess-oriented culture, from 6500 to 3500 BCE.[14] She may have been the psychological origin of the later Biblical Eve, since the myth of Adam and Eve is a reflection of the Osiris and Isis story. The Bible itself may have originated in the ancient Kemetic city of Byblos. Isis worship was the dominant cult in Rome before Christianity. It was also perhaps believed that she was a messenger from the Nile Valley civilizations of ancient Nubia and Egypt, the oldest known civilization with which we have some sense of continuity.[15]

To the contemporary Jungian clinician Isis's reemergence represents two images brought together. She is the Great Mother, but she is also human, with an earthiness in her. She was collectively worshiped for thousands of years for her fecundity on Earth, the bountiful harvest, the flowers, the living earth itself. She is clearly associated with sexuality, childbirth, and the whole feminine love and lust for life.[16]

Isis is also a dark or shadow figure who is hidden and reflects the collectively hidden in us. She may also, I believe, represent that first mitochondrial DNA mother in whose genetic pool all human lineages were crossed somewhere in Africa perhaps 150,000 years ago and whose legacy lives in us collectively today on both an intimate genetic and psychological level.[17]

As a reflection of the female principle, the goddess—in predominantly patriarchal times and cultures like our own until recently—has been largely repressed. Her reemergence coincides with our dawning collective need to renew the planet Earth, which as an ecosystem is clearly at risk. In a sense, Gaia, the ancient Greek word for the earth spirit, calls through the collective unconscious to us to heal the planet Earth and the living earth of human relationships in our own lives. This intimate and interconnected drama is not solely the product of New Age inspiration but is a living, *personalized,* and collective message from the genetic, biochemical, evolutionary, and primal levels of our being as a species. The body and mind sense and respond to deep ecological and evolutionary currents in the wider environment in which we all live.

It is perhaps no accident that the Black Madonna appeared at the dawn of civilization and self-consciousness in Africa, cast a shadow across the empires of Egypt, Rome, and India, and now reappears in our dreams in a world beset with a potentially holocaustic ecological and nuclear crisis. In this regard, it makes perfect sense that the image of the Black Madonna should be the symbol of one of the recent geopolitical world's more hopeful, successful, and liberating developments: the Polish Solidarity movement of Walesa and others. She is an unfolding dream from the racial, biochemical, and luminous depths of the brain. She represents the first mother, the Living Darkness, the sacred dimension of the female body, and the emergent redemption of Earth.

FAMILY DREAMS AND BODILY SENSATIONS

It is curious, given all of the somatic and psychological experiences occurring at the time of REM, that we do not perceive more connections than we do. In other words, our body is constantly giving us information or feedback regarding the way we are managing our lives. Sometimes in curious ways the dream and the waking states show a powerful cross-fertilization. This cross-fertilization often occurs in the process of the dreamwork. I am referring to those dreams that seem to tell the conscious mind of an upcoming physical or psychological difficulty that the somatic and psychological unconscious are struggling with. In some rare instances, a dream may be so powerful that it stimulates one of the senses, and the sensation carries over to the waking stage. In the following dream, in addition to the family dynamics, notice the operation of the sense of smell:

My father died suddenly in 1978 without my having had the chance to see him or to speak with him the year before his death. He had made a strong case for my coming to visit the year before and I accused him of being morbid and overdramatic but he claimed that he might not be around much longer. After his death I felt a great grief that I had lost the opportunity to tell him how much I loved him. In my dreams following his death I was always surprised to see him back from death and very sad to only make brief and unsatisfactory contact with him in my dreams.

In 1984 I had a dream that changed all that. The setting of the dream was in a kitchen of an unfamiliar house that appeared to have been built in the late 1800s. The kitchen had high ceilings and mostly antique furnishings. In the first part of the dream, which seems very separate from the substance of most of the dream, my mother and I are apparently alone serving food to the country western star Waylon Jennings and a few of his friends at a table in the dining room. My memory of this first part is fragmentary, as if it was part of an older dream I had been having which created the setting of the more important dream.

When we had finished serving, my mother reminded me that we had to attend another event and asked me why I was wearing her dress, the one she intended to wear to the next meeting. Completely surprised to find that I had her dress on, I looked down to find that I also had stained it. I apologetically volunteered to iron the dress and to clean the stain with a wash rag. I busied myself setting up the ironing board and began to iron the dress.

At this point in the dream I became aware of a complete and pregnant silence. The oddness of it or the meaningfulness of it caught my attention and I looked around at my mother. She was staring in respect and in shock at something beyond my vision in the dream. I nervously looked around to the other side of the kitchen and saw my sister Kathy and another sister Judith staring in the same direction as my mother.

When I looked back in the direction where they were staring, all struck in reverence, I saw my father standing beside the green kitchen wall. He was looking at me with his characteristic look of love and strong emotion. I had the distinct impression that he was there for me and in the dream I was aware of the distinct impression that this was not a dream. I was also aware that my father looked as if he had been dead for some time. His pallor was greenish, he was very slender and he stood looking weighted down and weak with his hand across his chest. There was a distinct Christ-like aura about the way he looked; he was nude except for a diaper-like cloth covering his loins. I knew in the dream that he had traveled a vast distance by the weariness of his face. I felt in the dream that he had not entered heaven (which was his supreme goal in his life as a devout Christian) and that we were in a sort of interim meeting place in a dream environment.

I recall looking back at my mother and both my sisters. Each remained dumbfounded or hesitant. Both of these sisters have threatened my closeness to my father as has my mother over the years. I was aware of a chance I wanted to take, that this was unusual and that I might not have much time. I assertively walked to my father, held his hands, and led him to a small table with two chairs where I sat and I leaned from the other chair toward him, very close, while still holding his hands. Never losing eye contact, I told him how much I loved him, how much I had missed him since his death, how sorry I was that I had not listened to him about his death predictions, and how grateful I had been when he had been with us. I told him that I was certain I would not have been what I am today had it not been for him. I could see that his eyes were bloodshot, but he was looking at me and smiling with tears in his eyes. The emotion between us was amazing and overwhelming. I believe I woke up at this point because I seemed to be crying as I awakened. As I became aware that I was awake, I had a sense that I had been with my father in a very real sense of the word.

Another interesting aspect of the waking up in the dream was that a distinct odor of my father seemed to remain on my hands and nearby after I had awakened. I don't know whether this was a memory pattern activated by the dream or not.

After this incident, I had a clear sense of finality that I would not see my father again. I've never been aware of dreaming of him again and I have had a clear sense of peace and resolutional closure. It is hard to express the nonverbal sense of "knowing" something, but I am clear that this resolves something for me in a very powerful and final sort of way. Nothing like this has ever happened to me before in this way. It is uncharacteristic of sorrow, loss, and guilt. If this is not a family dream but allusive dream, then it very creatively answered an unconscious need.

This dream, in which the autonomic nervous system stimulates or is stimulated by the subject and then is incorporated into the dream, is not unusual. What follows is another example of this type of experience submitted to the Family Dreams Research Project. Interestingly enough, it involves the interaction of one person's physical and somatic process with the intimate psychological process of someone else in the family and yet the distance between them is quite significant:

I was in the Air Force stationed in Athens, Greece in 1980. I'm sorry I don't remember the exact date or time. I was, at that time, very unhappily married and had just been involved in another violent altercation with my husband. He had stormed out of the apartment, and I was left sitting in the dark on the bedroom floor crying. I had very strong feelings against divorce. I could think of no other way out of that unbearable position, so I sat there in the dark and began to plan my own suicide. I was severely depressed.

As I sat and cried, I suddenly felt I had a hand on my shoulder, patting gently. It was a very warm hand and it comforted me. I immediately felt better. I thought no more of suicide, but was frightened because this was so weird. I got up off the floor, turned on the light, and looked in the mirror. There wasn't anything on my shoulder, but still I could feel the patting. I was afraid that maybe I was having a religious experience of some kind. This frightened me because I had never been very religious. I also thought that maybe I was having a hallucination and that I was having a breakdown. Still, I felt so much better that I laid down on the bed and went to sleep again. The invisible hand was still patting my shoulder until I fell asleep.

I didn't tell anyone about this experience because I didn't want to be locked up, until some days later (exactly the time it took to get a letter from home). I got a letter from my mother in Wichita and the very first sentence she asked me was what was wrong. She said that she felt that I needed her badly, but she couldn't do anything to help. (We didn't have a phone in our apartment or any way to be contacted.) The time and date she gave in the letter matched exactly with the time of my strange experience (given the time differences).

I know that this sounds unbelievable, but I swear that it is true. I have told very few people about it over the years, because I don't want people to think that I am a fruitcake.

I was not very close to my mom. I never had been. I wondered at the time if it had been my father, because we had always been closer. Also, my mother's hands had been very cold, so I didn't think it could have been her. After I got the letter, I remembered that she had recently had open heart surgery, and that my sister had mentioned that Mom's circulation had improved and that her hands were warm now.

Laboratory and clinical experiences have told us for several decades now that the emotional and subjective experiences of a dream state can have profound implications for the mind and body, and in some cases can be harbingers of physical experiences in the waking state. The above two dreams are somewhat dramatic instances of this. At the present time, these processes are not fully understood by clinical science. This is especially the case when the autonomic nervous system of one person appears to influence the autonomic nervous system of another emotionally related person, in spite of some physical distance between them and in the absence of direct communication between the two.

E. Douglas Dean and others have shown that a subject in an experiment will respond differentially on an autonomic nervous system level to stimuli about emotionally important people under certain conditions.[18] In their experiments, subjects were attached to a plethysmograph, which measures the volume of blood in a finger. The subject was presented with twenty cards. The first five cards contained names chosen randomly from a telephone book. The second five consisted of friends of the experimenter. The third five were names of people with whom the subject had close emotional ties. The last five were control cards and had no names. The recording mechanism was placed in another room with the experimenter and an observer. The experimenter shuffled the deck, chose the top card, concentrated on the name, and attempted to communicate extrasensorily with the subject, who was in a very relaxed state.

Dean found statistically significant data confirming that the baseline of the plethysmograph, a reflection of heart (empathic-affective) or cardiac and autonomic functioning, fluctuated more markedly while the experimenter focused on the names of people with whom the subject had a strong emotional relationship. This is an unusual finding and implies something about our subtle energetic interconnectedness with each other. Clinical science at the present time as we shall see next is much more comfortable with the dreams that seem to reflect or predict some physical calamity within the sphere of one's own body.

THE DREAM AND BODILY ILLNESS

Some clinicians[19] have explored the relationship between the dreamer's biology or body and their dreaming mind. They have focused on the biological and somatic dimension of dreaming as they look at catastrophic dreams of death and destruction provided by their patients with serious somatic diseases. Many have come to believe that dreams are a reflection of the psyche's attempt to libidinize, or try to make life affirmative, the mounting destructive forces of an organic disease. When the self or the ego is threatened, be it on a bodily or psychological level, it is expressed in dream formation. Other writers[20] have noticed the unusually large number of destructive and death-related images in the dreams of their patients with psychosomatic diseases. Much more interesting, however, is that others[21] have shown how dreams with such content seemingly increase in occurrence just before severe heart attacks among a number of patients. These dreams clearly would reflect an impending mass of somatic process.

Studies by Robert Smith[22] indicated that hospital patients with physical illnesses indeed have dreams that are *reactive* to their biological situation. He noticed that those men and women with higher incidences of death in their dream content had a much poorer prognosis and vice versa. For men the symbols were of death; for women the symbols were of separation. It is easy to see how an intimate biological process such as an illness would naturally have a profound effect on a person's dreaming mind. The body is largely unconscious. A large portion of the mind is unconscious. Here the mind is dreaming the body and the body is dreaming the mind.

There are many dreams in which this pattern of a massive autonomic nervous system arousal can be seen. The following dream series and summary is an example that appears often. Notice the sense of *physical* arousal and stimuli that occur in coordination with the imagery and information in this dream. It follows a typical pattern.

Before I go further, let me tell you that I have never used drugs, and I am part Indian on my mother's side. I don't watch T.V. nor do I indulge in science fiction or fantasy literature. I'm a college graduate. Now what brings me to write this letter is this. In April of 1985, the 21st to be exact, I had a nightmare kind of dream. It was about my mother. Her doctor and me were both involved. It was stormy in the dream and my mother had a very surprised, startled look on her face. I wanted to rescue her in the dream. When I awoke, I had a very overwhelming feeling that something awful had happened. It was that morning that I was told that my mother had died. After that I started taking note of my dreams. A friend of mine was pregnant, and I had a dream that she was crying and crying. She said in the dream, "It really wasn't a baby." Later on she had a premature baby with a severe birth defect. I had another dream in which a very dear friend of mine looked very gray, haggard, and sick. I found out later he was fighting a bout with cancer.

Though the exact dynamics are not known, what is clear is that a massive arousal of the autonomic nervous system is involved in dreams of this kind. Just as a person's physical symptoms can be expressed by symbols in the dream that contain meaning for the dreamer and their family, the body itself may express family dreams and family emotional symptoms and situations for the dreamer. Each is enfolded into the other.

DREAMS AND CREATIVITY

From the foregoing we can come to certain conclusions about the relationship between laboratory work and the autonomic nervous system and dreams, especially unusual dreams. REM, a process occurring in humans and other mammals alike, seems to increase both with individual development and with group or species evolution. It is not far-fetched to suggest that, since subjectively dreams employ the same principles of formal or formative intelligence and novel creativity that are used in the waking state, they therefore are as real to the body as the waking state.

Dreams have often been the springboard for deep inspirational creative work and have also provided true scientific insight and artistic creativity. We have only to remember the scientific work of Dmitri Mendeleev and the periodic table, Nobel laureate Otto Loewi and the biochemical transmission of nerve impulses, or Elias Howe and the lock-stitch sewing machine to see the power and creativity of an incubated dream. There is the musical genius of Beethoven, Saint-Saëns, Stravinsky, Brahms, and Wagner, not to mention the poets Blake, Milton, and Poe.[23] The dream and its powerful imagery, motivations, and psychophysical dynamics are intimately involved in the creative process. We can see from just the few dreams we have looked at so far that dreams are indeed another form of creative evolutionary intelligence, of the mind seeking wider and wider expression in humanity. It is not only in the waking state that we are creative and intelligent!

It must also be remembered that dreams sometimes are an attempt to solve individual, personal, and family problems. While we dream of each other we sometimes dream *for* each other, especially when trying to solve a problem in the shared system. Dreams continue to stimulate and develop the mind as does the world of the waking state. In other words, as we become older and more evolved, our dreamlife often becomes more evolved. We have seen how dreams sometimes warn of impending physical illness and can also reflect our preoccupation with physical illnesses. We have also seen how dreaming and its anomalous information processing can express a psychic dimension of our personality and our existence. When dreams of a profound revelatory or novel informational nature occur, there is literally an alteration in consciousness even in the dream state at this time.

Dreamlife, like family life, has a pulse on the life of the individual. Dr. Francis Crick and others are correct about the cyclic uprush of biological and subcortical processes into the system every ninety minutes that accounts for the rhythmic pattern of the dream. I disagree, however, with their assertion that the forebrain imposes an arbitrary order or meaning on this upsurge in life energy, or bioenergetic pulse. I believe that this pulse is an intelligent life force and the dream language is but another language of the mind that potentially opens beyond space and time and purely rational secondary elaboration. Indeed, the dream seems to point to something infinitely beyond the shifting structures of mind itself. Let us now proceed further into normal family dreams with all their stress and strain. What seem to be some of the underlying dynamics that we observe in these dreams? What are some of the various types of night dreams that different family members have?

5

Defining Normal
Family Dreams

The family molds the kinds of persons it needs in order to carry out its functions, and in the process each member reconciles his past conditioning with present role expectations. . . . In the struggle, the choice of particular defenses against anxiety is also selectively influenced by the family pattern.

N. ACKERMAN,
THE PSYCHODYNAMICS OF FAMILY LIFE

THE INTIMATE WEB
IS AWAKE

Family dreams and the intimate web they unfold encompass the whole spectrum of human emotionality and thought. We dreamed in the winter cave, we dreamed on the sun-warmed plains. We dreamed during the ice age and we dreamed in the deserts. We dreamed in the forests and we dreamed in war. We dreamed as priests and we dreamed as warriors. Throughout history, the characters that have populated our inner stages are those most intimate with us. As powerful themes and images emerge, intense motivation and wishes for love appear. Often fear and forbidden sexuality arise and give birth to guilt and shame. Pride and blame and power and innocence have all populated the inner landscape of the dream. Their faces are those of friend, family, and foe. When we share our dreams we see how we ourselves have looked and appeared to others in various roles as we move through the family life cycle. This can be awe inspiring, humbling, and intimate all at the same time. The vast majority of these feelings, often intense and sometimes bizarre, would still form the category of normal emotional expression. As we go through the following family dreams and emotions, note the similarity to your own.

Number 1

I dreamed of my first cousin on my father's side of the family and his wife (my dad's older brother's oldest son, whose name is Joel R.) and also his wife (Buela R.). They were sort of gliding down a hallway and had very dismal looks upon their faces. They parted and went into two separate rooms. The place was very foggy and there was no conversation at all. This is the first time I ever recall dreaming of them. I did not see myself in this dream, but I remember being very glad to see them at first, but after seeing them it felt strange. I then woke up.

Number 2

I dreamed of my Uncle Charles R. (my dad's older brother, father of the above first cousin). We were at my Aunt Elizabeth A.'s house (my dad's sister). He just walked through the house and was dressed in a baby blue three piece suit. He looked as though he had no emotions, a very stern look which is the way he generally looks; however, I have only seen him with one suit at a wedding and this was not the same suit. In other words, he rarely wears a suit. Nothing was said. My aunt just looked at him. I just looked at him and he appeared as though he did not acknowledge our presence.

Number 3

I dreamed of my Aunt Dorothy R. (who is the wife of the above uncle). She was standing in a long, flowing, baby blue gown in the middle of a lake, pond, or body of water. She had a sad look upon her face also. She spoke no words. There were other ladies in the water, but they all were a lot older than she is (45 years old approximately, they looked in their 70s). They were all dressed in gowns.

* * *

The significance of these three dreams was that they all occurred in one week and surrounding one branch of my family. I learned that weekend from my aunt mentioned in Dream Number 2 that my cousin and his wife mentioned in Number 1 were divorcing, and there had been a lot of quarreling amongst the family. This would definitely explain the nonhappy looks on their faces in the parting described in Dream Number 1.

The dreamer, obviously a good observer and record keeper of her own family dreams and psychodynamics, goes further:

Number 4

I dreamed of being in or near a swamp and that my Aunt Elizabeth A. (in Dream Number 2) and my cousin Melissa A. (her daughter) were saving me from being eaten by alligators. I, of course, felt very relieved, and they showed no signs of emotion.

Number 5

I dreamed of going to a warehouse of sorts where our father's side of the family was gathered. I was talking to everyone mentioned before and then some more relatives, but do not recall exactly who. My grandmother was there, too, and she is dead. The building itself was light green. There was a lot of food, like a reunion.

* * *

The significance of this dream was that my first cousin (mother's side) whose name is Joe B. and also lives with me and my mother told me a few days later that he dreamed that he and I went into a big warehouse of sorts. It was light green in color and many of my dad's relatives were there. As much as I could figure, it was the same night. He said that he dreamed in addition to that that he walked over to a certain room in this place where my grandmother's room was. She was not there and there was a typewriter that was typing by itself. This room was also light green in color and had a high bed. But he knew it was her room. He described it as being a shrine of sorts. I could not recall this in my dream.

One can easily see how the normal dynamics, stresses, and aspirations of family life can become involved in our nightly dreams. We see how we appear to others in their dreams of us as we all go through crises in the family life cycle. Some have a fleeting psi process implicated in them. Clearly, however, not every dream and certainly not every family dream is a psi-mediated dream. In fact the vast majority are not.

Dear Dr. Bynum:

I read an article about your research in family dreams. . . . It made me think of a dream my mother told me about once, so I telephoned her and asked her to repeat it to me.

She still remembers it clearly, even though it occurred 36 years ago. At the time, their own mother (my grandmother) had been dead for about one year. My parents lived in Windsor, Ontario and my mother's brother, Eugene, lived in Montreal, Quebec. Another brother, Edward, also lived in Quebec.

My mother had returned home at noon, from a stay in the hospital (gall bladder removal), and was still quite ill. The telephone rang numerous times during the evening, but my mother was too sick to get out of bed to answer it. My father was at work, so the telephone remained unanswered. That night, my mother had a dream (see next dream).

The next morning, the phone rang again and my father answered it. It

was my Uncle Edward, calling to tell my mother that their brother Eugene
had been killed in an auto accident the preceding day. It was Edward who
had been phoning the previous evening, trying to communicate the sad news.

I don't know if this will be of any use to you, but I wanted to pass it
along on the chance that it might be. This is a true recounting.

Here is the dream that this dream researcher's mother had:

There was a black panther running around and around our house, trying
to get inside. My brother Eugene was in the house with me, and he got a
butcher knife and said that he would kill it. I told him, "No, don't hurt it,
it's Mom. It's Mom!" I just knew that that black panther was our mother,
and that she wanted to get into the house, and I had to convince Eugene.
I woke up, sweating, with my heart pounding.

Notice the symbolism, the affect, and the motivational power of the
attempted message that was being communicated. Perhaps it was a psi-
mediated dream, but probably not. However, it is an indication of how
powerful normal family unconscious dynamics are.

Here are two other rather normal but emotionally intense dreams
that involve common modern metaphors for communication—the telephone and the mail:

My mother had had a dream that a close friend of the family (who at
the time lived in New York City; we lived in Virginia) was gravely ill. The
next morning she telephoned to see how she was. Luckily everything was
fine, but this continued to bother my mother. Later that day we received
a telegram at home that my grandfather on my mother's side, who lived
in San Pablo, Brazil, South America, had died the night before. We were
told that he had called for my mother quite a bit just before dying.

And now this one, expressed not through the medium of the telephone but through the metaphor of the mail system:

My sister sent me an article on your research which appeared in a recent issue of Omni, *the science magazine. This was sent to me in response to something that had happened to both of us.*

I wrote her a letter about a dream that I had about her: she was pregnant, and gave birth to a kitten. She wrote me a letter about a dream in which she had been arguing with a being that was generally half animal, half cat. Our letters crossed in the mail. This hasn't happened to us before, although we both are involved in our dreams. We write each other about our dreams very rarely (once a year or so), so perhaps it happens more often without our knowing it.

As you can readily see, sometimes an intense family-related dream is not as direct an expression of the external reality as the dream first seems to be. Sometimes, unusual corridors of information are expressed or reflected in dreams (e.g., one dreams the opposite of what is actually going to occur, or of a person or relative who actually symbolizes or represents another person in the relational web). We have seen this expressed so far in the dreams that have been presented in this study. The point is that normal dreams can sometimes be quite surprising. They can be irrelevant or even quite bizarre. Sometimes they can be a curious mixture of bizarre, spiritual, illuminating, and tragic. Notice the following example in which more than just two members of the family were involved:

Family dreams? Proofs? Yes indeed. My favorite example is one that occurred several years ago. On a Saturday morning (about 7:30 a.m.) I met my Uncle (Bill) in the dream state. He looked around in a rather bewildered way. Watching him I asked "did you die?" to which he replied, "I'm not sure." I called the name of a spiritual being who I was sure could help in this situation, and he appeared to us. With unspoken understanding he took my uncle to a place out west where my uncle was to spend three days "sorting things out." The place was one of the many national parks my uncle loved and camped at in his life.

I then woke up and wrote a letter to my uncle. I wrote of the dream plus an explanation about the person I introduced him to, as he (my uncle) was a devout Christian, and I didn't want him to take offense. I sent the letter, not knowing if he would ever get it. As it was, he did in fact die, exactly one week later. I found out through my mother (his sister) my letter was received the Thursday following his actual death. I thought I might make a hasty trip back to Illinois to go to the funeral, but then realized that I got the letter on the very day of the funeral. I decided to call my uncle's house and sure enough the whole family was there. I asked about my letter and my cousin went through the stack that was piling up on the table. She found it, opened it, and read it to the family. After reading it she commented that they all had had dream experiences in which it was clear that he was saying farewells.

You may well be asking yourself, what is the difference between this dream and a nightmare, and do they sometimes happen in the same situation? Also, how does the person know when they are dreaming and when they are actually having some profound and altered consciousness experience of a dreamlike nature but are actually in the waking state? These are all very difficult questions, but we do know something about the difference between dreaming, nightmares, and those other more unusual states of consciousness.

FAMILY DREAMS, NIGHTMARES, AND NIGHT TERRORS

In general, a nightmare is an unpleasant and high-anxiety-producing dream that usually occurs late during the night, often in the last three hours of sleep. It frequently unfolds in a long REM period of twenty to thirty minutes and is accompanied by blood pressure and heart rate increases.[1] Sometimes, however, nightmares occur just as the dreamer falls off into sleep. These are more properly called "hypnagogic nightmares." The nightmare is usually peopled by either unusual events, powerful frightening situations, or some combination of these. Often we will suddenly awake from a nightmare with an intense sense of fear or anxiety. Many different ways of working with the nightmare are common in the family and the individual clinical hour. The gestalt technique is a very powerful one. It involves working with, entering, and changing the dream content and process while awake. This can take place either in the clinical office or over the family breakfast table.

Children often have nightmares during a certain period of their development. These can come and go at different times. Adults occasionally will have nightmares when life stresses become very intense. Experiencing nightmares regularly as an adult is somewhat more unusual. In situations like this, the adult is invariably attempting to come to terms with a frightening event, memory, or anticipation. We will have more to say about this last aspect in the later chapter on the dreamlife of adult children of alcoholics (ACOA).

A night terror is something very different from both a regular night dream and its more brutal cousin, the nightmare. It also occurs during sleep. However, while a nightmare contains images and symbols, as does a normal dream, the night terror does not. It swims up from a deeper current of the night and we awaken only with a sense of overwhelming terror, awe, unearthliness, and dread. It is often accompanied by sweating, convulsive body sensations, and even screams. Often people on the brink of a serious psychological disturbance will have a night terror. At the present time, night terrors are treated primarily with medication. Night terrors are more common in children, who usually simply outgrow them without recourse to therapy or medication. They seem to occur in a deeper stage or level of sleep than dreams do, usually stage three or four. Night terrors are also associated with other unusual psychophysical symptoms that occur in deep sleep. These medical and psychophysical symptoms are the so-called parasomnias. Some of these parasomnias are activities such as urination, walking, talking, and other behaviors that when carried out in the waking state are quite normal, but are clearly problems when they occur in sleep. Some criminal activities have been associated with people in sleep carrying out illegal activities. They are dealt with in the clinical hour and in the sleep laboratory. When observed in the sleep laboratory, the heart rate and blood pressure have been noticed to double sometimes. The parasomnias occur within the first few hours of sleep and in that sense are thought of by some clinicians as disorders of arousal.[2]

The nightmare, however, is often a reflection of a family unconscious pattern of relationships and conflicts. This can be a normal transient stress that the family is going through or it may be an unusual and chronic stressor in the family. Often the child identified as the "patient" will have this nightmare, though this is not always the case. This first dream is a classical common nightmare dream of a mother and her children.

> I woke last night after having a terrifying dream about my 6-year-old son. At least once a month for the last year or so I have had dreams in which I lost or almost lost my son. These dreams are gradually becoming more frequent and much more terrifying. I have had very few but similar dreams involving all of my children. In these dreams I do not actually lose any of my children but there is a threat of loss or danger to them. The one child who is most threatened is the same one who is lost in frequent dreams. I had made up my mind this morning to call a psychologist or sleep disorder clinic.

This is clearly a family-related anxiety dream. With a dream like this occurring with increasing intensity, the woman's inner wisdom to seek external guidance from a professional was clearly called for. Her nightmare reflected certain family dynamics and would still be in the realm of a normal dream. The following dream is also a normal dream and is not classically a nightmare in terms of terrifying visual symbols. However, it expresses an emotional nightmare of rigidity and of feeling imprisoned while experiencing powerful emotions.

A little background: My father comes to Cincinnati from Baton Rouge, Louisiana for Thanksgiving 1985. I have two brothers and they come from Columbus and Winston-Salem. My father had not been well for a couple of years and had taken a turn for the worse after my mother drowned in June. He no longer cared for life. When I took him to the airport, I knew he wouldn't last long. A week later he was in a coma.

The dream came at about 3 a.m. on a Monday morning. In it, my older brother and I were frantically searching a hospital for our dad. We became separated and I searched until I opened the door and found them. I sat by his bed and began to cry. My dad had always been stern, hardnosed. He opened his eyes, looked at me and said, "Don't start any of that whoo whoo crap. Be tough." My brother and I sat tearless by his bed as he died.

I awoke and looked at the clock, 3 a.m. My fiancée also woke up and I told her of the dream. The phone rang at 3:15. It was a friend from Baton Rouge. He had sad news about my father.

FAMILY PATTERNS:
DREAMS AND WAYS OF ENFOLDMENT

These are powerful and unusual—but still normal—dreams that occur in a family context. They are to a certain extent predictable or normal even if they are sometimes a little unsettling. They tend to occur during major life shifts or life-change and stress situations. In our earlier discussion of the family unconscious, these normal dreams were certainly within the sight of Freud as he evolved psychoanalysis. Freud's awareness of family influence on the intrapsychic dreamlife of the individual was quite pervasive in his work. The earliest works of family-oriented thinkers and therapists have elaborated on the influence of family dynamics on the structuring of conscious and unconscious functioning. I wish to also emphasize the influence on somatic and kinesthetic reactivity. The family as a *living* psychosocial unit is well known and accepted. I would also go so far as to bring in the family as a *somatically influencing* organization. The experience and observation of certain primary images, emotions, and themes in action as a family develops over time is a formidable task to undertake but offers invaluable insight into one's own origins and subtle styles, both cognitive and somatic.

The family conveys or transmits styles, including characterological styles, attitudes, and personality traits, not to mention particular preferences and perceptual styles, in its everyday behavior. From these cognitive and emotional styles and character types we can begin to see that certain recurrent transactional patterns are preferred ways of relating and can lead to what we would think of as a stabilized energy system. Over time, these systems help structure, localize, and solidify relationships within a family. There is a covert group hypnotic induction process going on here. These systems are in a certain way enfolded in us. We carry these "deep structure" patterns outside and beyond the family. It goes without saying that our children pass them on to their children. This occurs regardless of whether these patterns are healthy or not, usual or unusual, or even if they sometimes reflect a quite disturbed emotional constellation. The unhealthy family can sustain intense delusions in the face of contrary facts when its shared family unconscious is deeply infused with a certain theme or themes. Unhealthy family patterns can manifest in family dreams or nightmares. However, as we have seen, nightmares can occur in normal families. In fact, most nightmares do occur within normal families. Also psi or parapsychological phenomena occur primarily in normal families.

There is much evidence to support the argument that the healthier a family is, the more likely they are to be able to communicate deeply about powerful subjects not only in the waking state but also in the dream state. These communications in all likelihood are connected to particular crisis points in the family's normal developmental pattern. These developmental patterns are expressed in specific stages of family development. Interweaving patterns of intelligence, energy, and motivation help us to see how these patterns are not located totally within an individual but within and between individuals in the overall family system. In other words, they are nonlocal. This interweaving of patterns and energy communication among family members helps us to view the individual psyche as an open system as opposed to a primarily intrapsychic or atomistic model. In the state of sleep especially, psychological and psychic boundaries are significantly relaxed. In this wider space, heteropsychic influences are more likely to populate one or another's subjective experience.

At times, our individual psyche appears to operate as an open field with networks of influence in mutual formation and information. During sleep in particular, the psyche is in a more expansive, relaxed, cholinergic condition. In these non-ego-domained conditions the psyche connects or reconnects with other psyches in the field. It should be noted at this point that the notions of discrete localization and fields are abstractions, and that the reality is of one undivided wholeness in flowing movement. In this relaxed state the psyche has a certain wave/field character. However, at other times the psyche seems to be contracted, tensed, and adrenergic or focused. In other words, in terms of great stress in our dreams, the psyche has a focus point or discrete particle aspect to its character. It is almost as if we "pulse" at a certain energy level or frequency that reflects our recurrent transactional patterns with ourselves and with others. These others with whom we have a high emotional or resonate affinity are the significant persons in our life. These various members of our significant family or constellation sometimes appear to share these frequency levels that operate through and within each individual psyche. This field comprises the matrix in which psyches at certain times appear to be separate points emerged from the field and at other times appear to completely identify with the person in the field.

This family unconscious system we are exploring, this field of relationships with strong emotional charges, has a certain established interactional pattern between focus points or individual members. These resonant affinities between focus points are constantly interacting with each other. The principle of resonance absorption provides a helpful analogy that operationally conceptualizes this issue. In this model we can see how an aspect of one field is taken in or admitted by the aspect of another field with similar structural properties. In resonance absorption, we see that in every frequency band or for specific frequencies within a band, there exists one or more natural or man-made resonators that seem to absorb energy within that band. The effects produced by the energy absorbed by a particular resonator depend on the characteristics of the resonator.[3] In this simple model, and again it is only a useful analogy, the interaction of electromagnetic radiation with matter is basically similar or parallel to the energy levels around and through the individual and family field in terms of absorption and information exchange.

What we do know for sure is that we are intimately connected with each other. On some level of the psyche we intuitively know that $E = mc^2$. We know that matter and energy are in constant interchange with each other and that we are intimately involved in this matrix. When a dream has a certain "tenacious quality" about it in the waking state, we can be sure that the autonomic nervous system has been deeply stimulated by the events of the night. Sometimes the events of the night have been stimulated by those with whom we are intimately involved yet who are physically at some great distance from us. When the overt correspondence between the imagery, event, and meaning of the dream symbols is very high, we refer to this as some form of psi-mediated dream.

Researchers have already performed experiments in the laboratory involving the autonomic nervous system reactivity of individuals as they respond to stimuli provided by emotionally significant individuals at a great distance from them.[4] There is also an extensive, replicated experimental literature in the laboratory on remote viewing, ESP or telepathy, PK, and other psi-mediated phenomena as they relate to dreamwork and similar events.[5] Remote viewing can occur while dreaming but also in the waking state and is an ability that can be cultivated. The issue is no longer whether or not this happens. The issue now is how it happens and what does this tell us about our capacities as beings? Some answers will be suggested in the next chapter, when we explore more deeply those normal, less common but still emotionally powerful dreams of an unusual quality. These are the classical psi dreams that have been alluded to throughout this book.

Extrasensory
Family Dreams

Everything in the actual world is referable to some actual entity. It is either transmitted from an actual entity in the past, or belongs to the subjective aim of the actual entity to whose concrescence it belongs.

A. N. WHITEHEAD,
PROCESS AND REALITY

Such experiences may indicate that psi is extraordinarily more complex than commonly realized. . . . One might speculate that human relationships may be guided and influenced by some fundamental underlying force that occasionally surfaces into consciousness as psi events, particularly during emotion-laden situations. Perhaps, during these times, a collective consciousness is formed between the individuals involved.

S. KRIPPNER AND M. ULLMAN,
DREAM TELEPATHY

FORMS OF PSI:
ESP, PRECOGNITION, AND THE SHARED IMAGE

Here is a scenario that thousands of us have experienced at least once:

I woke up from a terrible nightmare in which I was a man who was dying. The whole dream was one of extreme terror and had me repeating over and over to myself, knowing that no one could hear me, "I'm dying, I'm dying, I'm dying, I'm dying . . ." I woke up pumping adrenaline and checked the clock (not with purpose, it is just something I do when I wake up). It was 4:30 a.m. The next day I received a call from my mother that her father had died during the night sometime after 1 a.m. (Since I was in California and he was in Maine, you can see why I might shudder at the coincidence of the times.) Though he had not been ill, he was 87, and so it wasn't entirely unexpected, I guess. You can see, though, why I have never had the heart to tell my mother about this dream when she talks about her father having "gone peacefully in his sleep . . ."

What exactly is this phenomenon called "psi," and what are the forms that psi can take? Briefly and simply stated, psi is the situation in which information or influence is passed from one person to another in ways that seem to circumvent our ordinary constructs of space, time, and energy. We use terms such as telepathy, psychokinesis, and precognition to refer to these incidences, but as yet there is no scientifically accepted theory of their precise functioning. Freud was at times quite amenable to the notion that during the state of sleep, when the senses are quietly retired, psi and other latent abilities can come to the surface. In the yogic meditative practice of sensory withdrawal called "pratya-hara," certain psychic processes are known to unfold with skill and discipline as attention moves deeper into the regions of concentration and contemplation.

The dream that opened this chapter is what is known in the psychical research literature as a classic crisis telepathy dream. In this chapter, we are going to look specifically at several varieties of psi as they operate in family dreams. One type will be the ESP or telepathy dream that is scattered throughout this book. Another will be the related collection of precognitive dreams. A third will be the dreams in which there is a shared image or shared dreamscape but not necessarily of a tragic dimension. Examples will be given for each member in this family of dreams. One type of dream we shall not be exploring is the clairvoyant dream. In this type of psi dream, the dreamer does not necessarily communicate with another mind or dreamer but rather sees clearly a distant object, location, or event. Our focus will be apparent mind-to-mind communication in the open system of the family.

As we explore these dreams and the influence of powerful emotions and archetypal situations such as birth, death, marriage, and potentially catastrophic loss, an attempt will be made to clinically formulate how the ordinary and also the more unusual psi family dream operates. It should be noted that the powerful motivations of death and love are profoundly implicated in the family dreams of an unusual nature.

Some researchers claim that two out of three psychic experiences occur in dreams.[1] By very conservative estimates, if only 1 percent of our dreams were psi dreams, then in a lifetime of one hundred minutes of dreaming in an eight-hour night, with approximately 1,500 dreams a year, we would have at least a thousand such dreams in our lifetime! In reality it is probably much higher.

Death and illness and the *threat* of death and illness loom large in the pyrotechnics of the unconscious. An overwhelmingly large number of psi-mediated dreams involve the issue of illness, death, and impending death, with some researchers claiming that as many as 50 percent of all psi dreams do so.[2] Notice the dynamics of the following family dreams that were reported to the Family Dreams Research Project. They all involved crisis, the high motivation or need to communicate important information, and a certain apparent *coordination* of psychological and physiological states. Note the state of mind of the "receiver" of the information and the psychophysical state of the "sender" of the information. This combination of deep relaxation and high activation has been alluded to throughout this study in terms of the words adrenergic and cholinergic. It was mentioned in particular in chapter 4 on the psychophysiological parameters of sleep and dreaming. Death is certainly an archetypal event and one that sends profound waves through the psyche.

> My father had cancer from which he died February 6, 1985. Two years prior to that, I dreamed my father was lying on the ground with medical persons all around and they were saying that he was dead. I was screaming, "No, no. It is not the right time." Then I awoke. This happened on the Thursday morning at 8:30. That Saturday I called my folks. My mother stated she was just going to call me and she related that Thursday, two days previously, my father had a heart attack (which they informed me was brought on by medication they were giving him) and he had almost died. At first I didn't make a connection with the dream and then I remembered it and asked my mother what time this occurred. She said around 8 or 8:30 Thursday morning.

Here is an even more powerful dream in the sense that it involves not two but three members of the family:

> My dream had no physical characteristics at all. It was only a jumble of emotions and thoughts, not my own, but it was as if my soul was touched by another's. And we joined together in spirit and drifted through the darkness. In a distance there was an odd light. Suddenly I was feeling an indescribable feeling—fear and sadness and a great loneliness that was almost unbearable. At that moment I awoke and found myself leaning over the bed gagging and choking and crying and trying to cry out, but I couldn't. The powerful emotions that I had experienced in my dream remained for a few seconds. I was crying and shaking and knew that what had transpired was not of an earthly nature. I felt a deep sense of loss.
>
> Two days later, my father's body was found in the tiny upstairs

apartment he had rented. From the spattered blood on the wall beside his bed, it appeared as if he had awakened in the night choking on his blood and leaned over the bed as he vomited and choked. When I saw his room, the bed, the wall, I knew deep in my soul that it was his experience of death that I had felt.

My mother also had a dream on the same night as mine. She dreamed that she was asleep and was awakened by a shadow in the doorway. She recognized it was my father. He spoke to her then, saying, "If you had to do it all over again would you still marry me?" She thought about their tumultuous marriage and finally their divorce, and then replied, "Yes, I would. I love you." She reached out to him. He smiled then, but instead of coming nearer to her he drifted away.

The person who reported this dream and his mother's dream stated that both occurred on the night of his father's death ten years ago.

Here is a dream series in which the threat of death itself loomed large in the dream state of the individuals in the family:

While living in Maine in the spring of 1984 I had 3 days off from work so I decided to do a short backpacking trip with only my dog on the Appalachian Trail. After two days of rain, however, I deemed it best to head home. But once on the road I realized I wasn't really ready to return, so I set up my tent on a plot in a campground along the Penobscot River. It continued to rain most of the day, causing the river to rise. When I finally turned in for the night the water was about 15 feet from my tent, but I wasn't concerned since I was on a mound. However the next morning the river was only 8 feet away and I awakened to the campground owner yelling for me to get up and move my car. The car was parked behind the tent in what I thought was a safe spot but I guess the river must have made a bend just down stream, because it was immersed up to the bumper. Needless to say I hightailed it out of there.

That weekend I telephoned my parents in Pennsylvania who had no knowledge of my trip. My mom mentioned that the previous Wednesday (the night of the flood at the campground) she woke all upset from a vivid dream in which I was surrounded by water, and indeed I was.

I grew up closer to my mother than to my father and lived in her home (Mom and Dad divorced when I was 14) until the age of 20. We have kidded ourselves a number of times about ESP or the unexplainable little visitation inside each other's dreams a few times over the years, but two incidences stand out over the others.

First time I remember such an occurrence was in the summer of 1978. I was riding as a passenger on a motorcycle when the driver messed up in a turn, dumping the bike and throwing us off into the rocks by the roadside. I broke some bones in my knee as a result. The "dreamlike" part is quite a long distance one; it turns out the next day, as I lay in bed elevating my cast-covered leg, my mother, in Honolulu, Hawaii calls, saying that she had a dream the night before where I crashed in some sort of motorcycle or auto accident and had been either killed or severely injured. She had been awakened in the middle of the night with a terrible start as a result of this, and upon first light the next day she phoned my dad to ask him if everything was o.k. When she called me, I told her about my accident, and, although she was reassured, we had no explanation at the time regarding how she knew of the event. It was shrugged off.

The second (and the most amazing) dream link between my mother and me happened the following summer at almost the same time in August as the previous one did the year before. I worked long hours as a busboy at a resort about 14 miles away and was driving my mother's car home during a heavy rainfall at around 4 a.m.

At the foot of a long, steep hill, right before a corner was a depressed section of land filled with water. I was going around 75 mph and slowly getting ready for the corner when I hit the puddle and hydroplaned. I oversteered, skidded, and somehow made it around the bend without going over the edge of the road. I had, as I (understandably) remember, a tremendous surge of adrenalin during my split-second stirring save.

Reaching home, quietly parking the car and going into the house, I saw my mother at the front door as I entered. She was wide awake and wide-eyed as she came up to me, grabbed me at each shoulder, and asked me if I was o.k. I said, "Yea, why not? But hey, wait a minute, why do you ask?" and then I told her about the close call I had with the roadside. She then told me an account of how I was in a dream she just had suddenly awakened out of where I was driving **in the rain** *and crashed badly on the* **dark road late at night.**

Once again a life-threatening experience was superimposed into my mother's dream the exact instant it occurred to me. This one we figured down to the minute; it was 14 miles away. It takes roughly 15 minutes to get home and my mom woke up and had been waiting for me exactly 15 minutes.

These are indeed powerful dreams that reflect our deepest motivations and our deepest relationships in life. Sometimes a shared dreamscape in family dreams can be focused around a crisis situation, and often around a death or risk of situation. Sometimes, however, it can be focused around a shared image or metaphor that is more subtle in expression. This is less dramatic but actually more common than the unusual psi-mediated dreams. Note the dynamics and the recurrent transactional patterns in the following sequence of family dreams:

Many years ago around 1972, I was about 17 ½ and my sister was 14 ½ at the time. My younger sister went with my grandparents to Mexico for a family visit and to live down there for the summer. My sister and I have always been extremely close and we missed each other terribly. I bought a blouse for her, a striped red tank top, and also a blue one that I just liked for myself. I didn't tell her about the blouse because I wanted to surprise her on her return in three days. I left her blouse on her bed (we shared a room together).

That night I dreamed my whole family went to the country to look over a house we were planning to buy. Family friends by the name of Garcia stopped by and my sister and I showed them the second floor. The walls were yellow and had wooden cabinets and drawers. The house had a pool with blue tile, and my sister and I asked my cousin Raynee a question. She was sitting on a bench with her friend Becky. Raynee was wearing a checkered country-style shirt. We asked her where my parents were and she responded, "They went upstairs with the Garcias." So we went around the outside of the house where we saw a mailman who wore shorts a baseball cap [and had] long brownish hair and very, very blue eyes. In the dream I said to my sister "I just love blue eyes," and she said "I think I am going to really like it here." We went upstairs and joined the rest of the family. We sat across from each other and joined in the conversation. I was wearing my blue tank top and she was wearing her red one.

Two days later when we picked up my sister and grandparents at the train station she and I immediately paired up to catch up on the lost time (our parents used to call us Lucy and Ethel or Heckle and Jeckle). I started to tell her I had this crazy dream, and she asked me to tell her about it. When I did her eyes opened wide as she started filling in the spaces for me. She had had the same dream the same night I had. All the details were similar down to dialogue and wall colors. She even dreamt she was wearing the blouse, which she knew nothing about and dreamt I wore a blue one just like it. We dreamed about seeing the same people in the same places saying the same things and wearing the same clothes. She even beat me to the punch line about the mailman with the blue eyes and told me exactly what the mailbox looked like. What really struck us as odd was we saw things in our dream in perspective to our locations (e.g., when we sat across from each other she saw things behind me and the people on her left were on my right as I was sitting across from her). But they were the same people, same room, everything. At the time it gave us the creeps.

Thus the shared image can emerge in a number of different situations as the unconscious moves through our lives. One prominent sleep and dream researcher, Dr. Allan Rechtschaffen of the University of Chicago, has noted the high correspondence of similar images and themes between dreamers who are dreaming in the laboratory at the same time. Here, the possibility of simultaneous dreaming is occurring between emotionally unrelated people.[3] What happens, we ask, when there is a close emotional bond between dreamers? Here again is a situation from another family in which two family members shared the same dream image:

It was in February of 1979 that I had one of the most vivid and powerful dreams of my life. I had been unusually cranky that day and had had a difficult time falling asleep. When I did I dreamt the following: I was a small boy watching the T.V. It was not a modern T.V. but the old style, wooden console one we had when I was that age. I was watching my favorite program and enjoying myself a great deal. As a commercial came on, my brother, who appeared at his present age, came to take the T.V. away, telling me that a newer one had been found. I took the news very poorly, telling him that this T.V. was working just fine and that I didn't need a new one. While we were arguing, the T.V. began to go on and off, clear and fuzzy, with the sound becoming quite dim and then would increase in volume. My brother pointed out that I did indeed need a new one. He went behind the T.V. to unplug the old one and I began to wail. I pleaded with him and tried to interfere with his work. Suddenly, the picture became perfect and my brother even sat back to watch the picture. The commercial was still on but the voice coming out of the T.V. was not matching that of the picture. The voice was talking directly to me in a motherly, soothing way as to stop me from crying. The voice told me that the time for all things passes and that to rail against that fact was a waste of the precious time of life. The T.V. died. My brother replaced the T.V. I began to watch the new one calmly as if nothing had happened.

When I woke up I called in cancelling my classes for the day. I did not go down to breakfast but waited in my bed. My roommate came back in from some errand or other and told me that I had cried and shouted a lot in my sleep during the night. About 10 a.m. my mother called. Before she was able to tell me the news, I told her that I knew. I told her that I would make a plane reservation and call to tell her when I would come home for the funeral. She said that she was a bit surprised for my brother had told her the same thing when he had called. We were the only two immediate family members not present when my grandmother died. My mother told me that towards the end my grandmother had come in and out of consciousness, at times talking nonsense, at times talking just above a whisper and had even shouted once to my slightly deaf grandfather who had been dead for 18 years. She had at the end become completely lucid, telling everyone gathered at the bedside that she was at peace and ready to go.

My brother, who did not come to the funeral after all for his own reasons, told me later that he had had a bad night. He did not remember much of his dreams or of the night except he did recall needing to do some work for me and that when he awoke, he was sure something had happened to someone in the family. When our mother had called, he knew what exactly had taken place.

One of the more interesting aspects of this dream is a common phenomenon observed when people are dying from a long, drawn-out disease process. The dying person, just prior to death itself, often becomes *lucid*. One wonders how this brief *expansion* and *clarity* of their usual psychological and somatic consciousness is related to the psi event and its reception by the "receiver" in their relaxed, open state. Perhaps in this condition the individualized principle of consciousness is *intensified* and *projected* toward an agent with whom the person shares some resonant affinity. We will return to this theme and observation later.

The following dream involves a shared image and also heightened eroticism. It involves not the dream shared between family members but between people who have a close, family-like emotional relationship.

My dream began in a dwelling that was a series of connective tents. If you think of being inside card houses that would be close to this place. I was staying there with a group of people, and we were just getting up in the morning. That was the way to get to the shower and to get to use the sink.

The people I saw strolled around in towels and were comfortable with me and each other as if we knew each other well. The scene shifted then to another "tent" where I was having sex with two men simultaneously. Then again the scene changed to an outdoor setting. There were people sitting at small tables, about 3 or 4 people to a table. They were drinking and eating, and it was like a garden party. Everyone was white except for one black man who really stuck out. I stood up and took off my shirt fully aware that many people were watching me.

When Carol arrived that morning in Bozeman, she immediately began to tell me that while she was working in North Dakota she was having an affair with two different men at the same time. She proceeded to describe one man, and he matched one of the men I was having sex with in my dream. I stopped Carol in mid-word and told her that I had had an interesting dream the night before in which I had sex with two guys at once. I told her that she had just described one of the guys so now could I please describe the other man in my dream to see if it matched her other lover. He did, perfectly! A little bit later in the morning while I was in the bathtub I remembered two other parts of the dream. I didn't need to ask Carol about the first part, staying in a structure like a series of tents and having to share a shower, etc. I knew that Carol had been staying in a motel with the rest of her seismological crew. However, I told her about taking my shirt off in front of a bunch of people sitting at tables, and she got terribly excited. She started pacing up and down and waving her arms saying, "I did that. I did that." She took her shirt off in a bar and she told me that she did it knowing that certain people were watching her do it. She told me her inner thoughts while she did that action and it was just what I had thought in the dream. Then I remembered to tell her that there was a black man with their crew or on their crew. She said that they had picked up a black man hitchhiking and that he stayed for a number of days with the crew. He was there in the bar when she took her shirt off. I'm sure you can appreciate the scarcity of black men in North Dakota! This detail impressed me even more than the fact that I could describe Carol's lover to her just as if I actually had sex with the man.

PRECOGNITIVE DREAMS

Over time, many motivations and many scenarios enter the dreamscapes shared by people in close relationships. Sometimes these dreams are actually *precognitive* (i.e., family members have dreams of other family members, and the dreams then come true in the very near future.) In this situation, the usual boundaries of time appear to have been transcended by the emotional press to communicate with another in the shared system. Each example of a precognitive dream presented here is progressively more exacting than the next. They also have dynamics similar to telepathic family dreams.

> *I seem to be somewhere in Europe, a villa of some sort, as the buildings are very close set in. My own room in a house in Seattle has the same configuration. Some people are arguing on a terrace across the street. Suddenly the argument greatly intensifies, and I sense that one of the young men is about to jump to his death and I know that I cannot react in time to call out to him "don't jump!" All of a sudden he jumps and lands face down in a pool of blood. I call out the window and look at the spectacle below.*
>
> *The following day I received in the mail a letter from my father telling me that he was dying of cancer and he only had a short time in which to live. Two weeks later on April 15th he died after having been found in his bathtub, both wrists slashed, in a pool of blood.*

Another person offered this example of a precognitive dream:

> *Recently I experienced a dream prior to finding out my sister had been admitted to the hospital. The dream occurred at home as a setting. It was storming and Mom asked me to come home and watch the grandchildren. Upon arriving I immediately experienced a feeling of doom. My mother stated that she had to get to the hospital but instead of my sister being in the hospital it was my dad she was going to see. Well, in the dream*

I kept asking over and over what was wrong, but she would only say he was bleeding and she had to go to the hospital. This dream occurred on a Monday night. I had had no contact with my family since living on my own. Thursday evening I called my sister to ask a favor but I received no answer. I called home and asked about Sanya, my sister. I was informed that Sanya was admitted to the hospital Monday morning. This is one of many dreams I can recall but can't understand why my dad is usually the person that I picture or dream about who is hurt or in trouble. Usually, as in most cases, it is some other person who is hurt and not my father. There was a time when I tried to shut out these dreams, and other times I just hated knowing certain things. Finally I realized that it is a part of me and that I can't push it aside.

The reader may note the dynamics of this particular dream:

My son had had an accident and was in the hospital for several months. One night I dreamed that they had a fire in his hospital wing. The doctor I talked to told me that I was overly anxious after my other dream in which my son was injured. This dream had seemed to come true. He said I was just being nervous and that nothing would happen. But I signed the boy out of the hospital and took him home. Two days after, they had a fire in the hospital, nothing very serious, but it happened. The doctor did not know what to say.

This dreamer also has had dreams that are psi dreams but are not precognitive so much as telepathic. They resemble much closer the crisis telepathy dreams mentioned earlier.

Three weeks after the yearly visit of my dearest friend, an archaeologist named Dr. L., I dreamed that he was talking to me. He told me that he had died and since he had nobody else to continue his life research, he expected me to take it over. In the dream, he wanted me to promise him that I would accept. I experienced the strangest feeling. I did not want to hurt him, but I did not want to do it, but he kept on begging until I promised. At this time he was on tour so I could not reach him. For days after the dream I was overcome by an intense restlessness. I tried to find relief by taking long hikes. One day all of a sudden I felt very calm and at peace. A few hours later his son telephoned to tell me that his father had died, exactly the time when I calmed down.

Was the above a precognitive dream or a telepathic dream? Often the two occur in the same person and in the same family field.

PSYCHOKINETIC FAMILY MATTERS

We see that in the family a number of different kinds of psi-related dreams can communicate information in seemingly unorthodox or unusual manners. One is the typical crisis ESP dream. Another is the dream in which there is a shared image or shared dreamscape. Still another is the precognitive dream. However, there are other psi-related dreams of an even more dramatic but less well understood nature. Here matter, energy, and information become enfolded and then projected into the world of substance and events affecting various objects and forms. These dreams involve the possibility of PK. Interestingly enough, they often occur in adolescence. The clinical literature is ripe with these situations. It is also an area that in the past has been known to be populated by fraudulent individuals. However, it is much more difficult to fake such phenomena under the scrutiny of modern experimental research, which verifies the fact that these phenomena continue to emerge in the human mind.[4] As one might expect these phenomena also surround events associated with death.

In his book, *Mind over Matter,* D. Scott Rogo lists a number of phenomena that are associated with psychokinesis and death and their relationship sometimes to a turbulent or dynamic adolescence. Rogo cites a number of mysterious clock stoppings that seem to correspond to the time that someone significant in the family system died. Folk wisdom is full of this kind of phenomena, and it is understandably difficult to measure in a laboratory. Rogo cites the following dream record in which an object, in this case a watch, is implicated in the sign and symbol of a psi event. It suggests a subtle connection between image, emotional "charge," and significant object.

> One night . . . in our bedroom, we were awakened by a great noise; we had heard a mirror on the mantelpiece fall down, as well as your father's watch stand. I got up and found that the mirror had fallen upon the hearth; the watch had been thrown upon the floor on one side and the watch stand on the other. I thought that everything was broken, and, most annoyed, I must say, I went back to bed without further investigation. In the morning when we got up we found that nothing had been broken.
>
> However, later that same morning the postman brought us a letter . . . telling us of the death of your Aunt Boyet, your father's sister, who had died that very night in Montigny. What did this manifestation mean? The coincidence is at least strange.[5]

Death coincidences seem to flood this area. There is a famous book by Camille Flammarion, the French astronomer, called *Death and Its Mystery,* in which many such cases are reported. For instance, one of his correspondents in this book wrote to him about a friend of his who had been so ill that he had not been able to attend seminary classes.

> His illness lingered on for months. Now each student had his own personal nail pounded into the wall of the classroom upon which he hung his hat and coat. The sick student's space was therefore always vacant during this critical time. One day a fellow student decided to take advantage of the vacancy by placing his own hat on the nail. As a correspondent explained the following: Now one day between 11 o'clock and noon, while the entire class was attentively following the professor's course, the hat on the absent pupil's nail suddenly

began to turn, without the least possible reason being discernible. This motion was so energetic, and lasted for so long (almost a minute) that it drew the pupils' attention and even the professor's, and it made so much of an impression that they talked about it the whole day. Later that afternoon a cable arrived announcing the ill student had died at that very same time.[6]

In the same book and study another incident is noted. One of Flammarion's acquaintances reported the following:

One day his entire family was shocked by these incredible sounds during their evening prayers. He noted that "an extraordinary noise made itself heard . . . as though the heavy counter had been violently shaken, making the scales and everything upon it resound noisily." The family ran into the office, expecting to find something broken or at least disarray. Everything there was in perfect order, but news arrived later that evening announcing the death of a relative.[7]

In these very unusual cases of PK-related to family processes, the processes we know very little about, there are still embedded luminous secrets of the human potential. What to make of them, or where they will lead us, we do not yet know. We do know, however, that embedded in the family process, with all its powerful emotional factors, is the capacity to touch upon deep imagery that affects the psyche, the soma, and the material world. Here lies a latent power that is still unknown to us and untapped except for an occasional spontaneous expression in a dream or is perhaps displaced in a clinical symptom. Someday perhaps we will be able to draw upon this as yet not understood energy and capacity in the family and in the dreaming mind itself for individual and collective healing in the service of a radical expansion of human consciousness.

We do have ample laboratory evidence that these phenomena and such capacities do indeed exist.[8] By the very nature of their findings and their implications for our present-day conception of time, matter, energy, and science, these explorers will be met with a certain paradigmatic resistance and selective inattention by the narrow constraints of contemporary science. However, even these barriers are slowly eroding. Physicists, clinical psychologists, and experimentalists in various fields have begun to repeatedly find certain patterns in this psi phenomena work. The scope of their research includes telepathy, precognition, shared imagery, and PK. This last branch, PK, has been associated with adolescence and all its striving, powerful, intoxicating emotions, barely controlled motivations, and attendant imagery.[9] We do not yet know clinically what this means. However, we might draw a clue from some areas of experimental science.

A physicist, John Hasted, experimentally tested persons who apparently demonstrated the capacity to bend metal.[10] Not only are the results compelling if one approaches the idea with an open mind, but there are some clinical bits of evidence that can be drawn. One of the more important techniques that the metal bender might learn to employ when using sensitive experimental equipment, such as the strain gauge, is to psychologically avoid prolonged overintensification or over-concentration. Some researchers believe that in some strange sense the metal benders must learn to systematically release effort and attention at certain times if they want good results. This is strikingly similar to the reputed J curve that many believe exists in other forms of psi. At a certain point, one has to let go and stay with the roll of the dice rather than become fixated on a particular image or thought. When one becomes fixated on a particular image or thought, one's capacity to exercise these abilities significantly decreases. This general capacity to influence the physical world, sometimes at the quantum level, has been experimentally supported by other physicists and psychologists.[11] Indeed, the strongest and most powerful effects often occur when the individual or the subject relaxes completely after concentration.

There is as yet some unknown relationship between psyche as focus and psyche as field that might explain these results. There is much we do know, however, about these unusual family dreams and the paranormal phenomena that sometimes manifest in them. Indeed, throughout this chapter, special attention has been given to the emotional motivations, shared imagery, and recurrent transactional patterns and dynamics that seem to be alive in family dreams we have been looking at.

THE DYNAMIC FAMILY PATTERN
AS PSI UNFOLDS

Throughout this book, I have stated that the family is a psychosocial unit. I have stressed the fact that the family is an intense psychodynamic system, a shared matrix of energy, imagery, affect, and ideation. Further, I have suggested that the family unconscious field[12] is a vast sea of localizing energies that implicate and enfold each significant other in the field. These are all very useful maps and analogies, but as we all know the map is not the territory. What can be *clinically observed* in these situations and in the particular striking events that have been discussed so far? This is the question we must turn to now.

In each situation that has been outlined and focused on so far, certain recurrent transactional patterns appear to emerge in a specific context. It would appear that both the body, or soma, and the psyche are deeply implicated. While there is certainly some variation, we can begin to notice the following common themes or patterns:

1. A *shared* emotional and/or familial history and field is operative, a field we would call the family unconscious.
2. This field is characterized by some degree of empathy, not just hostility or fear or "pseudo mutuality."
3. The "receiver" of such information or meaning is in a psychophysiological state of relaxation or even dream sleep. We have referred to this numerous times as a cholinergic state.
4. The "sender" of such information who "starts it off" is in an agitated or highly aroused psychophysiological state of alertness,

or an adrenergic state. In other words their autonomic nervous system is highly activated and aroused. Often, this is subjectively experienced as fear or a similar intensified state of consciousness. It is often precipitated by the image and actuality of a major life event, the archetypal ones being death or impending danger.

5. Transference and countertransference feelings are operative on the part of both parties when they are in a clinical situation. This more often occurs between people not in a clinical situation but in a more friendship type of relationship that is very close. In the context of familial relations in particular significant others share a long-standing resonate affinity with each other; an inverse perception or representation of themselves seen and experienced in the other through a sense of shared identity as a family member.

6. Primary process mentation and imagery are implicated in the emergence of an overarching informational field and its relational meaning pattern.

7. There is a strong affect or emotion stemming from the sense of deep meaningfulness embedded in the process or event itself. It is sensed or felt strongly in energetic terms that the body experiences. There is a certain limbic resonance here.

This form of clinical and scientific *observation* is much closer to what might be termed "pattern recognition" or an algorithmic formulation than to quantifiable or actuarial science. It is a form of dynamic observation the clinician and the family member can put to the test either in the office or in their own home and family situation. One does not need to be a scientist in the strictest sense of the word to make these observations. The general pattern of recognition or constellation of events, both psychological and psychophysical, is what appears to repeat itself in many of these situations.

One can go so far as to incorporate this field of experience and mutually influencing processes into other laws of energy dynamics presently better known currently as the four fundamental forces of the physical sciences. In other words, the energy field we have been exploring manifests dynamics at various levels in their different but certainly identifiable conditions. This energy field would appear to be similar to other energy fields and interactions known in nature. It has a certain similarity to the ubiquitous gravitational force in that it appears to be primarily attractive in nature. It is similar to both the gravitational and the electromagnetic forces in the sense that it has infinite range and the possibility of exchanging what are termed massless "information particles"; it is similar to the so-called weak force of the atom in that it is extremely difficult to detect unless we are specifically attuned to it, since it appears to radiate from the organism much as the decay process does in the nucleus of the atom. We might even note that its *power* or magnitude appears to be similar to the inverse square laws embedded in those better understood electrostatic, magnetic, and gravitational fields, except that the field we are talking about is holonomic or holographic in nature and the "mass" or density of the "objects" is a function of historically shared affective-ideational intensity. In other words, it is the result of intensely relating people living together for a long period of time.

In a certain sense in these situations we see or feel ourselves in the other, especially the significant other. We all have a dim intuition or even memory of ourselves, for better or worse, being lived out in the life of another. On a deeper level this is positive for it helps us further recognize our own luminous and primordial substrate leading to a real and resonate affinity. This is most probably the root of deep compassion and the transpersonal or even psychocosmic foundation of ethics and morality that ultimately judges our own behavior.

Now if we were to try to clinically formulate what we see in the vast majority of crisis telepathy and shared imagery dreams, we could describe it as follows: What we might think of as the deepest aspect of the human being, that which we will call the Self, locates or resonates with an aspect of itself in the Self of another. The two or in some cases three or more share the field of what we have been calling the family unconscious. That shared emotional field of imagery, affect, and events becomes energized by the occurrence of an archetypal event such as death or near danger to one of those in that field. The whole process is then mediated and "transmitted" by the power or magnitude of a certain kind of energy field, which we will call a biogravitational field, that is associated with specific responses and activities of the usually unconscious autonomic nervous system. Biogravitation has a certain affinity to the well-established process of superconductivity and is at least theoretically possible in living systems and not only those systems near absolute zero in temperature. Each variable in the system constantly fluctuates in degree of intensity until the particular constellation of variables reaches a critical point at which time the psi episode transpires. This psi episode is a *discontinuous* or discrete process, in spite of the fact that the variables are all in *continuous* change from one stable state to another stable state.

In this field in a very curious way each emotional dreamscape is enfolded into and reflects or implicates each other dreamscape. A certain kind of holonomic pattern appears where each part can reflect and unfold all other parts slightly differently. During the dream state, it would appear that our "boundaries" and identities occasionally intermingle on an energetic and informational level with the significant others that we dream about. These energetic and informational processes seem to take a personalized and systematic approach when it comes to the dreams of people who are deeply and powerfully interconnected with each other over years and years and sometimes generations of shared events, feelings, and patterns of behavior, as occurs in the family situation. The deep primordial emotions of individuals in their shared histories with families makes this possible.

This certainly does not mean that families agreed about their different points of view, but rather, for better or worse, they shared and felt the same kind of emotions and reactions to the same intense web of events. As mentioned earlier, all too often in a dynamic family situation, such as family therapy, we implicitly ask not so much "*what* is the matter with you?" but rather, in the primordial African rooted sense, "*who* is the matter with you?" This dynamic process reflects an intimately *personalized* universe of symbols, symptoms, and events. Every family therapist implicitly knows and operates this way. Within this field of influence, and under certain psychophysical conditions that are a function of the body and the field of the family unconscious, we can observe a significant rise in the observation of these unusual dream experiences. The implications for clinical science are staggering and as yet only dreamed of. This is but one more indication of our intimate involvement with each other on many levels and the essentially transpersonal nature of consciousness itself.

PART TWO

Family Dreams and Healing

This section takes the exploration of family dreams in a slightly different direction. In previous chapters, the history, broad-context, and cross-cultural or transcultural aspects of dreaming and family dreams were discussed. Clinical and laboratory findings were presented—along with a classification system for dream process and dream information sharing—as we moved from an exclusively individual or intrapsychic focus to a family process perspective. In this section, we move more deeply into specific family dream styles that reflect familial patterns and life events.

The first chapter concerns the dreams of adults who had at least one alcoholic parent and reflects certain emotional and thematic constellations common to such families. The chapter on pregnancy and dreams reflects a different constellation of events and emotional patterns. Present in both are normal and unusual dreams that can be used in a therapeutic context. Embedded in both are shared emotions, nightmares, and symptomatic and somatic events. Some dreams of adults who had alcoholic parents or of family members who are pregnant have a nightmarish quality to them. Others express joy and hope. These chapters are intended to provide a deeper and clearer focus on the family and family dreams that occur in specific contexts. We must study, understand, and live our dreams. Indeed, we either pursue our dreams or our nightmares pursue us.

7

Family Dreams of Adult Children of Alcoholics (ACOA)

A Specific Style

I believe the depression we view as individual pathology is actually a response to a real perception of the pathology of others. It is an effort which is recognized as a failure to do something about the pain in the world.

C. A. Whitaker,
Midnight Musings of a Family Therapist

THE INWARD ASYLUM

This patient was able to recall a recurrent dream she had for many years. In this dream, she said the scene was very violent. She remembers a man chasing around a number of people and killing them by driving over them with a steamroller. The spikes of the steamroller periodically would catch her father and hurt him. In these dreams, the patient would hide under a bed as this man in the dream went around killing others. Apparently he flattened a dog in the street with his steamroller. The neighbors would look on. The patient was able to escape this figure in the dream but was never totally safe from his violent outbursts.

This dream was presented in therapy by C.D.,* a twenty-year-old college sophomore who was majoring in engineering and had referred herself for depression, anxiety, and violent outbursts. When C.D. became what she described as "overly emotionally reactive," she would sometimes be explosively angry for half an hour. It would sometimes take her as long as twenty minutes or more to calm down. She referred herself to therapy because she found herself becoming easily upset and was having increasing difficulty focusing on what she was concerned about in life. At times, she would cry quite hysterically and argue almost uncontrollably. Her outbursts of violent temper were focused around difficulties in her romantic life and also in her intimate family situations.

C.D. recalled experiencing these violent outbursts of anger since she was three years old. She indicated that in the ninth grade, she actually began to pull her hair out. This interesting symptom is clinically termed "trichotillomania." This is a symptom in which the patient, hounded by anxiety but also under enormous pressure to be in control, becomes "nitpicky" and literally pulls the hair out from her head, face, or other parts of the body. In therapy sessions, the patient associated this odd symptom with the extremely self-critical side of her personality. She indicated that she came from a family that had severe alcohol abuse problems on both sides. She indicated that on her mother's side in particular there was a history of "several alcoholics, anorexics, and neurotics." Family themes of volatile emotional relationships and alcohol abuse over several generations emerged in her treatment process. Her story and particular dream-life style, as we shall see, is not unique but reflects a particular pattern of family dreamlife.

---

*Not her real initials. All names and other overt identifications were changed in this text for reasons of confidentiality.

We have seen in earlier chapters how family issues and family styles profoundly influence the dream content and the dreamlife of family members. At various times earlier in this book, we looked at dreams in ancient cultures. We looked at the dreamlife as it spans the web of family relationships as well as intrapsychic and interpersonal relationships. We also touched very briefly on normal and unusual family dreams and on the contribution of the laboratory in discovering the presently known psychophysiological events that accompany dreaming. However, even without knowing any of these other aspects of dreaming, it is still possible to gain a grasp of one's own psyche—and the psyche of those others we are intimately associated with—by studying the dreams in our own immediate-family context.

The dream presented above is in many ways characteristic of those associated with ACOA families. In this chapter, we are going to look much more deeply into the dynamics, roles, and styles that seem to characterize, or be more noticeable in, the ACOA family and its victims. This is not to say that these patterns are unique to ACOA families. No particular theme is unique to any particular family. However, there can be a preponderance of certain kinds of themes in particular kinds of families. In the ACOA family, there are certain themes that the clinician, friend, or fellow family member can notice with alarming intensity.

FAMILY DYNAMICS OF ACOA

One of the most debilitating characteristics of ACOA is their intense fear of losing control. It underlies and motivates many of their defenses or internal security operations. Clinicians and other family members have noticed that ACOA family members have an extremely high need to maintain control of their feelings.[1] In addition to trying to control their own feelings and behavior, they must also try to control the feelings and behavior of others. This is done primarily out of an early, well-grounded fear and the unshakable sense that if they lose this control, then things will become extremely explosive. This was often the reality at home. They often become extremely anxious when control is not immediately available to them. As we shall see later, there is also a particularly strong fear of one's own deeper, more vulnerable feelings that are often cloistered inside, such as anger and sadness. These are feelings carried over from childhood that ACOA have progressively lost the ability to feel or express as openly and freely as they would like. In a large percentage of ACOA and their families, intense feelings of all spectrums are suppressed, even joy and great happiness.

ACOA are often noted to have a great deal of difficulty relaxing and simply having fun. They are famous for their extreme and intense self-criticism. Their difficulties with intimate relationships abound and are usually chronic. This is largely due to some of the explosive scenes and the painful themes that occurred in their childhood family situation. Often this is reflected in the area of sexuality. It is not difficult to see how the need for control can sometimes lead to often compulsive behavior and to living one's life from the emotional point of view of being threatened or constantly victimized.

One of the more curious difficulties here is that this adaptational style of emotionally anesthetizing oneself does provide some protection to the highly vulnerable individuals who find themselves thrown into a bewildering family situation. Unfortunately, in the future these individuals then tend to become more and more comfortable with this impending sense of chaos itself. They can move to the point where they seem to be getting closer to another person, then they confuse this intimacy with love and pity, thereby leading to a desire for fusion or codependency relationships. After that attempt at fusion, which of course usually fails, they soon experience the fear of abandonment. You might say that these individuals are suffering from a delayed-grief reaction of loss from years ago. They are survivors, and they identify themselves as survivors, which is mixed in with their fear of abandonment. In some, there is even a heightened tendency toward somatic or physical complaints. Below are some examples.

ACOA DREAM STYLES

M.A. is a thirty-four-year-old graduate student. In therapy, he told of numerous incidents involving his mother's alcohol abuse and her explosive temper. He related three different dreams concerning his family, his mother, and their shared ACOA-symptom situation. In particular, he remembers that his mother was someone who could be extremely rejecting, violent, and, at the same time, guilt inducing. He recalls having a very intense love-hate relationship with her and remembers that while she was alive, everyone lived in an intensely negative atmosphere, and negative self-esteem was reinforced in the family. After the mother's death, family members were able to free themselves a little bit, relax, and develop their own needs.

From that time in his life, M.A. remembers his mother being both an extremely sensitive and caring person and then, at other times, extremely angry and able to "suck the world dry." His father was remembered as always being emotionally withdrawn and removed from his own feelings in a rather passive way. Fortunately, M.A. was intelligent and insight-oriented, and in therapy he could see both of these aspects emerging in his own personality. He related several dreams that seem to be very much a reflection of this painful family style.

M.A. remembers having a dream as a child in which he was trying to run through water to get away from someone. He associated this situation with his mother and her negative influence. In another dream, he remembers being in his backyard, which was walled off from other yards by green hedges, and running away again from the same person, whose image he recalls to be his mother. In this dream, he was shot from behind four or five times. He remembers the bullets going through his body, but he was very calm and serene. Finally, in another dream, which was actually a recurring nightmare, he was at the bottom of a very steep rock chasm from which he could see the sky. From the ledge above, however, huge boulders were rolling down toward him to potentially crush and kill him. In all three of these dreams, themes of violence, pain, and seeming inescapability repeated themselves.

It is interesting to point out here that M.A. noticed his dreams could be so intense that they stimulated somatic or gastrointestinal tract difficulties. At times, he felt a great deal of tension and contraction around his stomach and his solar plexus. He experienced shooting pains in these areas as well. In addition, he felt constriction around his heart and sometimes in his throat. He even experienced tension in his ears and flushing sensations in his hands. On top of all this, he also suffered from Raynaud's disease, which involves difficulties in the heart or cardiovascular and circulatory system. At the end of each session, M.A. wanted my assertion that I understood his vulnerability and his need to make sure that everything was safe before he discussed things too deeply. He felt hurt and victimized by his past, and he was angry at the therapist who he felt did not recognize how victimized and hurt he was.

So here again you see that the themes of violence and explosiveness can oscillate between intimate and distance-creating family relationships. "Escape motifs" appear again and again in the family dreams of ACOA members. This is often interlaced with chronic low self-esteem and, in M.A.'s situation, a heightened sense of vulnerability and victim psychology. Also, there is often a great deal of somatic or psychophysiological reactivity that can be seen in the dreams of family members of ACOA.

While there are many different personality traits and styles that can be seen to proliferate across the dreams of ACOA family members, we are going to focus on a small, representative sample of ACOA and see how these themes repeat themselves in the family dreams of just one person.

We have just discussed briefly some of the characteristic personality styles and traits of ACOA family dreams. In particular, our focus is the issues of explosiveness, low self-esteem, guilt and anger, and perfectionism. All of these are accompanied by a strong need to feel in control. This is because the family's chaotic situation was so profound that it deeply affected the individual's sense of security and psychological boundary formation. Obviously, the intimate web of the ACOA family is an extremely hazardous place in which to open yourself emotionally.

What follows is a series of dreams from one ACOA family member that reflects some characteristics that I have been alluding to.

K.C. was the oldest of several children. He remembers the devastating effects his alcoholic mother had on the family. She eventually died of complications resulting from her alcoholism but not before she had deeply embedded feelings of shame and humiliation in all of her children. Even to this day, her children bear the scars of low self-esteem, fear, shame and guilt, and intense anger. K.C. even remembers his youngest sibling jumping out of a window in their apartment at the age of eight in an attempt to hurt or kill herself in order to escape from the family's intolerable situation. The siblings kept this a secret from the parents for obvious reasons. Not surprisingly, ACOA families are rife with many secrets. This familial style also cultivates myriad patterns and levels of denial.

K.C. remembers his mother being the focal point of the problems in the family, but he also recalls his father as being far from perfect. Nevertheless, even to this day, K.C. is extremely concerned about being perfect himself. He readily admits in therapy that this desire for perfection is related to his fear of losing control and to his profound feeling that his low self-esteem and supposed incompetence will come to the surface, becoming obvious to everyone. In both individual and group treatment, the heightened issues of perfectionism and self-control, along with the threat of shame and humiliation, were looked at and encountered over and over.

K.C. remembers two significant and recurrent dreams he had when he was growing up in his alcoholic family. Many of the themes of this dream series can be seen in the dream series of other family members of ACOA. One intense, repeating dream occurred when K.C. was between the ages of thirteen and fifteen. During this time, he remembers dreaming of standing in a corner of the unfinished cellar in his house, doing something. His alcoholic mother would come over and begin her usual round of intense criticism of him. He was not sure what the criticism was about, but the same scenario would repeat itself. However, during these dreams he would become extremely enraged at her and then physically attack her. He would pound and beat her head into the floor so furiously that there was obvious damage. At this point, he would wake up. Here, the themes of anger and rage are seen to proliferate through this explosive kind of family constellation.

K.C. also remembers having terrifying recurrent nightmares as a child. These would occur sometimes three or four times a week. The themes of the nightmares were always about K.C. being pursued, caught, and tortured by giants or monsters. He believed the giants and monsters represented parental figures. He recalled being "killed thousands of times," but each time he was killed, he woke up. In another dream, he was beheaded in an elevator. This is interesting given the fact that in his other recurrent dreams, he often would beat his mother's head into the floor until there was damage. To this day, he has anxiety about being in closed rooms.

Next is another dream in which nightmarish themes of violence, helplessness, guilt, and low self-esteem are played out. Instead of coming from a large family, this patient, K.M., was an only child with intense responsibilities. In addition to feeling that there was no family or community support for his father's alcohol abuse and physical abuse, K.M. felt that his poor grades were a reflection of his family's problems. He also believed that the family would lose more and more esteem in the eyes of others if he did not do well in school. At the time, K.M. had not told his parents that he was withdrawing from school for medical reasons. He did not know what he would say when his family found out.

K.M. indicated that he was very upset, but he did not indicate any suicidal thoughts. I was concerned about this and probed a little deeper. He indicated that suicide was not an option, given the fact that he was an only child. Also K.M. was clearly oriented to time, place, person, and events with no indication of bizarre ideation, hallucinatory behavior, impulsivity, or homicidal feelings toward his parents. His judgment was sound and his memory was intact. He was quite angry at his father, but he also felt helpless. In this context, K.M. reported the following dream, which occurred repeatedly when he was a teenager. In his dream, K.M.'s father, who is very angry and intoxicated, would be running around chasing his mother with the intent to do her physical harm. The mother would run away from the father and toward the son for help and protection. The son, however, was unable to help or speak, feeling that his hands were tied. His mouth opened, but nothing seemed to come out. He felt blocked. This dream seems to reflect the patient's triangulated emotional predicament, that is to say trapped between the struggles of his parents and himself. I gently suggested this to him and he agreed.

The dreams presented so far show the kinds of roles that can slowly evolve in this sort of powerful, but not very functional, family constellation. Some of these roles are used in non-ACOA families, depending on the stress and the situation. However, most of these roles seem to be localized in many of the families that are known and identified as ACOA families.

In a basically healthy, functional, and adaptive family, there tends to be open communication and respect for differences, along with a consistent pattern of loving discipline. This warmth and opportunity are necessary for growth and for fun. Expectations are generally clear, and limit setting is done within the context of support. However, in an ACOA family, the atmosphere is permeated by unpredictability, actual or potential explosiveness, denial, anger, fear, and guilt. Oftentimes if one spouse is drinking and the other is not, the nondrinking spouse is caught up in what is called a "codependency relationship," that is, they are caught up in the drinking behavior of the other spouse. The nondrinking spouse may demonstrate a great deal of frustration and anger toward the drinking spouse, but also a great deal of protectiveness as well. As a result, the nondrinking spouse is less emotionally available to his or her children. Mixed messages come from both parents. Out of this bewildering maze of emotional conflicts, ACOA family members essentially learn three rules for psychological boundary maintenance and strategies for emotional survival:

1. Don't talk, except about superficial things, since real issues are bound to get one in trouble.
2. Don't trust anyone. It is not safe, since you never know what will happen.
3. Don't feel, or at least tightly control what you do feel. It is much too painful, and you don't have much control over what others will do if your feelings come out.

Given people's needs and styles, they will all do different things with some of the roles that emerge out of alcoholic families. However, these roles tend to repeat themselves across ACOA families with a great deal of regularity. They are deep within the family's unconscious matrix and come out in each person's personality and dreamscape. Let us now look at some of these roles.

ACOA FAMILY ROLES

The first family role of course is the chemically dependent or "identified patient." This is the person who is usually most overtly drinking. Sometimes, it is more than one person. These individuals often appear quite charming, and yet they can be extremely manipulative and hostile and appear as though they feel the need to escape from the family for all kinds of reasons. While they may often have suicidal tendencies below the surface, sometimes these self-destructive tendencies emerge and are quite obvious. Sometimes others in the family share a secret, forbidden, guilty desire for the troubled drinker to successfully commit suicide.

The codependent, or mate of this chemically dependent individual, is another role in the family. This person is often called the "enabler" or "caretaker." This is usually the competent, responsible, or overresponsible member of the family. When it is not the spouse, it is often the oldest child. In an attempt to deal with a chaotic family situation, this member is often extremely self-reliant, self-directed, empathic, and sensitive to the needs of others and to the nuances of acceptable behavior in the family. At the same time, however, they are constantly repressing and suppressing an enormous amount of hurt and anger. They experience extreme difficulty surrendering their vigilance and allowing themselves to relax. They often are very controlling of others in a projected attempted to subdue their own inner anxiety state. Their positive aspect is that they often become leaders in the helping professions. However, the other side of this is that they often have difficulty accepting their own needs for support, tenderness, and empathy. These two—the enabler, or caretaker, and the chemically dependent—form the primary driving engine of the family. Most of the others in the family are reactive to this parental system.

One of the more interesting roles in ACOA families is that of the "family hero." These are typically the oldest children. They appear super responsible and are very success oriented. In other words, they are just the opposite of what you might expect from the oldest child, who usually identifies most with the parent. Often, they are extremely independent, while under the surface they are constantly seeking the approval of others. "Counterdependent" is the clinical term for this behavior. Their own addiction may come out in either alcohol abuse or workaholism. However, what is important here is that their style of adaptation is an attempt to be super perfect and to hide or contain their emotions. In the dreams presented so far one can begin to see that although the anger and rage in the family are repressed, these feelings do come out as powerful images in the dream.

The "scapegoat" is another common role seen and amplified in ACOA families. The scapegoat individual is seen to be acting out repressed and conflicted behaviors in the family. While this behavior is painful for the scapegoat, it provides family members with a distraction from the more dangerous and painful behavior of the chemically dependent individual. Fortunately or unfortunately, these individuals have extremely strong peer values. While they often become chemical abusers themselves, they also—in their own way—are trying to provide some relief for the family. They are more likely to run away, have difficulties in school, or have other problems that the family can sometimes focus on and call the "real problem of the family." However, underneath the surface, like many other ACOA family members, they feel shut off, angry, rejected, guilty, and isolated. Recall the individual discussed earlier who dreamed of a backyard full of fences and hedges that all blocked each other off and did not allow any contact.

Another role that seems to come out of the ACOA family constellation is the "family clown." Sometimes this person is called the "irrelevant individual." This is usually a younger child who acts very humorous and entertaining. These family clowns are the most loved and affectionate members of the family. They tend to provide some comic relief to lighten the tension in the family. They are also attempting, in their own way, to help the family move through an intolerable crisis. However, underneath, they experience a great deal of confusion and a heightened sense of vulnerability and frigidity. They often become artists and entertainers.

The "lost child" is yet another role that emerges in ACOA families. This role, too, is usually played by a younger child. However, these children try as much as possible to be invisible and generally do not act out. They make no waves and may be seen as shy and keep to themselves. However, their withdrawal is often an expression of depression and feeling inadequate and emotionally insignificant to others. This style also helps protect them from the critical eye of the addicted family member, who often is looking for ways to criticize, belittle, shame, and humiliate family members. It is an adaptive style, but one that is bought at an enormous cost.

J.A. was an extremely creative, attractive, and entertaining individual. She often presented herself in a very cheerful manner, even though at times she felt extremely confused, angry, and depressed. For many years, she felt it was important to present to the world the image of someone who was humorous, helpful to others, and in control. As she was struggling with issues of ACOA in a therapeutic context, she became less and less attracted to this mode of adaptation and more concerned with expressing herself and freeing herself from this painful family pattern. She had enormous difficulties setting boundaries and maintaining her sense of autonomy from what she experienced to be the intrusive influence of others.

As we see in many ACOA families, other members of the family can also be severely addicted to different substances. In J.A.'s situation, she had profound concerns about her sister's difficulties and endless complications. She recalled her sister also having difficulty setting boundaries with men, especially men who were friends, or friends of other friends. Therapy with J.A. often involved helping her establish psychic and psychological boundaries within herself, so that she would be more aware and able to express the necessity of having these boundaries with others. She was not a borderline personality in the classical sense. However, she did experience a great deal of anxiety and chaotic sexual feelings at times when she had to say no or set boundaries with others.

J.A. remembered her romantic relationships running "hot and cold." At times, she could be childish and provocative but then was confused when people would respond to her in a way that she felt she could not predict. This was accompanied by much anxiety and confusion in both social and intimate heterosexual relationships. She associated some of this to the angry, rejecting, and rigid authority relationships in her family. This particular pattern continued to appear as though it would affect her nonfamily relationships as well.

She remembers one dream that involved a supermarket:

I'm in a supermarket. I'm where the cashier was. For some reason, the cashier was giving a very chaotic lecture on art, especially the distinction between Vincent van Gogh and Picasso. Apparently, the cashier made a mistake and was attributing the images of Starry Night to Picasso instead of van Gogh. I wanted to correct her on this. However, I was trying to get in line using my automobile, as opposed to being in line like everybody else. Eventually, I was able to change this woman's mind, but not without a lot of struggle. After that, she drove out to California in the same car and picked up a number of people. These people seemed to be artists and others whom she found very attractive. However, all of these situations felt very chaotic and very anxiety-provoking.

J.A. indicated that she wanted to help these other individuals. She had absolutely no idea why things were so chaotic in the dream. This chaotic situation appeared in many of her dreams. When she more specifically examined the dream, however, she associated it with individuals she had recently met and with men she had just been involved with. In other words, she associated chaos in her dreams with the various relationships in her life. Curiously, J.A. did not mention at first that her mother was an artist. She did make that connection later in the session, though, recalling that her mother was a painter. Still, she continued to have difficulty making a connection between the dream process and her family process. Anxiety would arise, and her memory would fail her.

In another dream series, J.A. remembered being in perpetual conflict with her parents. She remembers trying to get in between her two warring parents to stop them from fighting, but she was never able to do so. J.A. was able to make some connection between her anxiety level and her difficulties interpreting the intimate clues of other people. She confessed to being very defensive when it came to intimate social behavior. She, again, would send out a signal that she was interested but then move away; at a later time she would send out the opposite signal and wonder why the person appeared confused. Remember, her relationships ran "hot and cold," according to her. Her own artwork had emerged as a way of both dramatizing and entertaining herself and others. But even her artwork often appeared chaotic and unpredictable to her.

In some families, the roles become so intense that individuals have a difficult time separating themselves from their roles. These roles can involve a great deal of pathology. Issues of guilt, anger, perfectionism, and low self-esteem are bound together, as are fears of explosiveness and the reactionary need to be in control and be perfect. Fear and escape motifs emerge over and over.

I.R. was a twenty-five-year-old college junior. She had lived away from home, as had her older sister, for nearly fifteen years because their mother had been diagnosed as both a paranoid schizophrenic and a violent alcoholic. Both sisters had lived with different people in foster homes. They have experimented quite a bit with alcohol themselves, using fake I.D.s and drinking to the point of almost passing out. Both were very concerned about being alcoholic. While they had both been in psychotherapy for many years, I.R. continued to have a history of alcohol abuse and auto accidents.

She described a number of very intense, fused, and volatile relationships with her sister, her mother, and her boyfriend. She actually moved around the country quite a few times, attempting to get away from these individuals, but somehow they would always locate her and the relationships would begin again.

I.R. indicated that living with her very erratic and explosive mother drew her and her older sister together. However, she said this closeness created another difficulty: a codependent relationship. In fact, the sister seemed to have entered into this fusion relationship with I. R. to the point that they would have complementary ideas, images, and dreams. At times, this was very interesting to them and reflected their degree of supportive intimacy. At other times, I.R. felt as if the relationship was suffocating her. The two sisters became so involved in their relationship that they had fewer and fewer friends and became progressively more isolated. I.R. in particular was quite concerned that her older sister seemed to be destroying their relationships with all of their friends. Issues of loyalty and identity kept coming up between them. As a consequence of these issues and I.R.'s growing sense of isolation from others, she felt that she needed to escape. Often, these escapes would involve attempting to become involved with another man. However, the men she became involved with often turned out to be demanding and absorbing individuals.

I.R. and her sister both flunked out of school several times, and they both had recurring dreams. I.R. dreamed a number of times that her mother was dead. Her mother was not actually killed in the dreams but would be found dead. She also reported dreaming a great deal about bees, wasps, and insects; she was very afraid of insects stinging her. I.R. also dreamed an unusually large number of dreams concerning automobile accidents. (Remember that this patient was often involved in minor automobile accidents, sometimes when she was drinking.) In these dreams, the patient would find herself being catapulted from the car and flying through the air beyond anything that she had seen before. She indicated that she also had "psycho-weirdo dreams" about her older sister.

I.R. remembers that when she and her older sister were growing up, they were extremely close. She idolized her older sister. Her older sister seemed to be better able to cope with her mother, but this did not turn out to be the case. The older sister was actually a "parental" child who took care of her mother, given the usual dynamics of ACOA. The older sister also tried to protect I.R. from her mother's explosiveness. However, the older sister herself became an alcoholic and developed a paranoid-schizophrenic style. In other words, the older, parental sister began to identify more and more with her own mother and was eventually swept into the destructive undercurrent of the family unconscious. This was a tragic situation in which the role of the family hero later became identified with that of the substance abuser. It is usually the family scapegoat who is more overtly identified with the family's chemically dependent person, but not all of these roles are rigid.

I.R. was very concerned about her own alcohol use. She had very mixed feelings about it, and these mixed feelings were intimately connected with her own feelings about codependency and her fear of isolation.

ACOA DYNAMICS: THE DREAM AND ART

The themes of fear, anger, guilt, and isolation have been used quite successfully by ACOA family members who went on to become great writers or artists. In the United States alone, William Faulkner, F. Scott Fitzgerald, Ernest Hemingway, and Eugene O'Neill all grew up in alcoholic families. Their literary genius was both deeply influenced by, and in deep conflict with, the ACOA family style. These writers were able to take the various roles that ACOA presents and turn them into literary works that described the intimate crucible of the family life in an ACOA constellation. Only fleetingly did they ever focus precisely on ACOA as a syndrome; yet such themes are quite obvious throughout their writings.

The self-destructiveness of other ACOA family members can later have repercussions on their offspring. Thomas Wolfe's classic novel *Look Homeward, Angel* is about an ACOA family and the seeds of destruction that grew from it. Jack London was also touched profoundly by the dynamics of ACOA. So was Sinclair Lewis, who was himself an alcoholic. Even James Joyce could not escape the bewildering power of the ACOA syndrome. The visionary twentieth-century painter Jackson Pollock would sometimes get roaring drunk, pick fights (or fake them), and proposition women endlessly—and he still managed to change the course of modern art. One could also list Hart Crane, Marjorie Rawlings, John Cheever, Truman Capote, and many others.[2] All these major American artists were singed by the flames of ACOA familial dynamics. So we can see the dynamics of ACOA are not controlled or transcended simply because a person or artist develops a creative outlet or expression for the pain they experienced in an ACOA family.

OEDIPUS AND ACOA

P.C. grew up in an extended alcohol- and substance-abuse family. His mother abused food in addition to alcohol. She had serious problems with her weight as well as mental and psychosomatic illnesses. P.C. initially had numerous difficulties with his sexual identity and his ability to move beyond the crisis of fear and tragedy into periods of serenity, clarity, and compassion for others. However, he eventually did so. He described how the intense love-hate relationship between him and his mother immobilized him. Their relationship had many levels of sexual feeling and emotional intimacy. P.C. had replaced his father as the mother's confidant, companion, and emotional supporter. She came to depend on him more and more, while both became more hostile and alienated from the husband/father. His mother eventually died as a result of her substance abuse when P.C. was in his latency period. This had a profound impact on his development.

P.C. remembers having recurrent childhood dreams of his mother coming to him and soothing him emotionally and physically when he was quite frightened. It was both a tender and erotic feeling. P.C. remembers a dream that repeated itself often. In this dream, he was chasing his mother with a dead mouse in his hand. His mother would become quite frightened, pick up a large stone, and attempt to crush P.C. with it. At the same time, P.C. would remember his mother in a dream fragment that presented him with the idea that "a way to forgiveness is to bring daisies." Thus, P.C. experienced an extremely hostile love relationship with his mother. This expressed itself in his other intense love-hate relationships. It took him years to overcome this sense of intimate violence and unpredictability in his family or in any other family he might be involved with. He developed many somatic and psychosomatic problems and needed to consult numerous medical experts for certain periods in his life. These were the result of his difficulty dealing with ACOA issues. At times, he was overweight, having developed an eating disorder that was identical to that of his mother.

THE ACOA FAMILY LEGACY

Given that the ACOA family teaches one not to communicate directly, not to trust, and, above all, not to feel, how do these unwritten rules and guidelines of family communication ultimately affect the personality and dreamlife of ACOA family members? I have already mentioned numerous times how patients' fears of losing control manifest in their dreams. I have focused on their sometimes overly developed sense of responsibility and heightened sense of guilt as being reactions to the fear of losing control of their own boundaries and violence. Living in a world of constant denial, including suppressing and denying one's own feelings and perceptions, cultivates a sense of not being in touch with one's own self and to a corresponding inability to control and maneuver smoothly in intimate relationships. At the same time, one is working overtime to control the roiling internal ocean of feelings. Fear, self-criticism, and living in the world as a victim permeate this lifestyle. However, more powerful than even this is the intimate relationship between fear and the cyclical desire to escape the fear.

Issues of intimacy and seduction and then reactionary violence oscillate in these intense love-hate relationships. The love-hate aspect itself goes back and forth. The ACOA member all too often has very violent and angry feelings toward the parent, yet these are only expressed in dreams. They cannot, and will not, be expressed openly in the family. These violent and volatile relationships seem to characterize the dark side of the ACOA family.

Denial has a positive side, at least initially, in the sense that it helps the psychic principle remain a little more stable and afloat in a chaotic emotional sea for these very vulnerable individuals. However, everyone is affected on a physical, emotional, and even spiritual level in these families. The constant potential for explosive behavior has a profound effect on the psychological defense patterns and the emotional reactivity of family members. In fact, it may be quite helpful at certain times to deny one's own feelings and strategically not trust, particularly if one feels excessively guilty, vulnerable, or violence prone oneself. This leads to feeling confused about the differences between intimacy and smothering, as well as the difference between deep relaxation and depression. These are all issues that ACOA family members must struggle with,[3] and they are the core issues and dynamics of what has become known popularly as the "inner child."

The subtle addiction to high levels of chaos is carried by ACOA into their own families later on. This is how the symptoms can be transferred from one generation to another. Guilt in particular is a difficult dynamic. In the ACOA family constellation, members have often learned to regard their own needs as an imposition on others. There is a subtle feeling that if they ask for something, they expose and reflect their vulnerability and others will use this against them. While avoidance of feelings can have a positive side, it is far outweighed by the negative side, since one can come to have a fundamental sense that feelings in themselves are wrong, bad, scary, or even dangerous.

In behavioral medicine, we have noticed that a large number of patients who come in for treatment of tension headaches, chronic fatigue, depression, colitis, or ulcers are often struggling internally with issues of ACOA. This is not to say that all people who experience these symptoms are struggling with these identical issues. However, we are pointing out that the ACOA constellation is a particular identifiable constellation that has a certain pattern of severe somatic repercussions.

CLINICAL FALLOUT OF ACOA

What are some of the repercussions of being part of ACOA families? What are some of the serious, across-the-board health costs and emotional risks? What about the spiritual damage done? The following are well-researched facts concerning children who have grown up in an alcoholic family.

In the United States alone, it is presently estimated that more than thirty million Americans have at least one alcoholic parent in their family. It is also well known that approximately half of all alcoholics have an alcoholic parent. Even more unnerving is the fact that one in three families currently report that at least one family member abuses alcohol. And finally, children of alcoholics are at a much higher risk of developing alcoholism themselves or becoming attracted to, and marrying, someone who is potentially an alcoholic.

The current medical research tends to support the idea that children born to alcoholics are the highest risk group for developing attention deficit disorders. At birth, they also have a higher risk of fetal alcohol syndrome and other alcohol-related difficulties. In an alarming statistic, alcohol is a significant factor in up to 90 percent of families in which child abuse occurs. Children of alcoholics are frequently victims of incest, child neglect, and other forms of violence and exploitation. This sad fact has been confirmed by the National Association for Children of Alcoholics. We have seen these dynamics expressed in the dreams of ACOA.

These ACOA make valiant attempts to adapt to the high levels of chaos and unpredictability endangering the sense of security in their families. However, this is often a losing battle. They too often only develop the inability to trust others. While they exhibit a very strong need to remain in control and to appear responsible, even overresponsible at times, the denial of their deeper feelings results in low self-esteem, depression, and extreme isolation, including a sense of self-alienation. Guilt, anger, and depression all seem to go together. ACOA have difficulties maintaining satisfying relationships and often become involved with other people who have alcohol or other substance abuse problems. These persist throughout childhood and into adult life.[4]

These developments remain unseen by others because the ACOA family has gone to great extremes to deny problems and appear normal. Except for those who are also acting out, the ACOA facade is often not even noticed. In most of the cases reported in this chapter, the individuals appear to others to be well adjusted and generous with very few problems of their own. This is particularly the case with the therapist and the artist discussed earlier. Both are very loving and very creative individuals; however, they often have profound difficulties in intimate relationships. They are always expecting the situation to become explosive and chaotic at any moment. This fear of chaos and explosion is endemic in ACOA family relationships, and it inescapably finds expression in ACOA's individual and collective dreamlife. The question to answer in these situations is not *"what* is the matter with you?" but again *"who* is the matter with you?"

Further adding to the complexity of this scene is the observation by family therapists first brought to our attention by Murray Bowen that the actual symptom pattern can express itself in one generation, then skip a generation, only to reappear in the next! This is known as the "multigenerational transmission process" and includes not only attempts at differentiation from the family of origin but the transmission of symptomology.[5] From our point of view in this book it is as though there were "waves" in the larger field of familial consciousness into which recurrent familial personas from time to time arise or descend and participate in the system.

SUMMARY OF ACOA FAMILY STYLES

We have seen in the family dreams and in the family unconscious matrix of ACOA families that there are certain patterns, roles, and styles that repeat themselves. We have observed from the dreams presented the volatile intimate relationships that emerge. Violent family themes are quite common. Powerful emotions of fear and a desire to escape appear repeatedly in these dreams. In the intimate relationships of ACOA family members, we often find them feeling very close to the substance-abusing member and then, at other times, they suddenly feel very far away. In short, they are never quite sure where they stand. This seems to fuel and complicate extremely intense love-hate relationships, which oscillate back and forth. There is usually profound anger, guilt, and resentment toward the ACOA parent; violent dreams and fantasies express this. There is a reactive desire to hurt those who have hurt you. However, there is also a great deal of emotional loyalty toward this family member. Rage, aggression, and anger are held in check by denial, depression, low self-esteem, and repression in the painful inner landscape of ACOA family members. Their dreams express this shared emotional matrix powerfully and deeply. And love . . . love is an avenging angel on the horizon with an injured wing.

8

Family Dreams during Pregnancy

Sweet weight,
in celebration of the woman I am
and of the soul of the woman I am
and of the central creature and its delight
I sing for you. I dare to live.

. . . .

Each cell has a life.
There is enough here to please a nation.

A. SEXTON, "IN CELEBRATION
OF MY UTERUS," FROM *LOVE POEMS*

THE OCEAN OF BIRTH: DYNAMICS AND THEMES

The body slowly widens and blooms like a great orchid. The generation and development of a new life is a momentous event in a family's development. After the intensity of conception there is a long period before anything is really known. Then, in the months that follow, the sleeping fetus elongates and grows. In the adventure of embryogenesis

139

the fetus develops. There are numerous biochemical and morphological changes occurring within the warm inner saline sea of a woman's body. These changes are paralleled by changes in the development of the fetus itself. There is no line of demarcation that is absolute between fetus and mother. Long before birth the fetus has gone through several stages of development that appear to have a profound effect on the subsequent dreamlife of this growing individual. Stanislav Grof, M.D.,[1] has traced this arch of development in the stages of the child's delivery.

The first stage actually encompasses most of the fetus's normal development. This is the stage of mostly quiet undisturbed intrauterine life. Our earliest human experiences in the womb are thought to be a mixture of positive ones (oceanic types of ecstasy, fusion with nature) and negative ones (fetal distresses, emotional upheavals of the mother, and spontaneous attempts by the body at abortions). These powerful, emotional, prototypical experiences will manifest later in life in the world of our dreams.

During the first stage of actual delivery, there is a rising distress within the fetus. It feels its world suddenly changing. The womb begins to contract. Feelings of engulfment and immense physical and psychological suffering may occur. The developing fetus may later experience dreams in which he or she relives the experiences of unbearable and inescapable pressures. Images of hell and feelings of entrapment may exist. These will have their expression in dream material of all kinds.

The next stage involves the slow movement and stronger contractions of the birth process. Suffering is intensified almost to almost cosmic proportions. There are powerful feelings of explosions, blood, fierce battles, and a literal struggle for life and death. This stage will have its expression later in life in dream images of various kinds with varying degrees of intensity. In particular, images of sadomasochistic and orgasmic sexual feelings may occur. Images of birth and death are constantly intermingling.

Finally, there is the actual physical birth itself. There is a rush and then an enormous sense of freedom and illumination. Images of radiant light, rainbows, and feelings of rebirth and redemption appear. All of these sensations manifest in the later dreamlife of the individual. While all of this has been developing on the inside, the mother and the family of this infant are having concomitant and parallel dreams on the outside.

These are precursors of the emotional life of the infant. The infant's family, however, is already intensely and consciously remembering, thinking, and dreaming about the emergence of this brand new person into their lives. Their dreams are also thick with intense feelings, anxieties, fears, and expectations. The intensity of these feelings can in themselves reach enormous proportions. Take the following dream submitted by a professor of clinical psychiatry:

We had been talking about having a second child for some time. We had been weighing the risks with the advantages. My wife and I both had concerns about her health. I had concerns about whether I would have enough to be a good parent to two children. I had recently decided that I wanted a second child if my wife's health was safe. It was at this time that I had the following dream:

I was in my car. I knew something was wrong. I did not know what was wrong. Then I was stopped by a state trooper. I can see his car in front of mine. He started to search my car. He found marijuana in the car. I was arrested. He and others went then to search my house. In my house they found pornography. They found dirty magazines in a trunk. They also found Polaroid pictures of my wife and me making love.

Next, I was on the witness stand at my trial. The prosecuting attorney was drilling me. He was twisting my words so that I had to agree with him. He questioned my wife's and my competence as parents. What were we doing with pictures like these and having children. His argument was so strong that I folded. I had lost.

The next image was outside. My wife was talking with a woman outside our front door. The woman had my first born in her arms. She was a child welfare worker. My daughter was crying, but she didn't say anything. The welfare worker was taking my daughter away. We had been found to be unfit as parents. My wife was saying goodbye to my daughter. I felt terrible. It was then that I woke up.

We can see many themes running through this very powerful dream. Many of these themes are very common for family members giving birth. There are themes of loss, loss of a child, fears of inadequacy, and also financial fears and health and delivery problem fears. This happened to be the dream of a father. Now look at the dream of a mother:

In my first dream I dreamed that I am flying very high in an airplane ready to jump out in a parachute. However, I am unsure or ambivalent about jumping. Would the parachute open? Was it not the time? Was it safe? I feel anxious and frightened at the opening to all this.

A quick analysis of this dream shows similar themes of fear and anxiety concerning the birth, making a change, and parental adequacy on many levels. This second dream was a dream of a woman in her seventh month of pregnancy of her second child. She was a professional woman and also a woman who had already had one birth experience. It is quite clear that having one birth experience does not necessarily eliminate all anxieties concerning the next birth.

Like other kinds of dreams, some of these dreams during pregnancy are very brief; others are very long and involved. In this particular chapter we will look at both types of dreams. We will also explore the dreams of *both* fathers and mothers and other family members and relatives when appropriate. By looking at the perspectives of many different people in the family, we will come to see the development of the family unconscious system throughout this spectacular period of family life. Each significant other in the family system will see and enfold the same event from a slightly different perspective, again much like a living hologram.

We will look at the dream content first from the perspective of the developmental periods or "trimesters" of pregnancy. Then we will look at this content from the perspective of the *common themes* that appear in our dreams during this period. There will be many extremely powerful ups and downs and changes during this time. The increase in intensity of emotions during pregnancy is well known. During this time, the family, and particularly the mother and father, are in contact with the elemental forces of creation, and therefore, inevitably, the forces of destruction. Contact with the elemental forces of creation and destruction inevitably leads to the contemplation or at least a passing reflection on the onset, duration, and termination of physical life. However, it arches beyond this to those fields of phenomena and experience that surround and infuse life, death, and the worlds that they encompass. Just as life and consciousness are known to exist prior to clinical birth, we know from near-death experiences (NDEs) and studies that life and consciousness appear to persist, if only for a brief period, after clinical death. Birth is not the exact beginning of consciousness, nor is death its rigid end. We can agree with Shakespeare that "we are such stuff as dreams are made on, and our little life is rounded with a sleep."

RESEARCH ON DREAMS AND PREGNANCY: THE TRIMESTERS

Dr. Patricia Maybruck[2] has outlined and examined hundreds upon hundreds of dreams submitted by men and women in the process of pregnancy. She follows on the heels of numerous other dream and pregnancy researchers—including psychologists, physicians, and experimentalists. These researchers also stress that dreams during the trimesters of pregnancy are more intense and different than dreams during other parts of the life cycle. It is not that the content of the dreams is radically different but rather that certain areas of the content are intensely magnified. These researchers all readily agree that dreams during pregnancy reflect the intensified emotional and biological life of the family.

Dr. Maybruck has outlined six particular themes that repeat

themselves and constantly overlap each other during the family's era of pregnancy. These dreams are focused around the themes of *physical deformity* or death, *inadequacy* of the dreamer, *loss* of one's mate, *difficulty* with delivery, *loss* of control, and *financial* burdens. The presence of these themes has also been confirmed by my own research. I would add three additional categories, however, that appear to reflect the consciousness of the dreamer concerning pregnancy. They are as follows: desires or *expectations for the newborn* in their own lives, *psi-mediated* dreams, and *mythological or psychospiritual* dreams. These emotional themes and motifs are strikingly similar to others that have been mentioned in previous chapters. In fact, you might even say that the expressions, images, and feelings during pregnancy are a particular bandwidth on the spectrum of the emotional scale and dynamics human beings are capable of expressing in their dreamlife. As this chapter develops, we will return to these categories and look at two or more examples of each one of these nine categories of family members' principal concerns during the trimesters of pregnancy. My approach to pregnancy dreams differs from other books and work in this area in that I will use dreams that explicitly make reference to pregnancy itself. This will decrease ambiguities of interpretation and make the significance of a dream more accessible to us.

Although themes have often been encountered before, the dream lives of all family members are greatly intensified and take on a dynamic new life during pregnancy. Pregnancy is a momentous and oceanic event in this epigenetic stage of family life. Birth, the risk of death, and intuition of rebirth loom large as primordial themes. There are enormous and elemental changes in the body of the woman. There are enormous changes in the body of the family itself, both psychologically and somatically speaking. Dreams clearly, powerfully, and vividly reflect this.

Here is the dream of a woman in her fifth month of pregnancy. She is having concerns about the continuation of her professional career, being an adequate parent, and making contact with her unborn child.

I dream that I am going shopping and hearing E.'s name come up in many separate places. There is no sight of him, only numerous references to his name and to his many needs. I feel some sense of urgency but cannot contact what it is that I am looking for. I can only hear it.

It is clear that this woman is struggling with normal themes and that accepting the identity of a new child is a problematic situation for her. The anxiety around loss and misplacement of the child is a common theme.

Eileen Stukane[3] has suggested that each of the three trimesters is accompanied by and reflects a different stage of dreaming for the family. Images of fertility and other elemental events naturally occur during the first trimester. Dreams may express images of flowering plants, vegetables, and other growing things. Dr. Robert Van de Castle's[4] studies of pregnancy during the first trimester revealed that many dreams contain tiny creatures, usually furry, cuddly little animals. However, there are also images of birds and fish and other aquatic animals during this time. In a sense, the earth and water elements predominate in the context of dreams during this period. Also during the first trimester, the beginning imagery of tunnels and rooms and roads and barriers begins to take shape. Coinciding with these images are the family's concerns about the health, safety, and conduct of the fetus during this time. This is the time when most of those spontaneous abortions alluded to earlier occur. It is also the first time that the couple or the individual begins to consciously realize the enormous responsibilities and the curtailment of personal freedom that are implicated with the arrival of a new life.

According to Stukane, it is the second trimester in which the actual image of the baby itself begins to populate the inner landscape of one's dreamlife. While the first trimester reportedly contains images of fertility and the generation of birth, the second trimester reflects the growth of the fetus and the looming reality of this fact in the emotional and psychological life of both the mother and father. The not-yet-born child, in a sense, begins to have a personality of their own in the mind of the parents. During the second trimester, women tend to describe enclosed areas and interiors in the imagery of their dreamlife. This is undoubtedly a reflection of the phenomenon of embryological development occurring within the womb of the mother. Men, however, are often known to dream of open spaces and exteriors, although this is not always the case. Many men concerned about the loss of traditional freedom may begin to dream about being trapped or encircled.

These differences in the content of men's and women's dreams have been studied by clinicians and researchers in the past and appear to hold fast even in these days of increased role flexibility for the two sexes.[5] They are summarized in the table on page 147. They reflect deep-seated differences in *tendencies,* relational styles, concerns, and attitudes between men and women. They are, however, tendencies and not absolute differences. Note the different emphasis each places on survival of the family, nurturance, and familiarity in relationships.

Along these lines, Dr. Cecilia Jones,[6] in her study of pregnancy dreams, found numerous references to large architectural forms. She felt that these architectural references reflected the dreamer's preoccupation with the uterine environment. She also noticed that a number of the architectural structures had been damaged in the dreams of pregnant women. In contrast, architectural structures that appeared in the dreams of nonpregnant women had less physical damage and fewer defects associated with them. She naturally concluded that these images and dreams of damaged structures arose from the anxiety of the pregnant mother, which was focused around her body image and boundaries.

During this period of time, especially with the arrival of the "personality" of the fetus into the emotional life of the family, other interpersonal and familial themes become quite intensified. Mother-daughter dreams apparently increase during the second and the third trimester. Dreams of the father and his own father and their unresolved issues arise. Dr. Van de Castle estimates that there are approximately five mothers to each father present in women's dreams during pregnancy. This may give us some idea of the concerns of the pregnant mother as

SEXUAL DIFFERENCES IN
MALE AND FEMALE DREAMS

Men's Dreams	Women's Dreams
Sexual contact with many unfamiliar people	Sexual contact with familiar people
Many sexual dreams, many themes of success and failure	More verbal activity and emotional reactions in sexual contacts. Increased moral and ethical concerns.
Overt expressions of aggression and hostility and competition	Subtle expressions of hostility, competition, and aggression. Higher sensitivity to rejection. More competition with women than men. Men seen as aggressors, women as victims.
More groups of unfamiliar and unrelated people. Work related themes more pronounced.	More familiar people, relatives, children, and babies.
Events occur in unfamiliar, outdoor and alien places.	Events occur in well-known, indoor places.
Dreams of animals more like reptiles, birds, and non-mammals. More aggressive creatures.	Dreams of mammals, soft, furry creatures, more benign, non-aggressive creatures.
More references to cars, weapons, tools, money, hair, size, speed, intensity, competition, power.	More attention to clothing, color, eyes, rooms, household objects, ornaments.

opposed to those of the father. These are apparently attempts to work through one's own family unconscious matrix of relationships.

Researchers have found that by the third trimester, because of the radically different shape of the woman's body and the obviousness of the upcoming event, issues concerning boundaries, attractiveness, sexuality, and financial pressures increase and proliferate in the dreamlife. The reactions of other family members become more and more prominent. Concerns about labor and childbirth take on increased urgency, since these are rapidly approaching realities. Dr. Robert D. Gillman,[7] a psychiatrist, has noted that often in order to deal with this momentous event, women will dream of having mature sons or daughters. This is an attempt of the mind to conveniently avoid the cataclysmic event of birth, be it positive or negative, and to move on to a more stable period.

Dr. Helene Deutsch,[8] the psychoanalyst, found that as the experience of labor, childbirth, and delivery draws nearer, women's concerns often shift from death and childbirth to more psychological issues such as the fear of separation. In her book *The Psychology of Women*, Deutsch reported that "in all women, the happy and the disappointed, the strong and the weak, the loving and the hating, the doubts, restlessness, impatience, and joyful expectation all conceal the fear of delivery, which is increasingly intensified with the approach of term." In all of these dream images, however, there are numerous and powerful references to the elemental forces of nature—birth and rebirth, the cycles and rhythms of life. Perhaps earlier in humankind's history, these rhythms and cycles of birth and death and rebirth in the natural world gave rise to the notion of reincarnation. It is certainly true that in primordial times, humanity was preoccupied with the mystery of fertility. In ancient times a strong and large baby would be considered a healthy baby. In dreams this often can be exaggerated. Note the following dream in this family by the mother of the mother-to-be.

> J.'s mother F. called and said, "The baby's arrived and boy was it a whopper." I said, "Really?" She said, "Ya, it weighed 16 lbs." In my anxiety I forgot to ask how J. (the mother) was.

Again the image/event/emotion is enfolded by another significant other in the family.

During the first trimester the mother can often experience enormous biochemical changes and imbalances that affect her dreamlife. Somatically these can also be experienced as nausea and morning sickness. In general, a pregnant woman recalls more of her dreams than a nonpregnant woman. However, a woman's menstrual cycle appears to increase her dream recall, with the greatest recall just prior to menstruation. In any event, during dreaming all women experience increased oxygen consumption, GI tract secretions, and adrenal hormones pumped into the bloodstream. The nipples become erect, vaginal temperature increases, along with blood flow, and sometimes contractions occur. Men experience penile erections while dreaming.

By the second trimester, the fetus may develop teeth and calcified bones and may begin to do some thumb sucking within the womb. The fingernails develop and kicking is felt. This kicking is a momentous event and is often experienced while the mother is dreaming. This is an unusually intimate situation. During the second trimester, blood volume and the metabolic rate also increase in the womb. In the final trimester, the eyes of the fetus open.

The fetus can respond to sounds and new or sudden sensations. *It is essentially conscious.* Research even indicates that the fetus has periods of sleep and wakefulness while in the womb! Contact between the mother and the fetus is certainly occurring. It is during the final trimester that the first preparatory muscle contractions for birth occur. These are the so-called Braxton-Hicks contractions. In the final trimester, the mother may develop, due to hormonal changes, increases in vaginal lubrication and a breast premilk substance, or colostrum, and the mucus membranes in her nose may briefly swell. These are all expressions of the enormous biochemical event that accompanies this moment of psychological, psychic, and somatic change. It is no wonder, then, that the parents become preoccupied with the psychological, somatic, and spiritual development of the growing fetus.

SIX COMMON THEMES OF PREGNANCY DREAMS

As you can readily see, the entire spectrum of human emotionality finds its way into the intensified and sometimes rarefied dreamlife of the family during pregnancy. However, this spectrum is not evenly represented.

Dr. Maybruck[9] and others have found that out of a whole range of human emotions, six overlapping themes appear to be more predominant during the pregnancy era of family dreams. I briefly touched upon this earlier. Capitalizing on her important and provocative work, I will present those fairly well-established themes and supplement them with my own observations. I will then present some representative dreams from each one of these categories. Again, these dreams are taken from the Family Dreams Research Project and include references from all three trimesters, from both the mother and the father and other family members, as well as from extended family members.

Concentrating on the intense but normal increase in preoccupation with the fetus during pregnancy, Dr. Maybruck noticed the six following streams that pour into the ocean of this experience: (1) dreams that the fetus or the baby will be *deformed* or die, (2) dreams of being an *inadequate* or in some way not-quite-successful parent, (3) dreams of *loss* of one's mate, (4) dreams of a *difficult delivery*, (5) dreams of *loss of control* in varying degrees, and (6) dreams of *financial burdens,* which may be more a reflection of modern times and pressures. Clinical research collected by the Family Dreams Research Project has tended to bear this out, as has the clinical research of others. However, in our own practice we have noticed three additional themes that seem to occur a great deal during pregnancy. These are dreams that concern what the parent *expects or desires* or wishes the child to be during the child's lifetime. Another series of dreams that can occur during pregnancy are *psi or paranormal* dreams. These are observations made by both laymen and professionals. Finally, there are historical and *mythological* dreams that refer to psychospiritual, cultural, and other universal concerns. Dreams representing each one of these bands on the spectrum will be presented.

Notice the elemental themes that occur in the dreams of this first-time mother in her twenty-ninth week of pregnancy. They are normal and powerful themes of deformity or defect in the child, even though other things in the dream appear quite normal.

I have arrived at a reunion for Three Mile Island, an Appalachian Mountain Club Family Camp we used to attend. I'm real excited to see some of the folks I used to know there. Actually they aren't very many of my old friends. I see Barbara W., who used to be there every single summer. I rush up to her, noticing how good she looks. A few others I knew but didn't like so well are there. Barbara and the others comment on my belly. I rub it proudly and discuss when I am due. Now I see movement in my belly, like I usually do, but this time I can see the clear outline of a face, nose and mouth showing through. I show everyone. We are all amazed. The mouth of the baby even opens up and I can put my fingers inside. This head (of the fetus) and mouth seem to grow until it becomes a long snout like a dog or a crocodile. It is actually full of tiny sharp teeth. It is still covered by my skin, but the skin goes all the way inside the mouth. It moves around a lot. I feel very concerned, especially since the skin seems to be tearing some.

In the following dream, submitted by a woman in her thirty-seventh week of pregnancy, the theme of deformity or potential deformity of the fetus again occurs. It is couched in terms of examination anxiety. A person seeks knowledge and guidance and security from her mate. All of these are normal themes.

I'm with a friend in a room full of moms and babies. They are discussing how after the birth I will be so limited in clothes, just two colors available.

I am anticipating when my water will break. I'm crossing some sort of street outside a modern-type building. K., my husband, has experience with this. He knows about water breaking since he has been through it. I want to hear of his experience and also realize his might be different from mine because he is a man. K. (I think) looks up the word amniotic in the dictionary. K. is then on the phone. We feel better now because the baby became a lot bigger, moves a lot, helping me feel relieved.

Suddenly I am listening to a program on the radio. I hear a description of the fetus's eye, as huge, unblinking, and streaked with blue. It is also

discussing how we can look and see whole fetuses. We see it as a whole
entity. When the fetus looks out its own eye, it sees only a very narrow
range. Its experience is very narrow.

A later dream submitted by this same woman reflected similar
themes. In this dream, public anxiety, medical examination, and concerns about self-evaluation during the whole situation occur.

She was born. There she was and she was nursing and she was really tiny.
I was holding her under my clothes. I was doing this because she weighed
only 2 lbs. Several days were going by and for some reason she was also
late. Then I was worried about taking baby pictures of her because it
seemed that it wasn't really her time to be born yet, that is to say she
looked like she was born too early and it was not o.k. to take pictures.
They say that right after the first hour of birth changes began to occur in
the baby.

This is a significant dream, and it is piggybacked by her husband's
dream.

It is Gallagher, and I associate to a Walt Disney dream. A doll is being
demonstrated at a museum amphitheater by a female assistant and a
male presenter. The man sniffs between the doll's legs and laughs, making
a joke about its action.

In these dreams it is clear that both parents are concerned about the
potential physical deficits the child may have and are either examining
it very closely or concerned that they may in some way harm it.

This next dream, submitted by a male professional, occurred during
his wife's final months of pregnancy, the last trimester. In this dream,
we see both concerns about being an inadequate parent and also concerns about loss of control. The sense of inadequacy comes from the
dreamer feeling like he may not be able to take care of the needs and

security requirements of his family. The loss of control has to do with the loss of control over the course and conduct of the situation.

This dream was actually stimulated by a real birth scene I witnessed in a movie. My wife and I are expecting a child. She doesn't seem anxious and is ready to let nature take its course. I am much more anxious and concerned and want her to get ready. She has some mild resistance to my pressure.

I consider making her or getting her committed to a psychiatric hospital because she isn't taking the birth and medical situations seriously enough. I appeal or consider appealing to a higher authority. I then awaken from this dream, reflect upon it, and then return to sleep. In the second dream, I dream of the feeling of pregnancy in the early stages. There are no images. I'm struck by this, almost in an abstract way. Then suddenly we are with our son. She and I are at a big event. She wants to take a long walk with him and me to the water or sea or the ocean. I do not and want to go home where we are safer. We then take our son, unexpectedly, to a family church situation that I don't really want to go to. We make a compromise, however, and I go.

As you see, the six themes are not separate from each other but often overlap and implicate each other on many levels. This male dreamer's feelings of inadequacy in terms of taking care of the family are apparent, as is his sense of losing control over the situation. The personality style that lends itself to manipulation and controlling behavior emerges and is intensified as an attempt on the part of this dreamer to deal with his normal anxiety. Interestingly enough, the wife of this dreamer had similar anxieties in the waking state about losing control and dreamed of going shopping several times and trying to find her son but only being able to hear his voice and see his image come up in numerous places.

Perhaps the most widespread and powerful themes that repeat across the spectrum of pregnancy dreams in families are those concerning the loss of a mate and difficulties in the actual delivery process. Out of these come powerful issues of loss, separation, and primordial anxiety. Two months before the birth of his second son, a doctor had the following dream:

> *My wife and I are out shopping for food with our son at a large super-market. We are going up and down the aisles, mostly the vegetables to the fresh fruit section. We are somehow separated, me by myself, my wife with our 2 and a half year-old son. While separated, my wife's labor pains begin and we are looking nervously for each other so that we can drive to the hospital. We finally do locate each other after an anxious search, rush to the hospital, but then discover they are only false labor pains. We are somewhat dismayed. Our other son is now curiously absent. We return home and are soon visited by a nurse carrying red flowers. The nurse really sees that pregnancy is still ongoing and is embarrassed by the lack of coordination. She smiles, drops off the flowers, and leaves.*

Here is another dream submitted by a woman in her thirty-eighth week. This dream reflects considerable anxiety, not only about the birth process but also about the supporting guidance of others. There are also subtle and clear references and themes concerning loss of control over the process.

> *I am in a large area with several other people all sort of milling around. It's quite dark. K. and I are here because a group of midwives (not our own) have suggested we come help with a woman's birth as a way to learn about what it is like. It's quite confusing. I can't really tell who is in labor at first. I figure it out and am sitting next to a woman who is next. I am touching her. There is some trouble; things aren't going that smoothly. I wander around some. Now I suddenly find that I am in active labor myself. I feel no pain, but feel myself dilating, opening up. One of the midwives checks my cervix. I can see her feeling it, as if she is holding my cervix up to the light. She is actually stretching it gently herself, smoothing it to full*

dilation. It feels fine, but I realize that we must call J., our midwife, and get home. This produces lots of feelings of tension and stress because we can't seem to reach J. We are in a small town and need to get to the other end of town.

This common theme of becoming anxious about the delivery has interesting clinical implications—implications for relaxation, that is. It is very common today to find relaxation and imagery procedures involved in the actual clinical process of birth. However, it was back in 1962 that Dr. J. V. Kelly presented his findings in the *American Journal of Obstetrics and Gynecology*[10] that when a woman became anxious or nervous, her tension caused her uterus to contract more slowly, perhaps resulting in a prolonged and more difficult delivery. Dr. Maybruck, Dr. Grantly Dick-Read,[11] and many others constantly emphasize the need for relaxation training from the very beginning of the birth process for this very reason. The emotional life of the mother has a profound effect on the emotional life of the infant. From the work of Stanislav Grof to the work of Thomas Verny and John Kelly, authors of *The Secret Life of the Unborn Child,*[12] evidence mounts that the fetus is indeed conscious and does respond to the emotional environment within and around it prior to birth. Thus, the emotional atmosphere surrounding the mother and the family unconscious system is of extreme importance during birth and has a powerful effect on the subsequent development of the personality of the newborn.

Notice the themes of loss of control and being overwhelmed that appear in the dreamlife of this professional woman in the midst of deciding whether or not she will return to work after the birth of her child. This occurred during the middle to latter part of the seventh month of pregnancy.

In the dream I am pregnant and swimming in a pool. Several people from my pressured work situation are at the poolside coming near me in the water. Next thing I realize is that I am under the water. I am over my head

and there are large concrete blocks over me. I can hear my husband and
son saying. "Oh no. Mommy, Mommy." Then I wake up.

This professional worked in management and did a good deal of training of other professionals and thus had a very tight schedule. During the latter part of her pregnancy, she experienced increasing demands on her time professionally and also in her family life. She used swimming as an exercise and a stress reducer. It is therefore reasonable that the images of swimming should appear in her dreamlife, both as part of the day's residue and also in terms of the elemental forces in nature involved with the oceanic process of birth.

Some dreams are frankly sexual. The hormonal changes experienced by the mother are often accompanied by an increase in sexual desire. Given the healthy dynamics of the couple, this may create an increased libidinal context for both of them. Increased libidinal contexts may affect them both in a slightly different way. The following is a father's dream:

I dreamed about my wife's vagina. I was exploring it in a playful sexual way while wondering what it would be like and would it be as relaxed and responsive when a baby's head came through it.

This father and lover's dream reflected not only some concerns about the sexual change of his mate, but also some normal concerns about the change of the body during the delivery process.

The following dream by a husband is along similar lines but adds the additional dynamic of comparing his wife sexually to other women:

Last night I dreamed that I was in a large shopping mall with my wife, who was not immediately there in my sight. I walked around the mall looking for her but could not see her. I was not alarmed, however. Soon I ran into a pregnant woman I had known in a work situation. We talked and soon there was some physical-sexual body contact with our clothes still on. I was aware of looking at her skin and her stomach and her sides and noticing that I felt pleasantly sexual toward her despite her pregnant appearance. Then my wife showed up who was pregnant. I was aware of comparing the two of them and noticing that while I felt sexual toward the first woman, I had more difficulty allowing myself to feel as sexual toward my wife. I was amused and intrigued by this comparison and wondered why I did so. In the morning when I woke up I associated the dream to a book I had recently read that stated that birth was also a sensual and sexual process.

Here is a dream that concerns a breech birth and is related to delivery and health issues. It creates a good deal of anxiety on the part of the mother and to a lesser extent the father. This dream occurred in the eighth month of pregnancy when the position of breech was confirmed by a sonogram.

I felt some "wetness" and when checked discovered it was blood from my vagina. My husband and an older man, a fatherly type figure, were there and were alarmed. They took me to the hospital. Some other type of "disaster" also occurred but I can't remember the details.

This woman had the following dream shortly after:

There was an explanation given by a physician as to why my two children were breech births. The physician told me that mothers secrete a hormone that is passed to the baby, causing the baby to turn itself into a head-down position. In my case, I secreted the hormone but babies did not "receive" it so they stayed in a breech position.

It is significant that this woman tried several alternative ways to "turn" the fetus. These included well-known medical procedures such as physical manipulation and also more experimental procedures involving certain herbal products.

Here is one more dream about breech births, this time from

the father's perspective. Notice the event, the symbolism, and the transformation.

> On 1/4/90 my wife and I went to Cooley-Dickinson Hospital at 10:30 a.m. for an inversion of the foetus. Dr. W.G. did it assisted by another female M.D. and an older male M.D. who was an anesthetist on call just in case. Several friendly female R.N.s were present. All assisted Dr. W.G. The foetus in her [belly] was physically moved around with some real effort. Several vaginal probes were needed. My wife was in the prone position. I held her hand. The procedure was successful. My wife was told that she "tolerated the pain well."
>
> On 1/5/90 I had the following dream: Two female neighbors were playing ball on our front lawn. They were throwing a ball back and forth on top of a large mound or hill in the front yard. The hill is a large bulge like a pregnant [belly]. They were having fun and all seemed well.

As we look back over the six major themes outlined in Dr. Maybruck's research and supported by the findings of others, we see again that family dreams during pregnancy tend to highlight certain areas of emotional life in particular. We have looked at dreams concerning preoccupations with the possible defects or deformity and death of the fetus. We have looked at numerous dreams about whether one is an inadequate parent or not. There were dreams that implicated concern about the loss of a mate. These appeared sometimes in the form of separation from a mate and sometimes competition with the newborn for the love and attention of the mate. Dreams of a difficult delivery are quite common and are often experienced concomitantly with dreams of loss of control.

Dr. Maybruck points out that dreams concerning financial burdens are relatively common for our times and may reflect the concerns of the modern age. However, there are also dreams that preoccupied humanity long before this so-called modern era. These are some of the dreams that we have seen in the Family Dreams Research Project. They seem to fall clinically into three areas: (1) dreams concerning what the parent and other family members would like the child to be, (2) dreams, occurring since primordial times, that involve psychic events in the dreamlife of the family during pregnancy, and (3) certain mythological, cultural, and spiritual dreams concerning birth and the foundation of a culture and civilization. We will look at each one of these briefly in turn.

THREE ADDITIONAL DREAM THEMES: THE HERO IN FAMILY, PSYCHE, MYTH, AND SPIRIT

The following dream occurred to a father during the eighth month of a pregnancy within the family. This dream reflects the father's preoccupations as a scientist and a researcher.

> I dreamed that either my pregnant wife or someone else or something else gave me a very special book. It was a large full book. The person who gave me the book was very close to me in feeling. When I opened this large book, out of its middle pages, on a large unfolding piece of paper, came a scientific chart. On this chart was a beautiful printout of the quantum relativistic field theory with all its interlocking equations and all other known forces of the universe.

The significance of this dream is apparent. The father is fairly aware of the family unconscious system and the desires and expectations he is projecting onto his offspring. However, the following dream is not so obvious. It occurred to a married man in the sixth month of his wife's pregnancy. It has some references to subtle experiences and at the same time some rather diffuse expectations of a child who would be born out of this kind of "subtle environment."

> Last night I had a long dream. In the dream I am an adult male and find myself on the campus of an institution of women. These women all know themselves and had a secret knowledge or wisdom or set of practices

unknown to me. I had the definite feeling that secret rites were practiced
in the hidden areas of the ground, i.e., in buildings, etc. Women's ways.

The grounds were quiet, well-kept and had an ancient feeling about
them, almost primordial. I, the only male present, was a guest or interloper.
These other women did not speak to me, but were more indifferent to me.
An unclear woman was my guide or companion among them. There was
no hostility or sexuality. I was not allowed to let my feet touch the ground!
This seemed to be because I was a male.

A child born of this "subtle environment" would have not only subtle spiritual powers but also embedded psychic powers not generally known to other infants and adults. This area of psychic influences has engaged the attention of professionals and laypeople for thousands of generations.

In his clinical study of psi in family processes called "psychic-nexus,"[13] Dr. Berthold E. Schwarz, a psychiatrist, relates that one day he was in a psychotherapy session with a young woman who had a diagnosis of hysterical character neurosis, and he was startled when she blurted out "I predict a boy for you." When he asked why she said this, the patient insisted, "I am positive you said your wife is pregnant." The psychiatrist was dumbfounded, since he had said nothing of the kind and was unaware of any such event in his own life, and her statement was said out of context in the session. While he was wondering if this was telepathy, the patient said, "Maybe I'm getting to be a medium. I associated to the time I was pregnant. I knew I didn't hear your voice coming out of the wall. I am quite crushed. How ridiculous. I feel I'll go back to my concealed tomb. You don't want me, telepathy interests me. When my son hurt his hand and when my mother died I telepathically knew it."

At the end of the session the doctor spoke with his wife about this odd session and was shocked to find out that his wife was indeed pregnant! A psychodynamic explanation was offered involving the patient's ambivalence, resentment, and sense of jealousy. However, clearly there was a reference to knowledge that the doctor did not even have that could only be picked up in a paranormal way.

Many phenomena such as this occur during pregnancy. Another psychiatrist, Jan Ehrenwald,[14] suggested that a great deal of psi or paranormal communication occurs between mother and offspring in the cradle. He refers to this as "cradle ESP." Long before this, Freud himself had suggested that humanity, prior to the development of language, had communicated telepathically. Carl Jung[15] documented numerous cases of psi or paranormal communication in his clinical sessions. He referred to the wider process of psi as synchronicity.

In the literature of the Family Dreams Research Project, there are numerous cases of reported psi or paranormal communication involving the theme of pregnancy during this phase of the family developmental process. This first one is the dream of the mother of a mother-to-be. This family had reported other similar communication.

I am thirty-three years old, and for as long as I can remember, I've had accurate dreams about family members (my parents and brother, and later on, my husband and my sons). My mother, who is sixty-two, is psychically gifted in many areas, and her dream experiences about family members defy normal explanations. One example that I can give you that impressed me at the time was about 8 ½ years ago. My husband and I had been married about seven years, and were childless by choice. We had made the decision, finally, to start a family over a late night of conversation, made love, and went to bed. I woke the next morning sick as a dog, and my husband took the day off to bring me to a doctor. I won't bore you with a long day's testing and probing, but the upshot was that he sent me to a local hospital for a pregnancy test even though I assured him that I had only had intercourse without using birth control less than 24 hours before. I took the test anyway, and later that afternoon, still at the doctor's office, the results came back positive.

Even though I was still quietly upchucking into any available receptacle, we decided to pit stop at my parents' house and tell them the good news.

At my folks', much to our surprise, was a big sign saying congratulations and my mother with tears of joy running down her face. She came running out to greet us, saying that she had a dream in early morning that I was pregnant and called to ask me if it was true. We were already out of the house, so when she got no answer she went back to sleep. She dreamt that we were at a doctor's office, that I was suffering morning sickness to the nth degree, and that as soon as I got a positive test result I would be coming over. My husband has been calling her a witch ever since!

This is indeed a very striking dream since it involves witnesses other than the dreamer. This next dream involves not only a psi or paranormal communication, but also intense psychophysical or autonomic nervous system arousal. It is accompanied by normal intense anxieties concerning these themes.

One day during my first pregnancy, I awoke from a nap with a pain in my foot. The pain was so intense I couldn't walk. I found out later that day that my husband had hurt his foot. This occurred several times during my pregnancy.

The other day I awoke, my wrist hurt so bad it felt like it would snap in two. I later found out my husband had hurt his wrist. I believe I may be pregnant again, and I am beginning to wonder if there is some kind of connection between my being pregnant and my feeling his pain. I don't remember now if I dreamed about him, but I always developed the pain while I was asleep.

This dream is similar to many other dreams involving paranormal communication, but it is different in that it involves a psychophysical situation. We are reminded again of the studies by Dean[16] mentioned in chapter 5 in which people who have an intimate connection with each other often will respond to each other on an autonomic nervous systems level outside of each other's awareness. These phenomena have been supported by similar experiments done in the laboratory. They indicate our profound interconnectedness with each other outside of the normal levels of awareness and the capacity of the mind to process information even when asleep. Certainly in the heightened, affectively potent state of pregnancy such emotional themes are intensified.

Perhaps the most expansive, collective, and universal dreams are those that involve the great spiritual and cultural issues of humanity. These dreams are mythological or spiritual in nature and indeed express the mythology of a people or a culture. They come from traditions all over the world. Dreams can also reflect the mythology each one of us has developed in our own personal history.[17] The shared or collective dreams of a people or a society make up the myths of that society. At one end, dreams are our individual myths, expressing our personal mythology, and at the other end, cultural myths express our collective dreams. In the following personal dream the dreamer has a spiritual vision of a child. This dream occurred not to the mother but to the midwife of the mother:

Our midwife went to sleep and had the following dream that she told us. She dreamed that our baby was talking to her. The baby seemed odd to her. She noticed that the baby looked like a little adult. She asked the baby why she looked like a little adult. The baby then said to the midwife, "It is because I am an angel."

What makes this all the more interesting is that later the baby was born with a small blemish on the inner left upper eyelid. This is commonly referred to as an "angel's kiss."

More striking than this personal dream, however, is the collective mythological dream. Part of it may have originally been personalized and true, but certainly much of it was composed and gleaned from collective dreaming. It concerns the mythological foundation of ancient Rome. If you will recall, Rome, a city on the Tiber, was founded by Romulus. As the legend goes, Romulus, the son of Mars and Ilia and the grandson of Numitor, the king of Alba, had a twin brother named Remus. The two brothers were thrown into the Tiber by order of Amulius, who usurped the crown of his brother Numitor. The boys were saved by a she-wolf, who raised them on her own milk until they were found by Faustulus, one of the shepherds of the ancient kingdom, who educated the boys as if they were his own children.

When the twins grew up and discovered their true origin, they put Amulius to death and restored the crown to their grandfather, Numitor. Later they undertook to build a city. They used omens and the flight of birds to decide who would manage the city. Romulus went to Mount Palatine and saw twelve vultures in flight, and Remus went to Mount Aventine and saw only six vultures. Because Romulus saw more vultures than Remus, he began to build the city. A fight ensued, and Romulus killed Remus. Later Romulus developed the city and took the counsel of the seniors called senators, and the myth of Rome's foundation was set. Romulus supposedly died as he was giving instructions to the senators during a full eclipse of the sun, which led to the legend and rumor that he had ascended into heaven.

This is a supreme cultural myth reflecting the pregnant dreams of a society about to give birth to greatness. Indeed, it was a pregnant dream for a people about to give birth to the greatest society of the Western world after ancient Egypt, or Kemet and Meroë.

An even more ancient and mythological birth dream is that of the Greek story of Oedipus, the dream that Freud used in the development of psychoanalysis. Oedipus, son of King Laius and Queen Jocasta, was the offspring and the prophecy of a dream. The king was informed by the oracle as soon as he married Jocasta that he would perish at the hands of his son (Oedipus). Jocasta, therefore, gave their son away to a servant so that he might be exposed to the elements on a mountainside and die. A shepherd of King Polybus found the child first, however, and educated him as his own.

When, as an adult, Oedipus consulted the oracle at Delphi, he was told not to return home, for if he did he would murder his father and marry his mother. Thinking his "home" was the one he shared with the shepherd, he went off in another direction hoping to avoid his fate. However, he ended up in the land of King Laius. They confronted each other on the road, and a struggle ensued, ending with Oedipus killing the king. Later Oedipus won a contest to unravel the riddle of the devouring Sphinx* and won the hand of the queen, Jocasta. He was unaware of Jocasta's origin, and she was unaware of her relationship to him as his mother. He and Jocasta had two sons and a daughter, Antigone. Later when Oedipus discovered his true identity, he was overcome with grief and remorse and blinded himself. He then took to wandering again. A number of other family dynamics were also played out in this myth, but in the final scene, Oedipus, unable to be saved by his family and increasing in age, dies and is buried in the countryside.

Here again we see the enormous influence of collective dreams and collective myths in the formation of a national character.

Finally, there are dreams of a frankly and overtly spiritual and cosmological nature involving birth and celestial expectations during pregnancy. The first of these arises from the Messianic Judaic tradition.

It is the story of Moses. In the traditional story, Moses is the son of Amram, the Levite, and Jochebed, and the younger brother of Miriam and Aaron. During a time of anguish and suffering of the tribe of Judah in the land of Egypt, the pharaoh ordained the destruction of all male Israelite children of a certain age due to a prophecy. The prophecy is told not only by the Hebrews but also by the Egyptian astrologers. The dream is that a "deliverer" would be born and would lead the children of Israel out of the land of Egypt. It is irrelevant at this point whether we consider the Jews to have been the chosen people in this situation or simply former Hyksos invaders who intermarried with and were later

_____

*It is interesting that the Sphinx, a great figure and symbol of older Kemetic Egypt, the land that many of the early Greeks looked to for science, medicine, and initiation into the sacred mysteries, would later appear in their dreams and myths devouring Greek heroes and Greek civilization. Many Greek legends held that their civilization was founded by Egyptian colonies ages ago. This is an example of "the threatened return of the repressed," with the repressed in this case being the knowledge of the African origin of civilization with all its implications in terms of politics, identity issues, power, and racism.

overcome by the darker skinned indigenous population. It does not even matter if, as the ancient historians and scholars Tacitus, Eusebius, and Diodorus believed, the Jews were originally a group of Ethiopians and Egyptians who left the Nile Valley and migrated to Palestine.[18] What is important is that both the Egyptians and the Israelite peoples had a shared dream concerning pregnancy and the arrival of the Messiah, or deliverer. This deliverer would have the power to free a people and would also have contact with cosmological and spiritual forces. This is especially interesting as a common dream if we accept Freud's[19] and others' assertions that Moses himself was actually not an Israelite initially, but rather a radical Egyptian priest!

The Jewish messianic tradition is further expanded in the mythology and the mystery surrounding the birth of Christ. Also during that time it was the prophecy that a Savior or deliverer would be born to the tribe of Judah, in the House of David. The time and the place of his birth were known to the astrologers of several lands in the East and Africa. It comprises one of the great, lasting, and monumental pregnancies and births humanity has ever witnessed. Similar events have occurred in other parts of the world, both known and unknown. However, the Avatar of Judea is perhaps the most spectacular and is paralleled only by two or three other such events. It is the case of a light in a dream coming to enlighten the world.

SUMMARY

As we look back over the whole spectrum of emotions and images that arise during pregnancy, we see that certain ones are amplified enormously and others are rarely mentioned. Each trimester invokes different themes that manifest in the content of the family's dreams. Drawing on the work of others and on the clinical work of the Family Dreams Research Project, I have noted, along with Dr. Maybruck, that the vast majority of dreams during pregnancy involve themes of *deformity, adequacy* as a parent, potential *loss* of a mate, *concerns around delivery* and health, loss of *control,* and that modern concern, lack of *financial* and social support. Beyond that, however, I have noted in the dreamlife of the family during pregnancy that there are also numerous, normal concerns about what this child *will be* when he or she grows up. There are also dreams involving subtle and psychic interchanges within a family unconscious system. Most often these are between mother and child, but not always. Finally, there are the great *cultural, mythological,* and *cosmic psychospiritual* dreams that involve pregnancy and the arising through evolution of a new order in humankind, life, and consciousness. All are expressions of the ubiquitous process of birth. It is an intimate, yet vast oceanic process that touches the most distant visionary shore in all of us because no one enters life without birth, and no one transcends life without death.

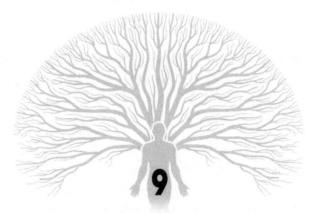

9

Family Dreams in Therapeutic Form

In dreams, when there is no actual contact with the external world, the mind alone creates the whole universe consisting of the experiencer, the experienced and the experience. Similarly, in the waking state also, there is no difference. Therefore all this phenomenal universe is the projection of the mind.

SANKARACARYA,
CREST-JEWEL OF DISCRIMINATION

Knowing the great, all-pervading Self, through whom is experienced the whole of dream and waking, the wise never become subject to sorrow.

KATHA UPANISHAD

KINSHIP BONDS AND
FAMILY DREAMS

Civilization—the arts, the sciences, and the religions with their subtle technologies—began in Africa. Then it migrated like humankind itself up out of Africa and across the planet. There are strong suggestions that the Egyptian pyramids and the sphinx were not created around 2500 BCE but date back to the time of Zep Tepi, the "splendid time of the first time," over 12,500 years ago, according to the Egyptian scholars themselves. Indeed, the lion body of the sphinx with its human head stares directly into the constellation of Leo the Lion on the vernal equinox of 10,500 BCE. Then this civilization, including its possible outcropping in Göbekli Tepe (in what is now Turkey), went into steep decline after 10,000 BCE for reasons unknown. Then slowly, slowly about six to eight thousand years ago on the banks of the upper Nile, then later on the Ganges, the Tigris, and the Euphrates, families and tribes were again worshiping their gods. These gods took to themselves favored families and favored cities. The voices of the family gods spoke to their members and were felt in their bones, in their blood, and in their minds.[1] Their voices bound the families together as much as the need for food, collective protection, and the perpetuation of their kinship lines. Perhaps we shall never know exactly the ways they worshiped and perpetuated their ancestors, the ways their early magic and myth matured into science and religion. But to be sure they felt the living current of the life force in all things, be they animate, inanimate, once living, or recently dead, back perhaps five generations. Theirs was a highly *personalized**
universe in which death as a final state was at best a mere abstraction. What they saw was the dance of consciousness manifesting in

---

*Personalized should not be equated with so-called archaic thinking or with states of prepersonal consciousness in the sense that Ken Wilber[2] and other transpersonal theorists use the term. It is rather the direct perception of a basic aliveness in all things and experiencing the world in terms of essences, consciousness, and personhood.

every form. Their dreams, so intimate and crosscurrenting, must have seemed as if they were embodied with a life of their own.

Today we live in a world paradoxically much larger and yet much smaller than in ancient times. Today's world is much smaller in that kinship bonds in general have decreased radically with the rise of individualist or self-centered consciousness. At the present time in the United States reportedly three out of four American undergraduates cannot even name all of their grandparents and supposedly only two out of three young children, when given a hypothetical choice between giving up television or their fathers, prefer to keep their fathers.[3] In ancient times, one may have traveled much less, and the world may have seemed no bigger than the village or the local tribe, but one's kinship lines extended one into the past and into the future. Today we travel around the world and yet seem to come from smaller and smaller families more isolated in space and time. In the past, the human mind seemed larger in that we could speak to gods in our dreams and in our waking life, while today we debate whether God exists and whether our dreaming life is even important.

Today we know that our dreams arise from within ourselves rather than from forces totally outside of us. Yet our dreaming life clearly has familial and even larger connections that join us to forces embedded in the natural world. We know that dreams occur in a specific state of mind, a specific state of body, and under a specific set of conditions. As shown in chapter 4, the laboratory has documented the numerous changes that occur during the dream state. We know about the changes in blood chemistry, body temperature, and brain wave patterns. We know about the REM and non-REM sleep cycles. We even know about how the immobilization of the body occurs and the numerous clinical situations that can arise from a disordered sleep and dream pattern. We know that dreams are accompanied by powerful images and themes that have a very intimate personal meaning and significance for the dreamer and often for the dreamer's significant relationships in life. We know we dream about each other and seemingly at times *for* each other. We know that crucial insights, both scientific and artistic, not to mention interpersonal and otherwise, can arise from the experience of dreaming. From dreams we have gained immense knowledge about the mind and by extension the transitoriness of the seemingly fixed states of space and time that occur in the waking state. We know that our consciousness experiences the dynamics of light and the force of gravity differently when we sleep and dream. Finally, our age is not the first to recognize that dreams have an immense potential for healing and therapeutic use and that this potential operates not only on the somatic or physical level but also on the psychological level, the psychic level, and the noetic or spiritual level. All of these are natural worlds that every human is privy to.

Certainly the ancients were aware of this and perhaps even in tune with the somatic changes that occur in the body, since the ancient world is replete with healing temples and altars to the images of the dreams that inhabit our religions. These no doubt worked in many instances. Their methodologies are unfortunately largely forgotten, but some small part of that wisdom runs through our modern therapies today. The power and effect of imagery on and in the disease process of the body is reflected in the new science of psychoneuroimmunology.[4]

In earlier chapters, we focused on the emotional and somatic inner landscapes of dreams, with their strange contours of space and time, and the profound impact they have had on the psychological development of humankind. We have looked at the way the ubiquitous process of dreaming has affected the family and the self through history, and we have seen the dreams in families range from the normal to the sometimes unusual and at times even bizarre. We have looked at the unusual communication channels that have sometimes occurred in the dreaming process. It was easy to see how individual dreams were very similar to and sometimes developed into cultural myths and shared cultural dreams. We saw how family dynamics and the individual dynamics of one's own emotions, images, and events are played out in the dreamlife of intimate emotional relationships. We delved into two specific examples of these themes and styles more deeply in the chapters on adult children of alcoholics and dreams during the pregnancy cycle. In both of these instances certain types of themes, emotions, and events were highlighted during developmental phases. Some of these brought joy, some brought sorrow. Some came out in the clinical situation; others were simply the record of family members dreaming.

All of these are acceptable ways of recording the natural occurrences of people during a certain phase of shared experience. Indeed, we all share the experience of dreaming and we all share the experience of family consciousness in some form or other. In fact, the modern experimental and experiential sleep laboratories of today were the temples, monasteries, and forest retreats of yesterday. But whether or not the people were at a temple retreat, a disturbing family gathering, a sleep laboratory, or the clinician's office, they all come from families in some form, facet, or fragment and bear witness to that level of consciousness enfolded within them. Alexis de Tocqueville, writing in the nineteenth century about the new emphasis on individualism in the United States, said that "our fathers did not have a word for individualism, because in their time there was indeed no individual who did not belong to a group and who could be considered absolutely alone."[5]

One can argue that while modern societies have increased individual rights, individual civil protection, and a person's autonomy, they have also contributed to the decrease of that most necessary of units, the family. In other words, self-centered societies have increased at the expense of kinship-oriented societies. Kinship societies offer more sanity, sanctuary, supportiveness, compassion, and warmth in general than individual-oriented societies. People lived together, suffered together, literally shared the fabric and matrix of dreams together. It was a loom around which one's identity was woven through life, and perhaps from life to life to life.

Even in our day, the family remains the most immense, intense, and permanent structure of relationships throughout our lives. It is perhaps, like the process of dreaming itself, a biologically rooted development in our species that we ignore at our peril. The large primates all live in families. Elephants and other large intelligent creatures live in families.

Elephants, primates, and all the other mammals also dream. Family consciousness does not seem to be limited to human beings. It is perhaps no more limited to human beings than intelligence and insight are limited to human consciousness. Kinship is older and deeper than we know. It speaks of field dynamics that are superordinate to individual dynamics. In other words, for a large percentage of the time perhaps the wave characteristics of the phenomenal world hold sway over the individual or discrete aspects of a field. This is true in quantum mechanics. It is often the case in culture and society. It may also be the case for our individual lives and our family lives.

What follows is a tour through the world of dreams that find their way into the clinician's office. As you will quickly see, there are several major arteries through which the fluid imagery and emotion of the dream flow freely with immense gain for the dreamer. It moves freely, as we do, through many levels of consciousness and form. Therapy taps into this intuitive, spontaneous nature of dreams and can glean insight from those that allow changes in the body and mind.

FAMILY DREAMS
IN INDIVIDUAL THERAPY

I mentioned earlier that the individual or the individual-oriented dream is a reflection of what is called the "intrapsychic realm." It is largely self-referential in that it reflects back on the individual's own needs, often without reference to others who are known to that individual. Most of our dreams are primarily intrapsychic dreams. These intrapsychic or individual dreams may be focused around a job, a trauma, one's needs, or other highly personal issues. Currently the most well-known system of approaching these dreams in Western culture is that of individuals in the psychodynamic and psychoanalytic field. However, even under such circumstances, the *analysis* of a dream may give rise to another clinical *method* of approaching that dream for therapeutic purposes. Take for example the following case:

A female undergraduate student in her early twenties presented herself to the mental health clinic during the fall semester. She was tearful and mildly depressed but evidenced no suicidal ideation or delusional material and was oriented as to time, place, person, and event. She was one of several offspring from a Pennsylvania farm family. The patient said that she had been having recurring "bad dreams." In these dreams, the patient's father, who had died suddenly about a year before, attempted to speak with her and somehow to "reach her." The patient described him as coming into her room, extending his hand to her, and uttering a few unclear words. His face, in the dream, was not angry or depressed. The patient also told the therapist in a tearful but smiling way that her father had been a turkey farmer and suffered a stroke and died on Thanksgiving Day!

During this one session, the therapist, after assessing the patient's ego strengths and defenses, including her capacity for humor and irony, employed dynamic gestalt techniques to elicit more affect and material. Using a fragment of the dream, the patient was asked to talk about the dream in the first person, to speak in the dream with her father and listen to him, and to speak about family-related matters that felt pressured, all in the active, present tense. Communication with the father during his lifetime was experienced as very strained. This technique,[6] used with compassion, elicited a great deal of affect. The therapist was well aware of the anniversary nature of the depression and the dynamic aspects of the dream material, as well as the potential transpersonal dimension of its impact.

The patient felt much relieved after the one-and-a-half-hour session. The therapist then requested that the patient, on her own, return to her father's grave site and speak with him there in her heart about what she experienced in the therapist's office. Several weeks later the therapist met the patient on the street in town, and she happily told the therapist of her resolution of the bad dreams and the lifting of her depression.

The foregoing dream is about a fragment of family relationships that were powerful. The approach to the dream was clearly in a dynamic, brief-therapy setting. However, there were transpersonal implications about the actual resolution of the dream in the sense that the therapist left the door open for the patient to resolve this powerful process on whatever level made sense to her deep unconscious. The usual notion of boundaries was not considered in this case since the brief clinical time together was not conducive to a fuller exploration of the psychospiritual dynamics of forgiveness and transcendence.

The use of dreams in brief therapy, not to mention in longer-term therapy, can certainly be an aid in setting a focus for treatment.[7] It is also tremendously useful in facilitating the expression of repressed anger, conflicts, and other trauma. Usually in this therapeutic approach to a dream there is a here-and-now focus on the emotional or affective level of the dream. We chose to work with the patient to try to locate the organic meaning of the dream for the patient as opposed to imposing the therapist's theoretical interpretation of a dream upon the patient. In this therapeutic approach, there is a behavioral implication based upon the insight derived from the dream. This keeps the dream active and functional and intimately related to the person's actual ongoing life experience. The following case involved another dream that has individual implications but is also a reflection of family dynamics and family processes.

The patient, a white nineteen-year-old second semester freshman, was seen at the beginning of the fall semester on a walk-in contact. Tall, lean, with long hair, he approached the therapist quite directly and extended his hand to initiate a handshake while he said his name with a clear and somewhat raised intonation. Eye contact was made.

In the therapist's office, the patient sat on the couch, tossing his books on one side and positioning himself near the edge of the other side. The atmosphere was charged and did not suggest small talk. The therapist began by asking what brought the patient to the clinic on this particular day. The patient slumped his shoulders slightly, his tension loosened and became less congested. He said that he did not know where to begin. The therapist responded by asking what had been "going on" recently. Tears trickled down the patient's face. He leaned back against the couch.

The patient told his story of the previous eight months. It was filled with turmoil. After successfully completing his first semester at another college, the patient was asked by his parents to care for his brother who had attempted suicide after undergoing a brain operation to remove tumors. He said that he did so hesitatingly. Occasionally, his brother was in good spirits; frequently he was depressed. The patient's life for six months was caring for his brother and bearing the burden of his moods and the threat of suicide. By the beginning of the semester his brother's condition had stabilized and the patient began to think of returning to school. He decided to transfer in order to save his family money and to major in Special Education, a program not available at his previous school.

When he arrived at college, he quickly began to feel agitated, lonely, unable to concentrate, guilty about being away, and worried about his family. Matters became worse when he was not able to enroll in a particular course and heard rumors that his program might be dropped because of shifting university priorities. He denied any suicidal ideation. He reported that he had been having trouble eating and sleeping for several days; he was scared. During a discussion about his insomnia, he reported the following dream:

> Brother and I are together on a road in the country. My brother is uneasy and frightened by lots of things. A car comes down one of the hills. My brother jumps out in front of it. The car runs him over. I thought he was killed. But the car went over him without hurting him. I woke up.

This simply stated, unelaborated dream was experienced by the therapist as stark and anxiety rousing. The care and burden of responsibility was clear in the context of what had been discussed before the dream report as well as his brother's suicide attempt. Yet the therapist felt something else. A troubling angry wind was in the dream as if removed from the rest of the scene. The patient said that the dream had been bothering him for the past couple of days. What concerned him about the dream was that his brother had continued his suicidal potential. He felt very guilty that he was not home to help his parents and to watch his brother.

The therapist was quite supportive of the feelings captured by the dream. These feelings were linked to the events of the past eight months including the frustrations at school and the mixed feelings about leaving home. When the notions of loss and trauma were presented by the therapist, the sobs that followed were filled with pain and relief. Another session was scheduled for later in the week.

The patient arrived on time for the second session and reported feeling much better. He said that he had talked more to people during the past several days, felt much less anxious, and was able to sleep. No other dreams were remembered. Essential focus was framed by reviewing the dream presented on the first contact that emphasized the notion of his being traumatized. When the notion of being angry with his family for disrupting his life was also introduced, it was initially rejected by the patient with marked intensity. These two matters became the themes of treatment over nine sessions. In this case, the initial presenting dream was especially useful in facilitating the expression of repressed affect and setting a focus. The behavioral implementation emphasized was staying at college over the weekends rather than going home. Here we can see how dreams, even within the dynamic setting of brief therapy, can have behavioral and familial implications.

When dreamwork is combined with biofeedback, or psychophysiological information, a whole new dimension of powerful treatment and exploration can be added. With biofeedback, both subtle and not-so-subtle organic and psychophysical processes can literally be mirrored back, shifted around, and resymbolized to the client as a reflection of how the mind and the body mutually influence and perhaps enfold each other. In this way a patient's dream can be directly associated with body movements and functions in the *immediate present* and can become an active process of reowning disowned or negatively projected bodily functions. Biofeedback helps recognize areas of psychological and somatic conflict or concern and extends consciousness into a region of maladaptive repression. Insight comes to rest directly in the body as shifts of tone, feeling, and experience are worked through.

A postsurgery patient was referred to the clinic because of prolonged somatic and psychological suffering. Much of her GI tract had been removed, causing her great distress in terms of self-esteem, sexual self-image, and intimacy. The person was a gifted writer and scientist who experienced vivid dreams. By selective use of biofeedback to reflect autonomic and other somatic processes, the patient was able to use her dreamlife, including some lucid dreams, to reown and relibidinize these negatively perceived and somewhat dissociated and conflicted areas of her bodily functioning. The techniques involved *actively dreaming* about these bodily areas and functions, keeping *attention focused there* in treatment, and gradually bringing a warm, loving, *primal feeling back* into these areas and functions. Psychotherapy and dreamwork here were active and led to experienced shifts in bodily and emotional feeling and experience.

There are other dreams, however, that reflect another level of consciousness. This level is referred to as the collective unconscious. In situations like this, the clinician attempts to interpret the dream in a therapeutic fashion and help extract its personalized meaning from the more universal archetypal expressions, which are felt to have surface manifestations in various more-specific or localized images and situations. It is more like the deep structure versus the surface structure, or the latent meaning as opposed to the manifest meaning. These dreams are usually evocative and even spiritual in nature. Jung[8] felt that they are an intense aspect of human consciousness and that they exist because of a human need to work through the deep and eternal problems, conflicts, and situations faced by humanity. More than a disturbance of surface waters or the personal balance of an individual, they reflect the primordial concerns of the human species. We have touched upon these collective unconscious dreams in earlier chapters.

In the situation of the individual or personal or intrapsychic dream, and in the dream of the collective unconscious, the individual or personal issues—*including* their physiological or somatic correlations with the life of the family and the life of the individual—are expressed. In fact, given the reality that the human consciousness lives *simultaneously* in the world of logic and structure *and* in the world of mythology, the world of energy, and the world of spirit, a larger assessment range or profile is needed to evaluate the entire range of issues, from somatic to noetic. Appendix B contains an assessment profile referred to as the "Kemetic Imagery and Healing Assessment Protocol." It takes into account not only the personal and the familial concerns of an individual but also the archetypal and the somatic concerns of an individual. It focuses on images in terms of clarity and meaningfulness. It is only by looking at the entire range of human functioning and consciousness that we can help construct an appropriate series of images or metaphors that will have dynamic psychophysiological effects on human consciousness.

Finally, it is important to mention, at least briefly, the other dream cultures that use dreams and the sharing of dreams for individual and tribal healing. The Senoi people in Malaysia are the most famous, even though they do not use dream interpretation as widespread as had been formerly reported. The Native Americans of the North and Southwest United States are another instance, as are the shamans of almost every lineage and the legendary, nearly mythological, Australian Aborigines of the Dreamtime.

FAMILY DREAMS
OUTSIDE OF THERAPY

Now let us turn our attention to the dynamics that occur in the systems of family dreams.[9] In previous chapters, numerous examples have been given of family dreams and fragments of family dreams that occur in the psyche of every individual. We have also seen certain dreams and dream images that repeat themselves in families and in individuals over time. Some of the dynamics seen in dreams that involve the family involve the dynamic process of projective identification.[10] In the process of projective identification while dreaming, a trait, attitude, or feeling experienced by the dreamer is psychologically denied in themselves and is then projected or located in the psychological landscape of another person who is usually emotionally significant to that dreamer—an inverse representation of oneself in the other, you might say. Often feelings of anger and rage are denied and projected outward toward others. Sometimes feelings of love and tenderness are recognized in oneself and also projected and recognized in another. The family unconscious has enough room for both extremely positive and extremely negative emotions. It is a shared field or larger matrix of dynamics on which these are painted as opposed to individual dynamics.[11] These, too, have powerful psychophysiological effects upon the soma of the individual, as we shall see later. Take this instance of a dream fragment presented by a preadolescent male who was not in therapy.

S.W. was neither a patient nor in family treatment. He reported to me the following dream that occurred several times around the arrival of his younger male sibling. He dreamed that M. turned into a large bird in his crib. When he did this, he would then fly away. This is a common sibling-rivalry dream in which one sibling in competition with another wishes the other sibling would disappear or go away. What made it difficult for S.W. was that the child, his younger sibling, died suddenly (crib death), and he was overcome with guilt and grief. It is significant that his mother also dreamed that her own mother, now deceased, had come and taken the dead child away, ostensibly to help the child. The mother experienced guilt also but none of these feelings were directly expressed until years later. This is an example of a family field sharing the same imagery and emotions around a traumatic but normal family event each from a slightly different perspective. Remember the hologram. Now observe the next dream that is significantly more dynamic, but in which similar field dynamics are operative.

For several nights, a woman was repeatedly and painfully presented with intense dreams. In each dream, her family figures would appear in odd and also sometimes familiar situations. In one dream, which occurred on a Tuesday night, two Chinese individuals led a procession of mourners to her front door. They called her "Mrs. Jefferson" and said how sad they were. For rather complicated reasons, this woman, now living several states away from her parents, had not really spoken with them for a number of years. A few days after the dream, her sister called and informed her that her parents had just had the "unveiling" of her brother's tombstone. This is a Jewish custom in which a ceremony is held on the anniversary of a death. The brother had died in an auto accident a year and three months earlier, so the unveiling was three months late. While the family was home with the mourners, the parents were emotionally very intense, the mother even passing out. The dreamer was totally unaware that the unveiling had been postponed for three months. The unveiling was held on the same Tuesday that the dream occurred. The deceased brother had had two significant romances with Chinese women in his life and his name was Jeffery!

It seems that this dreamer had somehow unconsciously touched upon a deep collective image or bed of information within this family system. Everyone in this family seemed to have a particular perspective on the idea and emotional informational field that all members of the family share. You might also notice that the members of the dream were intensely powerful in their emotions and that, during the actual unveiling, the family was in an agitated psychophysical state. We see how powerful emotions and images can affect the physiological processes of the body, including the body of a physically distant dreamer. It would therefore be very useful to have a way of assessing and then later therapeutically structuring various images, emotions, and associations for their capacity to influence psychophysical processes.

DREAMS IN COUPLES THERAPY

Dreams are useful in working with couples also. Individuals in intimate living circumstances can derive a greater benefit from their relationship by discussing their dreams. Clinical focus simply brings into sharp relief what is already a natural therapeutic potential embedded in any relationship. The following is a dream that actually occurred in couples therapy. It is reported by two clinicians, Dr. Richard Perlmutter and Dr. Raymond Babineau.[12] One of the therapists had been working with a couple for eleven previous sessions. In the twelfth session some dreamwork was done. The context of the following dream is this: Alice and Bob were discussing their plans for the future, a future that involved the eventual termination of their relationship with the therapist. In the final moments of the session Alice offered this dream:

Alice: *I dreamed that friends were dying on me and stuff. I had to call this girl I went to high school with to make sure she was still alive.*

Therapist: *A friend died in the dream?*

Alice: *Ya. I guess it is frightening to change, to grow, to be different even if you don't like the way you are. The last time we were talking about being grateful to people who had done things for you.*

The therapist then reportedly asked Bob what he was experiencing as he heard Alice repeat this dream she had. Bob spoke about his past memories of his younger sister when she would wake up upset by thoughts of death.

Therapist: *The dream had something for you, too.*

Bob: *Well, this is putting my own interpretation in it, but thinking about the fears we have right now, we could grow apart too.*

Alice: *No, that's not it (pause), but part of getting close to Bob meant growing apart from Judy (the high school friend in the dream).*

Bob's interpretation expressed recurrent transactional themes for this couple. Issues of intimacy, termination, and loyalty were recognized by the therapist.

The same authors later discuss a dream-sharing session with another couple. The therapist reports that this couple was in their late thirties and that they were coming back to therapy as a prerequisite for moving back in together with each other. The wife apparently had been in turmoil for years about her ability to commit to this marriage, and the husband manifested a very rigid obsessive-compulsive style. These recurrent transactional patterns had eventually led to their initial separation. At first, the wife reported a dream in the session that made her husband quite angry:

> **Wife (to the therapist):** *You, my husband, and I were going to school; we were married and living in campus subsidized housing. We were very happy. I remember looking back at the house . . . and I am feeling very happy about my relationship with my husband . . . and I look at the house; it was this ramshackle thing like in the neighborhood I used to live in. Then I thought: "Boy, is that an ugly house." And then we went to pay the rent, and you were the landlord, and I thought: "That devil, he tricked us!"*

The husband became very angry upon hearing the dream. Competitive feelings with the therapist and loyalty and attention issues with his wife emerged. Underneath these surface emotions, deep feelings of dependency and fear of abandonment were eventually uncovered. In connection with this, the therapist guided the wife toward looking at her own ambivalent feelings about men in her life. These feelings were worked with in the transference and the countertransference process. Six months later the couple discussed the very process of dream sharing itself:

> **Wife:** *I enjoy relating dreams that are interesting. My husband doesn't want to hear about them.*

Husband: *Boring! Her family can tell you about dreams, that they usually have to do with animals . . . I can't stand it. First of all, I don't remember dreams . . . I don't know why dreams fascinate you.*

Wife: *They do because the feelings that you have in real life, whether they are positive or negative, are intensified in a dream.*

Husband: *Crock!*

Wife: *Well, they are for me! Maybe I have special dreams. It is just like greater awareness, like you could almost touch a feeling in a dream.*

This along with some additional therapy, eventually led to a healthy dream-sharing culture in this couple. I have encouraged families to share their dreams as a way to become more intimate and paradoxically differentiated from each other at the same time.

In a nontherapeutic situation a dream culture that is shared can increase the intimacy of the husband and wife. Take for instance the following dream:

After a sleep-filled night in December, my wife and I mentioned our dreams to each other, as is our custom. I had dreamed a strange dream in which a "grandmother type" was trying to reach or catch me. She had "mixed feelings" of protection and also somehow of "getting me." Also in the dream the "grandmother type" attempted to steal or cut off a pickle I had! Having a somewhat Freudian lens, I made note of the sexual aspect of this. I later woke up with a slightly eerie feeling about the dream, but not tired.

On the same night my wife dreamed of my grandmother (L.G.) who had a necklace with a moon-shaped crescent locket. The locket fell partly from her neck but not completely, and turned into a knife or sharp edge. My wife then wondered in the dream, because of the shape and opened locket as it hung around my grandmother's neck, whether the grandmother was "gay."

In the above dream, it is worth noting the correspondence between grandmother images, sexual feeling, and the action of cutting. Certainly this is an extremely high correspondence. Neither of the dreamers had discussed their grandmothers for a long time and they could not remember any recent events that would account for the dream process in terms of day residue.

This particular kind of episode happens quite often. The eminent dream researcher Calvin Hall estimated that in an average lifetime a person experiences approximately a hundred thousand dreams.[13] One percent of those dreams, on a conservative estimate, are statistically thought to be psychic in nature. Thus the average individual may have a thousand psychic dreams in their lifetime. We have discussed this process of psi and dreamwork in the family and in individuals in earlier chapters. As the couples in therapy become more clear and warm in their intimacy, there tends to be an increase in the recognition and experience of psi-mediated dreams.

DREAMS IN FAMILY THERAPY

Now let us turn our attention to a much larger canvas, where the boundaries defining relationships, and the connections within and between relationships, are much more varied and expansive. This includes psychic and psychological boundaries between individuals and also the permeable boundary between body and mind within an individual. Because it is like a ripple wave across many generations, a transgenerational theme can be seen to have a certain binding and unifying effect within a family constellation.[14] It also can be a potent method of expanding one's own individual mind and individual perspective. The following dream is reported by a psychologist interested in transgenerational themes:

I remember going to sleep and in a dream having dinner with my father.
In the dream I sat down with my father, soon my father's father joined us.

It was then that my father, myself and my grandfather were present. Soon after this, in a somewhat shadowy form, my grandfather's father appeared as if he was looking over my grandfather's shoulder. My attention was drawn to this. Finally my grandfather's grandfather appeared in an even more shadowy sort of way. I reached my hand across the table and across the others and managed very briefly to physically shake his hand in the dream. He was not a depressing figure, but was a shadowy and distant or legendary figure. I felt some important knowledge was communicated to me. It was clear that my grandfather's grandfather in this situation was a slave but a slave who felt like a free man.

Several years later, this same psychologist found himself the guide or the focus of large multifamily therapy sessions. In these sessions, several families at a time would get together to have a large group family therapy session. The dynamics in this situation were significantly more complex than those others in that several family systems had events simultaneously occurring. In this situation, generational themes and transactional patterns could be seen to repeat not only in the lives of individuals but also across many generations at the same time. From this vantage point anyone who looks deeply into their own family ancestry and history going back multiple generations has seen not only the repetition of names and similar faces, but also stories and claims and seemingly individual characteristics. One cannot escape at least the sense that individual styles and perhaps even individual family souls appear and disappear in and out of the height, width, depth, and time flows in this four-dimensional familial matrix from another or fifth dimensional level. It appears as though there are "waves" in this sea of familial consciousness. Important archetypal family dreams may move from one wave crest to the next in this sea, from one generation to the next.

In other words the body has dynamics and processes that apply to it that obey natural laws, even if we do not fully understand those laws. Medicine is fully aware of this humbling truth. However, what we experience as the mind and its body are not exactly identical even if we accept that mind is a more "subtle" form or expression of matter. We know clinically and experientially that mind and body can be experienced as vastly separated from each other at times by way of autoscopic vision, out-of-body experiences, remote-viewing experiments with later-verified accurate information processing, and the various forms of clinical dissociation. Different laws appear to govern these realms and regions of experience.

Mind in a sense, from this perspective, incarnates into the body. The soul or aspect of consciousness that "descends" or unfolds out into the familial present-day consciousness in a sense incarnates into that familial psychological and emotional field from perhaps a higher enfolded order. In turn it has natural laws that govern its dynamics in these regions of experience, even if again we do not fully understand them. These regions of experience may be quite difficult to capture in our current vocabulary of space, time, matter, and language-dominated mental conception. However, it would be presumptuous to assume in the current era that we understand all the laws of matter and consciousness.

Even if this idea remains speculation and intuition for many people, the operation of the family unconscious itself is certainly clear, at least for the present generation of family members. There are recurrent transactional patterns of affect and behavior and values that can be observed and stand out. They at the very least function as a wave form over the discrete functions and behaviors of individuals within the system.

In multigenerational family therapy one need only have a grandparent, a parent, and a child present. This form of therapy has been found to be extremely useful in issues involving substance abuse. It is also extremely helpful in working with characterological and neurotic styles that manifest over generations and when looking at illness and disease patterns of families. The therapist can begin to notice in certain disease processes that sudden and subtle bodily and psychological associations and states of mind are held by members of the family across many generations. A way of assessing this in terms of body and mind, family associations, physical associations, and others would be extremely useful. In that sense, any assessment profile used would need to expand to the full range of human associations and needs.

Beyond this, the awareness of multigenerational themes can foster the sense of differentiation and liberation within the family, while maintaining deeper bonds that are necessary and that connect us to individuals, relational systems, tribes, and even nations. This is the dynamic interplay between the individual principle and the group, or collective, principle.

In working with this family unconscious system, the generational themes are elicited by the therapist in the same way that individual themes and relational themes are elicited in family therapy with a group emphasis. It is extremely important in this form of uncovering that the work of the dream be approached in the first person and in the present tense. This allows for the dreamer's body, mind, and senses—*the whole visceral self*—to be involved and in turn gives rise to bodily associations, information about family illness processes, and the unique language that each person uses in the dialogue with themselves.

Procedures and techniques can be drawn from any school that is congruent with the family and the therapist's own values, inclination, and worldview. Some prefer a more classical dialectical approach that can be seen in some forms of gestalt dreamwork. Others prefer a psychodrama approach in which voices are given to different aspects of the dream. As long as these are complementary, they will help elicit the simultaneous and corresponding roles that are acted out and reinforced within the family systems. Projected or disowned aspects of one's own self are reabsorbed into the personality. The process of projective identification is also decreased. In the process, the family myths, family roles, and useful or dysfunctional rituals can be assessed. Usually a family myth, much like a cultural myth, emerges to express a family's belief or way of perceiving being in the world. In such circumstances of dream reporting and dream sharing, the process stimulates similar family dreams and family-oriented dreams with other members of this extended group. Such authors as Robin Shohet,[15] Phyllis Koch-Sheras,

E. Ann Hollier, and Brooke Jones[16] have used this procedure with great effect. They have recognized along with Montague Ullman and Nan Zimmerman[17] that the dream and the group process lead to the unification of the personality on a deeper level.

In the multigenerational theme and dream that opened this section the clinician picked up on and identified the past family myths and family motifs. In that situation, it was the motif of liberation, first played out in a social-political way, then in a family way, and then finally in an individual and psychological way.

GROUP DREAMWORK

There are ways of working with dreams in groups in which participants are not members of the same immediate family. This is group dreamwork. In this particular context profound and evocative feelings are elicited using some of the same procedures and techniques used in group and family therapy. Later on in this chapter I will outline specifically what some of those questions and directions might be. For now, let us look at a representative way in which a group might deal with a dream presented to it. In the process of reading, notice how *the group makes the dream its own* and in so doing uses its own projections and not those of the dreamer. The desire to help is strong, but there is also a great degree of concern for the privacy and protection of the dreamer. This session comes from Montague Ullman, a long-time theorist and clinical practitioner of group dreamwork.

Doris's Dream

I'm at my friend Betty's house. I phone to make an appointment to get my hair highlighted. I speak to the receptionist at the beauty parlor in a Russian accent. I say I can come in in a couple of days. She asks, "Are you sure, because we are changing things around here," implying it won't be good if I change my mind and cancel the appointment. I realize after speaking to her that I don't need to have it done yet because my hair hasn't grown out. But George and I go to the A Train to the beauty parlor. The train travels outside through a neighborhood that I have never seen before. George gets out at a stop as if he nonchalantly is doing something. The train leaves without him. I wave to him and feel bad that he is not on the train.

Feelings expressed by the group: *I feel pressure, feeling rushed. I feel as though I am acting a role when I put on the accent, a role I like. I feel challenged by the receptionist; she knows some things about me. I wish I could make up my mind. I am annoyed; I wish my friend Betty would help me. I feel better having George with me. I am frightened being in a strange neighborhood. I don't know what I'm getting into. I feel abandonment by George. I'm insecure and have to take George along with me.*

Images discussed by the group: *Hair is the dominant image; minor external changes seem important. I'm disguising myself. I'm trying to feel beautiful and loved. I do take the A Train to the Dream Group. My dream thoughts will be brought above the ground; I have mixed feelings about that. The Dream Group will be messing around with my head. The hair represents my feelings, feelings that haven't ripened yet. George is preoccupied. I want some highlighting and not to be left alone. I want to draw attention to myself.*

Doris's response: *I'm embarrassed that the dream has so much to do with my hair. I knew I would do a dream tonight. It has to do with how others see me and how I want to be seen. I wouldn't normally pretend I was Russian with someone I didn't know. I resent it when the receptionist asked me if I was sure. She reminded me of my chiropractor's receptionist. Lately I have felt abandoned. I feel as if I am watching George's life and his concern over a profession more than I usually am.*

My hair has been cut short recently. When I'm getting my hair cut I usually don't like it right afterwards. It's important to me how people see me. We do take the A Train to the Dream Group. Yesterday I was with Betty. I don't have to be embarrassed with her. I can admit that I want to look nice and there is no question of being judged. I feel angry at George for getting off the train, yet I certainly don't want him at the beauty parlor. Lately our feelings of sharing together have been pushed aside. The strange neighborhood? Perhaps new things will have to be confronted. I want the Dream Group to accept me; I don't want to be judged.[18]

In the give and take of this group dream session it is remarkable how much emotional material is available after the process is underway. Individuals spontaneously offer their own experiences, their own intuitions, and their own projections, all the while owning them and not assuming that they must be true for the dreamer. This helps the dreamer feel protected, accepted, and able to unfold. This could easily go in the direction of psychodrama,[19] or in a dialectical process, depending upon the theoretical orientation and the tendencies of the therapist and the group. While working with the dream, members of the group, be they one other individual, a family, or a formal group setting, must really listen attentively to what the dreamer is saying. This lets the dreamer know that the group appreciates and recognizes the importance of the expression of the dreamer.

The dream is largely the dreamer's construction, a construction of reality that other people are implicated in. The dreamer is encouraged to define and to describe and then eventually express in as straightforward a manner as possible the exact dream imagery itself. In the process the dreamer is reinforced and encouraged to connect his or her emotional or felt sense to what is actively going on in the dream.

In our work a physiological correlation and a somatic association are made to the dream wherever possible. This is really using one's own body to let the dreams do their work. Some work along this line has been explored by Gendlin.[20] With the potential of the body's own expressions, the somatic associations and repercussions of emotional states are clearly in evidence. Appendix B holds the Kemetic Imagery and Healing Assessment Protocol, which contains a way of assessing the activity of various bodily functions. It also provides a way to assess the capacity of personalized imagery, affect, symbols, and images to influence emotional and bodily states. When used as a guide in an individual or family context, it reflects certain recurrent transactional patterns over time that have an intimate correspondence to the dreamer's own inner world of body and mind.

Other researchers have indicated that dreams often forewarn of physical illnesses occurring in the body.[21] It is known that before going to surgery, some individuals have massive changes in the perception of their body that is reflected in their dreams.[22] This is a normal reflection of a heightened sense of vulnerability and anxiety. There are even dreams in which family members have been known to be able to foretell the disease or the illness or the physical accident of a family member either at the same time that it occurs or sometimes weeks before the actual diagnosis of a problem. They appear to be trying to warn or protect, heal, or offer a solution for the afflicted family member. This process, in conjunction with other ways of profoundly relaxing the psychophysical body, has immense therapeutic potential, especially when the dreamer attains lucidity in the dream. We will return to this in the next chapter.

KEMETIC IMAGERY AND HEALING ASSESSMENT PROTOCOL

Throughout this chapter and in earlier chapters I have alluded to the necessity, when dealing with clinical issues, of assessing a person's emotional and physical reactions across the full spectrum. This is also a procedure for expanding the awareness and the conventional boundaries of a person's emotional life and their interaction with others on many levels. I mentioned how Gendlin[23] has used the body directly in letting the dreamwork take its course. This procedure was actually used in ancient times by the Egyptians, Greeks, and Romans. It was quite commonplace to assume and perceive that certain "gods" or "neters" and certain natural forces held sway over specific systems in the body. This, however, was not limited to the broad Mediterranean world. On the Indian subcontinent, such practices were well-established, particularly among the Dravidian peoples, the same people known to be India's original dark inhabitants and yoga practitioners long before the Indo-Aryan invasions of the North. In the African empires of the sub-Sahara, such practices were in operation for thousands of years.[24] In fact, the ancient Kemetic Egyptians and the Dravidians shared a great deal with each other historically in terms of trade routes, psychospiritual beliefs, and genetic lineages. All were aware of the power of directed feeling and imagery to affect the body.

We are generally aware today that the two hemispheres of the brain have developed specialized functions over time and that, somewhat simplistically stated, the left is associated with linear thinking, logical functions, and sequential modes of adaptation to the world, and the right is more highly associated with global thinking and perceptions, imagery, intuition, artistic creativity, and emotionality. However, modern neuroscience has also suggested that our consciousness-controlling processes are centered in the frontal lobes, or the prefrontal division of the brain, which belong to the tertiary zones of the cortex. This is the location of the decisive and *purposeful formation of intentions* and programs that influence the subtle regulation and verification of highly complex human behaviors, including *symbols* and other context-dependent behavior such as interpersonal interactions.[25]

An important distinguishing feature of this prefrontal region is its dense, rich network of cortical connections to the lower levels of the brain (the medial and ventral nuclei and pulvinar of the thalamus) *and* to nearly every other part of the cortex, including the sensorimotor and somatosensory systems. These prefrontal lobes, especially the medial and basal portions, are connected by particularly well-developed bundles of ascending and descending fibers with the reticular formation, and these regions of the neocortex receive extremely powerful streams of impulses.[26] Thus, by a two-way street, the conscious, cognitive, and symbol functions can profoundly influence and be influenced by the sensory and visceral aspects of the overall system. In order to do so with volitional control and skill, the system must be relaxed and focused. This will allow the increased upward flow of individual, familial, and collective unconscious images from the brain and brainstem pathways that were mentioned in chapter 4 under "Pathways of the Unconscious: Dreaming, Biochemistry, and the Brain."

In the Kemetic Imagery and Healing Assessment Protocol there is, for purely technically reasons, a profound need to relax the physical and the subjectively visualized or psychological body. The patient is introduced to the technique of diaphragmatic breathing with emphases on the exhalation phase of the breathing cycle, and then two other techniques, alternate nostril breathing and then focus of attention at the top of the lip/bottom of the nose, to quiet the activity of the autonomic nervous system and to bring equipoise and quiescence to the state of mind. The bombardment of sensory stimuli is quieted and attention is slowly turned inward. This is similar to certain phases of sensory withdrawal employed in yoga and other forms of meditative practice.

The person is then brought to a subtle but definite sensation of "living" and flowing experience in the body itself. With some training and work, this living current can then be applied and focused very directly in both waking and dreaming states to the bodily processes themselves. The intuition cultivated is that the breath is a living force. The assessment profile allows different areas of a person's lived experience to be assessed and then maximized in some cases while delimited in others. Direction of this living experience practice would be the clinical work of the therapist. The gentle focus of this living current appears to awaken a certain integrated, rejuvenating feeling process within the body-mind and as a direct consequence decreases the biochemical stress reactivity of the body, decreases the overactivation of the autonomic nervous system, and helps bring the many levels of the mind to a quiescence and healing focus. The immune system is strengthened in terms of white blood cell, phagocyte, prostaglandin, and "resonate" pentenes functioning. In the final stages, it helps the individual, the clinician, and the group find a functional healing metaphor that can enfold the psychological and emotional aspects and the powerful imagery and experience on the body for clinical purposes. At the very end are well-known ways and techniques to arrive at some mastery over the visualization and the control of one's internal imagery process. This is merely to make explicit what has been known implicitly in a fragmentary way for eons.

GUIDING QUESTIONS TO UNFOLD IMAGERY AND HEALING PROCESSES

What are some of the questions a family or a friend or even a therapist might ask to help elicit the kind of powerful affect, imagery, emotion, and neurological processes that I have been outlining?

An atmosphere of safety and unwavering support of the individual is encouraged to connect their physical bodily feeling with images and events that happened in the dream. Again, it is important to always tell the dream in the first person. The group or family never tells the individual what their dream means. Rather they say what the dream means for them and ask the dreamer what their experience is. Any names or particular events should always be noted. Beyond that, it is very important to know what issues or situations seem to occur in the dream, and better yet, what situations repeat in the dream. What feelings and emotions are involved? Are there any connections with things that have recently happened, especially the last two or three days? The group is always interested in what the story line of the dream is. Can it be stated in a mythological format or even in a matter-of-fact format? Are there any associations and analogies to the body or bodily processes? What images and symbols, particularly images of family members and symbols of cultural importance and religious importance, occur? Are there any themes in the dreams that don't make any sense at all? If you were writing about your dream, what would you call the dream sequence?

These are all questions concerning the structure and the form of the dream. From here one can proceed to other areas of the dream to be explored.

As one moves away from the form and structure of the dream and from recent day residue and other factors, one becomes more involved in the dream on a personal and meaningful level, focusing on the appearance of those particular individuals within the family system that one is emotionally close to. There are often situations that are *repetitive* in this context. Family myths concerning the role and function of intimate family members arise here spontaneously. There may be more of a focus on the "meaningfulness" of the dream and on a bodily emotional sense in family therapy sessions than in group therapy sessions when dreamwork is used. In this regard, it becomes easier to draw closer correspondences between aspects of a dream, images of a dream, and the dreamer. Conflicts with others take on a greater and sharper focus. Childhood memories arise spontaneously, as do concerns about sexuality and even psychological, psychic, and spiritual enfoldment.

The assessment profile covers this entire spectrum and in that sense does not focus on or tend to reduce things to intrapsychic psychodynamic consequences. In the last context, the noetic or spiritual issues concerning psi, NDEs, psychic and spiritual experience, and related matters are accepted as real and valid. The universe becomes much more a living and consciously participatory universe than a universe in which one is walled off within the context and the confines of one's own ego.

Working with dream imagery and dream symbolism in a family or a larger group situation greatly expands one's own boundaries, yet maintains a sense of external cohesiveness and integrity. This often stimulates similar processes in others. One can begin to see how an issue in one's own life is stimulated and unfolds systematically in the lives of others with whom one is intimately involved. This occurs on both a psychological and a somatic level. Through this whole process the dreamer is again encouraged to speak in the first person and to be as simple and emotionally and physically evocative and participatory in the dream process as possible. In this way consciousness expands, and we touch the dreams of our ancestors from ages ago and send messages to our children's distant children eons from now.

10

The Dream
of Infinite Life

*The Further Reaches of
the Dream in Family and Self*

*They say we have been here for more than 60,000 years,
but it is much longer than that. We have been here since
the time before time began. We have come directly out of
the Dreamtime of the great Creative Ancestors. We have
lived and kept the earth as it was on the First Day.*

ROBERT LAWLOR, *VOICES OF THE FIRST DAY:
AWAKENING IN THE ABORIGINAL DREAMTIME*

*Far from being mutually exclusive, the Universal and
the Personal grow in the same direction and culminate
simultaneously in each other.*

PIERRE TEILHARD DE CHARDIN,
THE PHENOMENON OF MAN

Not for a changeless littleness were you meant, not for vain repetition were you built. . . . Almighty powers are shut in Nature's cells. A greater destiny awaits you in your front. . . . The life you lead conceals the light you are.

S. AUROBINDO, *SAVITRI*

Luminous beings we are, not this crude matter.

YODA, *THE EMPIRE STRIKES BACK*

ORGANIZING IMAGES AND BEHAVIOR

A thirty-five-year-old writer had the following dream:

An exceedingly wonderful dream. Partly vivid, partly devotional, and largely allegorical, it took place in a modern city area with myself, a man (Gary) who we met while trekking recently in Nepal, and my wife.

The convoluted plot focused around the "quest" for meaning and purpose, which brought in aspects of philosophy and a pervasive devotional, somewhat religious or bakti sense to the atmosphere. In the dream I had a "clear light" experience and had just come out of it. It was thus a dream within a dream. My emotional state was elated, cheerful, and also ballooning to the "I" sense. I watched myself attempt to reorganize my "I" sense while I was cheerful with the elated afterglow of the setting, my head on a desk as I sat down near the home my wife and I lived in. Two clear statements spontaneously appeared to me in the process of the dream within the dream:

Every profound experience, waking, dreaming, or sleeping, enormously expands the "I" sense, pervades it with the sense of truth and eternity.

Our ultimate identity is realized in ecstasy and light.

The power of dreams to express emotions, motivations, fears, desires, trauma, and creative ideas, and also to open up to the noetic or spiritual dimension, has been a central thesis of this book, woven in with the other central thesis of family interconnectedness. Indeed, the dream and the dream process in many ways provide an undercurrent or shared reality for both the family and the individual within the extended network of the family. In previous chapters, we looked at the dreams of individuals and how powerful they can be. We looked at dreams as they occurred in families and saw the reflecting and organizing capacity they have in terms of family relationships. We have even seen dreams in culture and society and the collective dreams we refer to as mythology. Indeed the collective dreams and myths in movies, art, and various other forms of gigantic imagery provide one of the major motifs for the twenty-first century. That motif is the capacity of large-scale organized imagery to motivate the emotions and influence the current of intellectual ideas and group behavior for humanity. One need only look at massive, highly organized imagery and the propaganda systems of the modern state. The cult of personality and its mythology is one of the examples of the capacity of imagery on a large scale to organize and direct social and political behavior. The twentieth century was replete with heroes whom the cult of personality favored and disfavored relatively quickly. Mao Tse-tung is one example. Adolf Hitler is another. Remember *Triumph of the Will*. In a more benign sense, the Reagan era in the United States was a cult of personality.

In earlier chapters, we have seen the capacity of dreams to reflect deep individual and family processes during certain phases of family life. The chapter on the dreams of ACOA clearly demonstrated the reflective capacity of dreams in the context of painful family dynamics. On the other end, we have seen dreams as they appear in pregnancy and all the rich possibilities and the positive emotional turmoil that they can sometimes stimulate and reflect. We have also seen the interconnection between dreams and certain paranormal events. This latter capacity was well known by Freud and Jung at the beginning of the twentieth century.

An aspect we have not touched on too deeply is the fact that we experience familiar places as well as family members in our dreams, and our family has shared familiar places in our collective dreams. This is more support for the living reality of the shared dreamscape. Its implications are far reaching, as will be discovered shortly.

Dreams can be about other dreams, and dreams can and do stimulate the memory of other dreams. It is one theory of déjà vu. It, too, reminds the dreamer of some prior image, event, or memory. Whether or not family members are present in the dream, symbolically or directly, many locations have correlating familiar feelings and associations. This is also true for the waking state. In both conditions implicit memory can be unclear, and our tacit assumptions about reality can be rather vague.

Indeed, unless we actually reflect on our condition, waking or dreaming, we simply assume certain laws and dynamics to be true and in operation. There appear to be two sets of these tacit assumptions about the dynamics of the experienced universe, and we simply accept the state or condition we are operating from at any moment as a given. We rarely ask, when awake, are the physical laws of the universe operating here? When dreaming, we rarely ask, are the mental or psychical laws of the mind operating here? We simply take it for granted. Each in its own way is a certain kind of dream. What we *know* is to a significant degree dependent on our state of mind.

Beyond all this, which, despite its power is still largely subjective, is all the "objective" information we now have about dreams. The laboratory data on dreams and their imagery has revealed the changes in blood rate, thermal effects, and brain and neurological processes during dreaming. The relationship between the prefrontal lobes of the brain and every other cortical system, including the sensorimotor and somatosensory systems, and their extensive connections to the deep thalamic regions of the brain in the conduct and possibly conscious concourse of intentionality, symbol behavior, and imagery has been alluded to before.[1] Yet while much about dreaming is known, why we even dream at all is still an enigma. In concert with this is the deep mystery about the capacity of dreams to enfold information and the range in influence of consciousness itself.

Family dreams have the capacity to express family myth—myths that touch all of our lives. Repeatedly, the dream within the family was shown to reflect implicitly the enfolded relationships of all the significant members within the family. This has been termed the "family unconscious" by some authors[2] and the "familial unconscious" by those in the Swiss movement. The latter movement drew a great deal from earlier assumptions surrounding the science of genetics.

Out of the family unconscious evolved the observation of both the family psyche and the family soma, where the ubiquitous effect of similar or shared imagery, symbols, and other powerful indicators of emotion or stress were seen to affect the body in a clinical way. The need to gather information about family images, symbols, and even family deities has been brought into this assessment process. In order to evaluate the whole spectrum, I developed the Kemetic Imagery and Healing Assessment Protocol. I pointed to the notion of interconnectedness among intimate relations. These relations are not only within the individual but between individuals and sometimes between the somatic systems of individuals who share a common history. In other words, the group wave form can and does exercise an influence over the behavior of individuals. One look at family illness processes lends strong support to this observation. However, the observation is not made in isolation. Modern science is replete with intelligent interconnectedness emerging in many areas of science from neurology to quantum mechanics, from family relationships to economics, ecology, and the unified living field of the earth, which is known as Gaia.

Family dreams and individual dreams are deeply implicated in the healing process of not only family but self and community. Indeed, political myths and religio-political myths are as powerful in organizing human emotions as are individual and family dreams and myths. Powerful political or religio-political myths have enormous consequences for world political order. In the early part of the twenty-first century, many myths are crumbling on a vast political scale and new myths and alliances of interconnectedness are emerging. These will have enormous political and scientific implications as we emerge with a new vision of ourselves and our identity in the coming years.

There is no doubt that the family on many continents and many countries is at risk. This is not only due to the usual economic and political pressures, but also to the fragmentation of kinship feelings as individual and self-oriented values have become predominant. With this fragmentation has come an increase in the emphasis on autonomy and separation. The effects are seen not only in our political and philosophical life but also in our theories about the role of individuation and autonomy in clinical practices of various kinds. Dreams reflect the processes on an individual and on a shared or group level. They also, as we shall now see, reflect the intimate connection between death, family communication, and the more subtle realms of order and intelligence.

FAMILY DREAMS AND DEATH

Death is an inevitable part of life. Death and life may be cycles or consequences of a prior existence or a deeper reality. In other words, the perception of death and its apparent opposite, embodied life, may both be projections of some deeper, more subtle order of intelligence, energy, and consciousness. That prior or deeper reality implies a certain interconnectedness, one that is often expressed in intimate or subtle communication in dreams. Earlier we explored some family dreams that pertained to death. Just as dreams of pregnancy have a certain style, a certain focus on imagery and symbols and motivations, so also do dreams of death as they occur in the family context. Common symbols of death in dreams are shrouds, burial grounds, images of nightfall, the end of the stage act, the drawing of the curtain, and so on. These are normal images in dreams. Different cultures may have different expressions of these symbols, but the symbolization process in all cultures is the same.

Often in normal grieving, past loved ones are seen or even sought out in dreams. Painful emotions sometimes recur along with feelings of resolution, guilt, or frustration. William Boylin[3] has shown how the family's conflicts are intensified during the grieving process. Reflection of family conflicts in the family's dreaming is normal and occurs quite often. There is also a classification of normal dreams, however, that does not occur as often. These are those dreams of families in the grieving process or that involve the family in deaths that have a certain "uncanny" feeling about them. These are explored next, one level at a time.

As mentioned above, normal grief dreams have common symbols of shrouds, burial grounds, and so on. There are, however, family dreams occurring at a deeper level that are much more unusual in their emotional and subjective feeling aspect. Some of these dreams we might classify as "visitation dreams." These are dreams in which dead or recently deceased family members appear to the dreamer. Often the feeling in these dreams has a certain numinous quality about it. Here the deceased person is often experienced as wanting to communicate a certain emotional or sometimes even factual message to the living dreamer. These dreams can be clearly differentiated from those of someone dreaming about a dead person they were close to but do not try to communicate with in the dreams. There is a clear difference in feeling, tone, sense of intimacy, and meaningfulness, and a certain uncanny or unearthly quality to them. At best it feels like contact with benevolent spirits or guides. At worst it feels like unwanted contact with the living dead.

The crisis telepathy dream mentioned in chapters 1 and 6 is another level of common family dream concerning death. In this kind of dream, often at the moment of death, the person who is deceased "appears" to someone close to them in family relationship and emotional tone. The communication may be direct or it may come through in a more symbolic way. The dreamer clearly has the felt sense that the person in the dream has just died or is deceased. There is often the feeling that the person in the dream is hurt or is endangered in some way. In this case, it is not death, per se, but the risk of death that is communicated.

Finally, on another level, there are those dreams in which there is the anticipation or premonition of one's own death. Abraham Lincoln's coffin dream is the most famous. One might refer to these as precognitive dreams as I have done in earlier chapters on paranormal dreams. Sometimes death can come very quickly and yet the dreams can still prophecy or warn of it. In her brilliant book *On Dreams and Death,* Maria-Louise von Franz[4] reports the following dream. It is from a young woman who was suffering from an incurable disease and had died unexpectedly during a surgical operation. Prior to the operation she dreamed the following:

> *I find myself at the edge of a lake with my husband and some friends. The lake is very deep and the water is clear, transparent, clean and blue. Suddenly I see a black bird in the depths of the lake; it is dead. I feel great sympathy and want to dive in, search for it and save it. I cannot stand to think that it is dead. My husband intervenes lovingly but firmly and asks me not to do it, because, he says, it is right this way. I look into the lake once more and see the eye of the bird; it is a diamond that shines brightly. Whereupon I awaken.*

Von Franz believes that the dead bird must be symbolic of the extinguished life spirit of the body which the dreamer must abandon, otherwise, she would be contaminated with the dissolving powers of death. In other words, she must keep herself free of the dying body but at the same time look into the diamond eye of the bird. In Jung's psychodynamics, the diamond is an alchemical variant of the self as an indestructible core of personality. This may indeed be so. In the Freudian approach to the understanding of death, the unconscious is supposedly unable even to conceive of its own death. But we certainly can conceive of the death of loved ones in an abstract way in dreams. We can even conceive of the impending death of ourselves in a dream. Indeed, there is some sense that the dreaming self does not believe in death. Whether it is true or not, the psyche certainly believes in life after death, both for us as individuals and also for those in our family. As far as clinical science can tell we are actually to some extent conscious prior to our physical birth, and emergency room experiences and the NDE confirm that we are conscious to some extent after clinical death.

There are numerous possible reasons why the psyche does not accept or believe in its own death. Perhaps the psyche is so full of denial and wish fulfillment that it cannot even conceive of a final end to itself. Maybe the psyche overtly identifies with the body and thus cannot imagine a condition of no body. The most intriguing possibility is that on some level, perhaps, the psyche peers intuitively into its own deeper reality that is not located in external or objective space and time and realizes that death is a projected illusion of an eternal consciousness in which it participates and has its transformations. It is no wonder that the psyche can summon up in certain states of consciousness the "departed" psyches of intimate family members who are believed to have died.

It may very well be that reincarnation and other afterlife survival theories about ourselves and about our families are the intuition of a radiant current of ceaseless life and its various forms circling and cycling through the great shared luminous matrix of a common identity that is neither created nor destroyed, but rather changing constantly from state to higher state, using the constructs of space, matter, and time to manifest itself. Freud stated almost dogmatically that the unconscious cannot conceive of its own death. This may well be because death is not in the realm of the unconscious at all but is a peculiar dynamic of the transconscious that is beyond space and time as we know it. "Objects" are in space and time, have solid form, and come into existence, and therefore in principle must go out of existence. Consciousness, which is more closely akin to the energetic process of reality, uses space and time, objects and form, but is more an undercurrent or source of space and time than its consequence. This appears to be the case in quantum and relativistic physics with matter and energy where matter, by way of

$E = mc^2$, is trapped or enfolded energy. Space and time are seen as ways in which matter and energy express themselves in the unfolded or overt universe.[5]

Dreams and certain meditative states may reveal the matrices and dynamics of energy, intelligence, and consciousness beyond the body-object dynamics expressed in the denser processes of birth, embodiment, and death. Indeed, it may be that as the consciousness associated with the physical body decreases during the process of death, the energetic aspects of the mind that are more associated with "light" are progressively liberated from their embedment in the psyche. The embedded light begins to outshine the more dominant body consciousness to the extent that awareness is flooded, transformed, and eventually outshone and identified with the supraliminal level of our being. Whatever its dynamics, clearly those who have died have entered a realm of phenomena that those of us who are still living have not. When those who have entered this realm are very close to us or have been close to us emotionally in the past, a whole new range of dynamics are operative at the time of individual and familial death. They have shared with us similar events, meanings, and familiar locations, both waking and dreaming. This memory and intuition is the origin of ancestor worship and prayers to the dead. Note the following family death dream submitted by Carl Jung:

> He meets two . . . guides who lead him to a building where he finds many
> people; among them is his father, step-father, and his mother, who gives
> him a kiss of welcome. He has to go on a long climb ending at the top of
> a deep precipice. A voice commands him to leap; after several disparate
> refusals he obeys and finds himself swimming "delirious into the blue of
> eternity."[6]

The man who submitted this dream to Jung was an aging man. Jung interpreted this dream as a preparation for death and pointed out to the dreamer the Hindu belief that the dying rise upward to the cosmic

Atman. Jung said that "there is no loneliness, but allness, or infinitely increasing completeness."

FAMILY DREAMS BEYOND DEATH

It seems that on some level of the mind we all intuitively believe that $E = mc^2$, that from light to light and from life to life do we go! So many curious anomalies surround us in this age of materialist science that we cannot help but sense that something else is going on besides our romance with matter, mechanics, and mathematics. These anomalies are scattered about us like the vestiges of a once-vibrant civilization that we have all but lost and struggle daily to keep forgotten. Yet like some deeply buried secret or trauma, their reality from time to time infuses our daily waking life along with the luminous corridor of our sleep.

There are at least ten if not more areas of perennial interest that are the offshoots of ancient sciences and disciplines that focus on the realm of death, dreams, intelligence, and consciousness as active modes of operation after physical embodiment is transcended. The Bardo Thodol, or Tibetan Book of the Dead,[7] is a traditional account of the journey or adventure of the departed family member or oneself through the consciousness of death. It is a Buddhist text with admixtures of even earlier Tibetan psychoreligious practices and beliefs. Because it is a "map" of phenomena and processes that occur between one "birth" and another, it is really more accurately referred to as the book of the "in-between."

Even earlier than this and strikingly similar is the ancient Kemetic Egyptian text, the Egyptian Book of the Dead.[8] Its purpose is much the same, and indeed it may have been the original teaching later spread by civilization to India, Tibet, and other areas of the world. Again, the title "Book of the Dead" is less accurate than its original title, which is the book of the Coming Forth by Day and the Going Forth by Night. This text was the focus of helping departed family members and others we shared consciousness with through the phenomenal worlds of death and beyond. It was the crest-jewel of the temple mysteries at Karnak and Luxor at least seven thousand years ago—that appear to be the remnants of an even earlier civilization. And it was the primary mode of African transcendental religion until Arab jihads swept out of Arabia over North Africa and repressed the indigenous religion and culture of the region, only to have it resurface in some variation in the religions of other peoples, particularly those in West Africa. This belief system later spread to the Americas in the guise of voodoo in Haiti, Umbanda and Candomblé in Brazil, Santeria in Cuba and Puerto Rico, and to other areas of South America where slaves were brought over in the African diaspora.[9] Actually, this would be the second wave of African influence in the Americas since there is considerable historical and archaeological evidence of an African presence, especially in the ancient Olmec culture, which gave rise to the later Maya, Aztec, Toltec, and Zapotec cultures. Clearly they were not slaves, but explorers, mariners, and merchants on the eastern coast. See John G. Jackson's *Introduction to African Civilization*[10] and Leo Wiener's *Africa and the Discovery of America*. In general, however, the attitude of Western science toward these religious and psychospiritual disciplines, with a few notable exceptions, has been intensely negative.

Beyond these cultural and psychoreligious disciplines and beliefs there are another ten or so offshoots of these that are studied and classified, somewhat inaccurately, in Western terms. They are generally referred to as a branch of the "psychic science," or parapsychology, though strictly speaking are *not* a part of parapsychology, but rather of religion. The paradigm of mind and consciousness is radically different from the ego-psychological models of Western science, especially in regard to psychic energy, boundary formation, and the reach of information processing systems. These ten areas are: (1) the formal study of parapsychology or psychic phenomena, (2) traditional or indigenous religion, (3) mediumship, (4) the study of discarnate entities, (5) spirit "possession," (6) so-called spirit photography, (7) past lives phenomena, (8) Kirlian photography, (9) NDEs and out-of-body experiences (OBEs), and (10) eschatology, the branch of theology concerned with final events or death.

Contact with deceased family members and others is termed "mediumship," which really became a large movement in America and Europe in the late nineteenth and early twentieth centuries.[11] A related field is the study of discarnate entities seen by others who are not necessarily practicing mediumship. This, too, reached its zenith in the nineteenth and early twentieth centuries.[12] Another area of study is possession, more commonly associated with the psychoreligious practices mentioned above. Technically the person is not really being "possessed." In actuality the person possesses or embodies the gods through appropriate disciplines. The person is volitionally involved in the process, at least initially.

There are other areas of interest, however, that are more prominent in studies of our own day. The interest in past lives is very high at the present time. This is interesting in the light of long-held African and Tibetan beliefs that we are the reincarnated souls of long-departed family members. There is a field called "spirit photography" that claims, at least theoretically, to capture the photographic image and energy field of related or unknown entities.[13] Again a large percentage of the images are of relatives of families in some context. This has some relationship to the science of Kirlian photography where the energetic form of a living or recently terminated life form evidently can be captured on film using special techniques. In the latter, the "energy" is not parapsychological at all, but rather classically electromagnetic in nature. These Kirlian methods, based on the work of Semyon Kirlian and his wife Valentina, allow one to make a photographic print on any electrically conductive object by using the corona discharge that surrounds the object's surface. It is *not* an "aura" or "spirit" photograph, but rather an electrophotograph that can have medical-diagnostic uses.[14] It is related to spirit photography in the sense that the psychophysical and electrically conductive human body and the reputed psychoenergetic spiritual dimension of ourselves are *both*, in some permutation, forms of energy and are, for a time at least, localized in the same human frame and space-time. In some "subtle" form, therefore, this energetic dimension may be able to be detected. However, one is parapsychological and the other, Kirlian, is not.

More interesting and more "clinically" relevant than these last two fields of study, however, are cases seen by physicians, nurses, and other clinicians. These are connected to parapsychology, also, but are not, technically speaking, a part of it. They are the NDEs, OBEs, and death-bed observations. In the NDE, individuals have been clinically dead and then medically revived. They very often report the experience of light, intelligence, and the appearance of deceased relatives who contact them in a helping fashion. These people have the experience of leaving the physical body (an OBE) and moving down, along, or up through a long tunnel where deceased family members come out of the shadows to greet them, comfort them, and guide them along. This has been attested to by so many thousands of people that the phenomenon itself is no longer in question.[15] The question, both clinically and psycho-religiously, is, what does it mean? All kinds of explanations have been offered, and while none have been proven beyond a doubt, the reality of the experience is beyond dispute.

Finally, there are what are termed "deathbed observations" made by physicians and nurses. There is a long tradition in medicine of observing the dying process. In one exhaustive study, more than 650 nurses and physicians recounted a record 753 cases of patients whose mood greatly clarified and elevated just prior to their actual death. We encountered this phenomenon before in the section on crisis telepathy family dreams. There were 888 reported "visions" of a nonhuman nature and nearly 1,370 persons reported the apparition of dead relatives and friends. These patients were not in a confused state but rather were fully conscious, clear, and alert.[16]

It appears as though in the dying process, as we are progressively disengaged from the physical self, we have greater conscious access to that implicit, enfolded level of our shared consciousness we call the family unconscious. Moving deeper into the death or dying process, this family unconscious opens or unfolds and those with whom we have shared life events, symbols, ideas, dreams, and locations, both waking and dreaming, emerge again into wholeness. The universe becomes radiantly personal again—alive, conscious, and indescribably luminous.

DREAMS AND REALITY

Freud believed that dreams were a subpart or a secondhand reflection of waking experience. He believed the dream mixed distant and recent events in a particular dynamic of dreamwork that led to certain kinds of subjective experiences. This theory considers the dream to be less of a reality than the waking state. The Tibetan yogis hold just the opposite point of view, regarding dreams as a closer approximation to absolute reality than the waking state! Others have suggested instead that both dreaming and waking are on a par.[17] In other words, it is not that in the waking state we suddenly realize a dream was not reality and therefore have a better understanding of the world. Rather, it is that in unreflective dreaming and in unreflective waking, the individual does not know which state is more real at the time that they are experiencing it. When someone is dreaming and they are not reflecting on their dream, they assume that this is as much reality as when they are awake. The connection and differentiation between the waking state and the dreaming state are based not on specific or concrete memory traces but on abstract rules of logic and intuition. This is true *unless* the dreamer or the waking person reflects upon their experience in a critical fashion. How can this be done? There are some useful ways to differentiate these parallel reflections of reality.

The first aspect of these methods is to realize that, as we stated earlier, waking and dreaming tacitly assume two different sets of laws that govern the experienced universe. After all, the experience of light and gravity are different when awake versus dreaming. We can defy gravity, even consciously at times, when dreaming, and light can be conscious and communicative in a dream. When this occurs we generally assume it is the normal operation of things. If we examine some of these briefly, we can get a feeling for the different tacit assumptions of the waking (W) state as contrasted with the dreaming (D) state, both of which are states of aware consciousness.

W: Assumes linear space and time; Aristotelian logic; $A \neq B$.

D: Assumes a multidimensional space-time matrix; both $A \neq B$ and $A \geq B$ and vice versa. Space can be curved, and time can "move" at different speeds.

W: Time, place, and persons are discrete.

D: Time, place, and persons can change, reverse, and enfold/implicate each other.

W: Beings, things, and persons are either alive or dead and can only go from being alive to being dead. Most things are not "alive."

D: Beings, things, and persons can move from life to death to life again in circular or simultaneous ways. Everything can be alive.

W: Thing $A \neq B$, and it takes A "time" to signal B, even at the speed of light.

D: Thing $A \geq B$ and/or $A = B$. There is a basic interconnectedness between A and B. A and B can communicate perhaps instantaneously (faster than light).

W: The "dead" are truly dead and cannot communicate with us. Consciousness is discrete, separative.

D: The "dead" may be able to communicate with us. Consciousness is continuous and fluid.

If we summed up these two sets of tacit assumptions or laws for waking and dreaming reality there would undoubtedly be areas of overlap. The waking state is capable of seeing and *thinking* on an archaic and fluid emotional level but actively suppresses this. It is capable of logically *seeing* in a quantum-relativistic or even holonomic way, but rarely *feels* it. It thinks $E = mc^2$. The dreaming state is also capable of *both* archaic thinking and quantum-relativistic and holonomic logic. It *feels* both. It *feels* that $E = mc^2$ and observes, visually, its endless transformation. Both waking and dreaming emerge from a deeper, enfolded order of intelligence in which consciousness, energy, and meaning are totally and luminously coextensive.

THE DISCIPLINES OF SLEEP: LUCID DREAMS AND YOGA NIDRA

The disciplined study of sleep and dreaming holds enormous potential for the individual and the family and the widening experience of awareness. After all, our body and brain do operate somewhat differently depending on when we are awake or asleep and dreaming. When lucid in our dreams our brain waves are actually at their fastest, with frequencies as high as 50 Hz or cycles a second—the gamma range—versus our usual 14 to 40 Hz when awake, and down to between 4 and 14 Hz when we sleep. So things change in lucid dreaming and yoga nidra. We will look at these two particular techniques—lucid dreaming and yoga nidra—as ways of disciplined exploration and expansion of consciousness. These can occur on an individual basis and also have potential for experience and expression on the family level. What will be presented next are different levels of self-reflection or awareness during the dreaming process. Each dream and sequence will be able to reflect an *increasing level of self-awareness* of the two states from the perspective that enfolds and incorporates both the waking state and the dreaming state. The dream sequences will be presented within the context of one particular individual's process. They will start with intense or vivid dreams and move through to the actual use of lucid dreaming and yoga nidra.

Two related persecution dreams evolved last night. In the first one, I was persuaded to "help" capture and legally restrain some criminals for the local government or authorities. The criminals (organized crime figures) were more organizing than the police and eventually came after me. The police then were useless. Somehow I was a writer or reporter for a newspaper. Anyway, after some close calls on my life I had to put my whole life in the hands of the Absolute. I surrendered to that on top of a tall building. Just in the pinch of time a change of national-community attitude occurred and I was no longer "alone" in fighting the criminal forces. My legal identity was changed by the government, much like the witness protection program in the U.S.A. I was given a new location, my wife joined me, and somehow I was saved.

The second dream occurred as the Japanese military of World War II were invading Manila in the Philippines. As they came into and overran a town that I was in, I "trusted" that I could lift myself up and fly away. With effort I flew up and away as the army, in amazement, fired bullets at me. I escaped to a nearby area. It was not a lucid dream, however, only vivid and uncomfortable.

The following is a dream that involves a *little more* self-reflection in the dream process. It is not a lucid dream but rather a "prelucid" dream. Notice how the element of flying is a useful first indicator of this process.

Another rather long, involved flying dream. I find this is unremarkable. However, again, I was acutely aware that I was flying by effort, which was unusual. However, I did not take the next step in self-consciously saying, "I am dreaming."

The following is a similar prelucid dream with a false awakening:

I dreamed a couple of days ago, before my recent thirty-eighth birthday, that I was about to fully awaken in a dream. In the dream I was talking with someone in a somewhat "clinical situation." As they spoke, I was aware of also reading their monologue as they spoke on a tablet or book I was holding. I said that this was unusual and that therefore I must be dreaming. I then tried to prepare my body for full concentration and meditation by attempting to lay down flat on the couch. Prior to this as I was on the couch, my back was not straight. I felt a strange perceptual shift during the actual reading of the monologue. For some reason I did not or could not straighten my spine and retain the lucid-minded condition, and it faded out.

What follows now is the same individual adding lucidity and thereby recognizing the dream state and holding on to it a little longer.[18] Note the relationship between recent events as stimuli and the reasoning process within the dream.

Last night I suddenly found myself in the midst of a lucid dream. Friday evening I watched two episodes of the new T.V. series called the Twilight Zone. *In both episodes, the theme of dream reality was central. In one, a man was caught in a recurrent nightmare of his own legal trial and execution. He was aware of the dream reality, the exchangeable other characters, e.g., the judge, prosecutor, jailer, priest, etc., but they were not. My wife and I had discussed ways to escape such a situation should it ever occur to us that we were in the midst of one. In the other T.V. episode, there was a positive aspect and some future travel by an opera singer and her dying sister. In this one, things were sad but hopeful.*

Anyway, I awoke into the lucid dream apparently from the state of dreamless sleep and not from any cue in the dream itself, such as flying or any other odd situation. . . . I emerged from this condition of dreamless sleep into lucid dreaming. This is the first time this particular sequence has become conscious to me. In the dream, which was generally uneventful, I was conscious of maintaining a lucid condition over a long period of dreaming time. I was able to consciously fly and glide through a tall building as I followed a person. It was an intricate passageway through the heat pipes and corridors, yet I was able to do so and quietly sustain lucidity. Again the general dream content was bland.

Finally when, after a long time, I decided it was time to begin formal meditation in the dream, the dream ended or I lost lucidity. I can't remember.

Now notice the next dream where a particular practice called "yoga nidra" is employed.[19] Yoga nidra is the discipline of going from the waking state to the dreaming state without loss of consciousness. This is different from lucid dreaming in which the dreamer may realize the dreaming condition by recognizing a certain image or cue in the dream that stimulates the self-reflective process that makes them become aware that they are dreaming. In lucid dreaming there is a slight break in consciousness. In yoga nidra there is an unbroken continuity of consciousness.

Last night and early this morning were filled with vivid and lucid dreams of one variety or another. The early evening dreams were unremarkable. When I awoke to use the bathroom later, I went back to sleep afterwards with the practice of Yoga-Nidra as I laid down.

It began with a loose fantasy I consciously entertained of being in outer space, flying, and some sort of communion with the vast spirit of the universe. Anyway, I then drifted in and out of dream sleep, but the same theme line remained intact. A good deal of primary process mentation occurred along with an entangled story line of various cameo appearances of family members, especially my sister C., and a tumbling collage of scenes and locations from the backyard of my hometown to the parking lot of Stop and Shop in town here.

Eventually the theme became more clearly and intensely one of my own death and divine communion with the unseen but increasingly personified radiant spirit. This occurred in the dream state and also out of the dream state. The two were flowing back and forth fairly easily.

At the tail end of this process, I was intensely psychophysically engaged, i.e., my autonomic nervous system was aroused, breathing was a bit labored, I felt heat very intensely in the body. I was aware of feeling that I was dying, and was telling the divine to absorb me into its vast domain. I was aware that it meant the final dissolution of the "I" sense, yet it felt benign and uplifting. I laid dying, on my back, intensely and preferably inviting the unseen but all-felt intelligence-benevolence-light to absorb me as I surrendered into its vast field. For some reason my sister C. was there at my side humbly watching my process, but was not in terror at all, only awe and quiet acceptance.

Soon my body seemed to vanish into the air. Whatever it was, the witness state immediately associated to the psychophysical-spiritual deaths and translations into light of certain figures I had come across, namely the "gentle mystics" from the movie Dark Crystal and the stories of Sai Baba, the saint of Shirdi.

The witness state was then aware of going out and up a tunnel-like whorl of speckled, shimmering light and consciously enjoying the sense of freedom, ecstasy, flight, and lilting joy of the "experience." Slowly, "below" me, the light began to condense into darker almost cloud-like formations that seemed to slightly open. A brief movement toward them was quickly halted by a strong "no" from the witness state. In some strange association, the thought of rebirth arose. The witness state then focused "upward" and began the mantra "Amen." I was clear, but somewhat unsteady, yet remained in concentration. This process was enough to direct the overall sense of motion upward. Soon after this I awoke and immediately associated to the rehearsal of death.

The above-mentioned dream experiences are examples of vary-ing degrees of *increasing* lucidity, with the last one briefly entering the divine light. The waking and the dreaming states and their abstract principles can be seen more and more as tools of an abstract intelli-gence. This abstract intelligence is embedded in every individual and can be heightened or decreased in intensity by discipline and study. Family openness to such phenomena greatly increases its likelihood in an individual. Note the following dream as an example of the conscious state and its dynamics associated with waking-ego properties and the unconscious state with its associated dream dynamics, as both condi-tions are interwoven into an emergent third state.[20] This third state can be seen fleetingly at times to enfold or embrace the dynamics of the waking state and the classical dreaming state.

Last night at 4:50 a.m. I awoke and went to the bathroom. I also noticed that I left on one of the kitchen lights and so went downstairs to turn it off. It was then that I noticed the time.

Upon return to bed I began to practice Yoga-Nidra techniques in order to enter a lucid dream state. After two or three unsuccessful attempts, I used the highway driving-airlift technique and successfully attained lucidity.

Almost immediately I recognized successful flying dream phenomena and stabilized myself emotionally and psychologically. It was then that I consciously began to meditate on flying upward. I lifted higher and higher upward through a series of levels or planes of phenomena. Initially the whole body was involved, then eventually the "I" was released through the top of the skull. There was a kind of "body," but it was more ephemeral than the usual dream body.

The higher I consciously went, the more controlled ecstasy I allowed myself to filter into my experience. I was conscious of the recent Shirley MacLaine movie on spiritual seeking aired on television, and witnessed some sort of silver cord attached to the body below me. However, I am not clear whether this was my experience or my memory of her experience! In either, it was a brief observation.

The higher I went, it seemed as though I went through different realms. The first was merely a dream realm of images, sensations, etc. The second realm was entered through my going through a hole or small aperture at the top of a dome. Through it I went. It opened into a realm of light that was similar to a shattered chandelier of light fragments. I whispered to myself to be relaxed with myself both physically and psychologically and "don't contract." The passing thought arose that I might induce a stroke (CVA) with all this intensity. I quickly let this go this time.

Finally, I seemed to go through and up, wordlessly into a realm that was akin to a warm ocean of bliss-light intelligence that swept around and enveloped me. The light was not blinding and oddly enough seemed less pronounced than the light of the prior realm. However, it was a wordless, seamless realm of intuition-intelligence, a womb (?) or cosmos of radiance.

After an unclear duration of time, the "I" began to move back "down" through the prior realms in exactly the same way and route that the "I" had arose in the realms previous to that. I was aware of descending a great height and becoming "embodied" again. Finally, I re-entered the dense dream realm of images, lingered a while, and gradually lost lucidity. Later I awoke.

From the aforementioned sequence it can be seen how the critical faculties of intelligence that underlie the dynamics of the waking state and the dream state can be enlisted as tools and how the observation, discrimination, and amplification of a state of consciousness that is prior to and enfolds both waking and dreaming states is possible. This is clearly and certainly the dynamics available to all individuals. Also, an extremely creative realm is potentially available not only for ideas of a scientific or an artistic nature but also for the healing process as it relates to the psychophysical systems of the body. Somatic conversion in the body is fairly common and the neuroplasticity of the brain is real. Imagine the possibilities of bodily healing when some day we are able to attain lucidity in a dream and then, by biofeedback methodologies, focus this heightened awareness on specific systems and areas of the body and brain.

CREATIVITY AND DREAMS

Dreams have a lineage older than recorded history in the development of human ideas and aspirations. Much of the collective history of humanity is of shared dreams and individuation. Men and women dreamed in the caves of Europe during the ice age, on the open plains of ancient Kemetic Egypt, at the river mouths of the Ganges in India and the Tigris and Euphrates in the Near East, and in the forests of Mesoamerica. Of the billions and billions of human dreams, a certain percentage have had a remarkable effect on the course of human history and development.

There is a well-detailed history of the use and purpose of dreams in scientific, artistic, and religio-spiritual experience. Many great insights in the area of science alone have been traced to dreams. Einstein traced his theory of relativity to a dreamlike experience he had when he was an adolescent. In this dream, he was reportedly riding on a sled. As he went faster and faster, the stars became distorted. This intuition stayed with him and, after a series of mathematical transformations years later, emerged as the theory of relativity. As he slept before a fire on a cold night in 1865, August Kekulé dreamed of a twisting snake biting its tail. When he awoke, he suddenly had the solution to the molecular structure of the benzene ring as a closed carbon ring, which revolutionized modern biochemistry. René Descartes went in and out of sleep in 1637 to dream parts of his *Discourse on the Method*. In America, Elias Howe was inspired to create a design for the lockstitch sewing machine after dreaming he was in a caldron and was surrounded by cannibals who kept thrusting spears at him. And finally, in a spectacular case of dream incubation, Dmitri Mendeleev developed the structure of the periodic atomic table of elements after working on it for three days without sleeping. He then literally dreamed the near-perfect solution to the chart. Each one of these individuals had a dream, and then their particular training helped them "decipher" the meaning of the dream.

In the area of artistic creation, Robert Louis Stevenson dreamed the plot of *The Strange Case of Dr. Jekyll and Mr. Hyde* in which the doctor character saw a picture of a jackal just before his transformation. Mary Shelley based her story of *Frankenstein* on dreamlike hypnagogic imagery. The epic poet Dante claimed that he received both the form and much of the content of his great book, *The Divine Comedy,* from a series of dreams he had while traveling. And finally, another great poet, Samuel Taylor Coleridge, reportedly transcribed large sections of his epic poem *Kubla Khan* almost directly from an opium-induced dream he had before he was interrupted by a salesperson. Thus, it is possible to see or create or observe information and intelligence directly in the dream state. Like the waking state, the dream state is intelligent.

Given that dreaming is a predominately visual experience for most people, dreams have a high profile in the visual arts. Yet like the experience of dreaming itself our visual, auditory, and movement senses are all interwoven in the dream. So from music to dance and sculpture to poetry and painting, dreams and dreaming in the arts can express multiple levels of meaning and emotion simultaneously. In the great mass art of film, the dreaming mind is on vivid display (see appendix C).

In politics and religion, similar striking observations have been made. Eleanor Roosevelt saw full and elaborated sentences in a dream that she later incorporated into the charter of the United Nations. The great spiritual leader Muhammad is reported to have had a long and extended divine or revelatory dream in which many parts of the Qur'an came to him directly. There are other innumerable such instances lost to modern history, not to mention those that have occurred in the ancient cultures of India, Africa, Japan, and Mesoamerica. Their culture and the evolution of their societies were intimately associated with collective dreams and collective metaphors, just as they are in the modern world.

In families, these individual and family dreams can also provide solutions, create marvelous new ways of thinking, and offer insights into difficult situations. Sometimes they can almost prophesy other situations, both good and bad, that occur in a family among intimate relations. Just as there is not an apparent end to energy in the universe, there is not an end to the range and reach of energy, intelligence, and light in the universe. Dreams, as forms of intelligence, are certainly part of the living informational and radiant matrix of life that we all share.

DREAMS, IMAGERY, AND HEALING: A RETURN TO PERSONALISM IN SCIENCE AND THE UNIVERSE

Since primordial times, we have known that the body and the myths of the body inhabit the inner corridors of the mind. Methods of healing the body and mind have been scattered throughout the development of civilization, from the pyramid tombs of ancient Nubia, the oldest known centers of civilization that were south of the first cataract of the Nile, to the temples of the Near East, Greece, and Rome. From Abu Simbel in ancient Egypt to the modern laboratories of major international cities, research on the body-mind dance remains a firm interest of humankind. Theories, techniques, and metatheories may shift in terms of attributing cause and effect to various gods, higher or natural forces, or the intimate processes of neuroscience and body chemistry. However, certain methods comprise a commonly accepted wave front over the various separate and distinct theories and techniques.

We know that activation of the mind by imagery, powerful emotion, and invocation to higher intellectual, cortical, or other functions is essential in the healing process. We know also that rhythms, entrainment, and vibration are intimately associated with imagery in healing. This may be due to some of the processes discussed earlier. In particular we mean the relationship between imagery, emotionality, and the dense cortical connections between the right hemisphere and deeper levels of the thalamic regions of the brain that have been emphasized. At the present time, research moves from focusing on the endocrine system to special functions of the immune system and to various other areas, all in the search for the elusive metaphor of healing that actively affects the somatic and psychological aspects of our being. Much is already known about the relationships between psychological states of mind, in particular depression, and the suppression of the immune or health-maintaining systems of the body. Much is known about the relationship between the central nervous system and the immune system. However, an ocean more is still unknown. The whole field of body-mind interaction is really an ancient one. In modern guise it goes under the term of "psychoneuroimmunology."[21]

We know already that the states of mind have an effect on the somatic and disease processes of the body. In fact, dreams have been known to predict various states of the physical body before the self-conscious part of the individual is aware of them. Sometimes after a physically or emotionally traumatic situation, the body informs the psyche, which correspondingly reacts. The gateway between the two is not fully understood and may in fact be in a constant process of shifting within the same individual as he or she goes through various experiences and developments. In whatever fashion, human intuition has been aware of this since time immemorial.

In the halls and temples of ancient Egypt and Greece, the initiate was often helped to have a certain kind of powerful dream. In these dreams, symbols, gods, family members, and ancestors would approach a person with healing solutions to their physical and emotional problems. For a thousand years, this practice was known and written about throughout the ancient Mediterranean and North African world. For thousands of years before that, it was practiced in the Nile Valley. These healing dreams were often assisted by the presence of priests, powerful family spirits, and tribal deities. In most instances, a certain trance state was entered. (Today we use hypnosis, sometimes facilitated by music, to help enter this state.) At other times, different techniques and procedures were used. The ultimate aim, however, was to enter a profoundly relaxed state in which the mind was focused and concern with external matters was significantly decreased as attention to *internal absorption was significantly increased.*

As yet we do not know the full effect of imagery on the healing process; we only know that it is a profound one. A dream is a domain of imagery that is already associated with powerful affect. When we learn how to harness imagery and dreams in a conscious fashion, we will have taken a quantum leap in the capacity to heal ourselves and our significant relationships. In the healing trance, in the healing dream, the fire of intuition and attention is focused on the process of awakening the disordered or diseased function or area of the body and the system. A new organizing and healing image combined with a more soothing awareness is brought to the hidden and unknown areas of the body-mind. The sense of division and fragmentation is decreased. The sense of connectedness, warmth, and acceptance is increased. Illness as an alteration in consciousness becomes less and less dominant. Eventually this fire of intuition and attention is drawn into the ever-greater and widening process of awakening.

Other mammals dream. Other primates experience intelligence, cognition, and mentation on some level. All human beings dream, and their dreams are intuitively and intrinsically important to them. We now believe that in some function and in some form, families share intimacies and communicate with each other periodically directly or indirectly through dreams. Dreams are obviously deeply and intimately involved in the life forms and in the life current of intelligent creatures on this planet. Everything is alive in a very real sense. This makes the essence of beings into a *personal* reality infused with life, purpose, and meaning. Intelligence, relationship, consciousness, and essence are all enfolded and localized in each individualized situation. The world process is neither a purely material one nor a fully spiritualized one. Both of these aspects are actively present but grounded in a living, personalized realm. The dream and family dream are but another expression of this in an extremely intimate and personalized universe.

In this view of personalism pervading the universe, the individualized principle inherently moves toward harmony of not only body, mind, and spirit but also of society, culture, environment, and the wider rhythmic entrainment of the ecology. This is a natural trance and again sends a harmonizing wave over the separative behavior of individual acts and tendencies. This higher-order harmony reaches at times into the generative order of the Divine Persona in whom we are all mysteriously alive.

Our personhood is at the center of our intimate daily and moment-to-moment encounters with reality. It is even deeply embedded in our scientific theories *about* reality. Our personhood or intuitive apprehension of phenomena profoundly influences our perception and interpretation of the sensory, spiritual, and logical data of reality. There are at present at least eight different interpretations of the quantum theory.[22] They range from the Copenhagen interpretations of Niels Bohr and Werner Heisenberg to the many-worlds interpretation of Hugh Everett and John Wheeler to the undivided wholeness of David Bohm and more. Each theory can predict and account for all the quantum mechanical facts we can measure and, by extension, a lot more. Each of these divergent interpretations of the "facts" leads to a widely different conception of the material and the energetic universe. The interpreter's consciousness and personhood influences the perception of the "objective facts." This is not confined to the esoteric and almost bizarre, dreamlike logic of quantum mechanics.

There are at least six divergent, highly articulated interpretations of the phenomena observed in clinical hypnosis. They range from ego regression models to social learning paradigms to altered states of consciousness views. Here, too, each theory can "explain" most of the observed facts and behaviors and influence the phenomena in the course of interacting with or "measuring" it. What it all intimately means to us is that it turns on our personhood—not personality dynamics, mind you, but our naked contact with the flesh of reality.

Similar situations can be seen in theories of personality, psychopathology, and even schools of economics. Sometimes new data arises that ushers in a new, more inclusive paradigm or way of seeing the data, but this is not always the case. In any event the new paradigm almost immediately gives rise to new questions, perceptions, and expanding interpretations born of the encounter between the intimate personalism of the observer and the reality they live. This *immediacy of experience* is foremost in our contact with reality since each area of the unknown, which is *most* of reality to us, is encountered, structured, and made meaningful in the realm of our personhood. This is how one can appear to evolve a knack or uncanny skill or relationship with a particular kind of project. It is how one demonstrates a consistent but seemingly unexplainable ability to interact with the "objective" world of medicine, mathematics, or mechanics. It is also how one can come to directly sense a personal relationship with God, a force of nature, or an orisha and to communicate with them while awake or in the fluid labyrinth of a dream. There appears to be a progressive, albeit discontinuous, unfoldment of intelligence and consciousness as we move deeper into the more subtle orders of matter, energy, and luminous spirituality. These at times are in intimate contact with human experience.

It is not such a large step from here to see the members of the human family as the conscious dreamers for the collective life force of this planet. The integrated biochemical and ecological living system of this planet is now an accepted reality. It was a known and assumed reality of the ancient world, and we have in recent decades discovered it again. It is referred to as "Gaia." Could it be that humans are the conscious dreamers for the evolution of our world? Perhaps consciousness participates as much in us as we participate in consciousness. Perhaps as objects and forms emerge out of the matrix of energy that is neither created nor destroyed, we emerge out of consciousness, have a form and personal history, and finally dissolve back into the underlying energetic current of consciousness that also is neither created nor destroyed but is infinitely transformed. Perhaps this is the radiant intuition the dreamer has at death. This is a question someday each of us will intimately come to know. In that knowing we may come to realize, in consciousness, that the dreams of birth and death are themselves but the children of infinity.

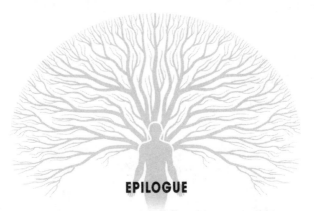

From Matter to Dream to Light

It would appear from this brief overview of family dreams and the individuals whose psychological and psychic fields make up these families that indeed we are not the creatures who, once self-conscious of ourselves, dream no more. Rather we are the ones who, once conscious of ourselves, move toward unfolding ourselves endlessly, reflecting back upon ourselves, seeing our essential Self in every object, form, face, and name.

We are not the ones who, seeing ourselves in the mirror and family of faces, no longer seek the origin of our souls. Rather we are those whose own souls are echoed in the heartbeat and gesture of nameless other souls with whom we share consciousness and transformation from age to age, from life to life to life.

Our nightly dreams are the easily entered temple for exploring and realizing this. For just as we go back and forth from waking to dreaming reality until we touch the state beyond this known by many names, so we go back and forth from embodiment in dense matter to death to subtle matter to embodiment again, or so-called reincarnation, until we reach the condition beyond this as beings of light. As we learn in the NDE we are rooted in what is beyond waking, dreaming, and deep sleep. And when in our ultimate moments we pass through death and encounter the great light and review our own lives we see how our waves have interacted with innumerable other waves we have encountered, for good or ill, and realize we ourselves are our own ultimate judge and jury. This is the root of cosmic morality and ethics, suffused in luminosity, preparing us for the next stage in the evolution of our species.

The "new physicists," like the ancient metaphysicians, keep telling us that all we see, all we touch and feel as sensible objects, are in reality patterns of life and energy locked in a moving corridor of space and time. Indeed, they are dreams or apparitions before our eyes, there but not there, real but less real than the energy vortex out of which they swim. Vast and indifferent, yet intimate and deeply personal, this tissue of matter and dreams makes up the latticework of our nerves, our blood, our thoughts, and our breath.

Birth, embodiment, laughter, and death are but permutations of an infinite, luminous, and inherent existence. Since $E = mc^2$ is really true, whatever is, in some energetic variation, will always be. Interconnectedness and the supraliminal are everywhere the case in our highly personalized, shared universe. Consciousness is prior to matter; intelligence is senior to form. Chaos is the name we give to the physical wisdom of God that as yet makes no sense.

And so we send out our dreams to family, friends, enemies, and strangers; they catch them and echo back from constantly shifting shores. This was the case from ancient Kemetic Egypt and Nubia to India and Asia and Europe and the Americas. We literally are our ancestors in mind, blood, and spirit—interconnected, conscious, and vibrant. In this context it should not be surprising to witness recurrent family souls arising and passing repeatedly through the generations, changing roles and learning the lessons of the soul. Across all the ages and races of humanity, matter and spirit are connected by the arch of the personal. Our universe in this sense is indeed quite personal.

It is my own intuition and belief that just as there are ripples in the fabric of space-time itself, vast gravity waves that one day we will master and travel, there are waves in the sea of consciousness that the individually trained mind can experience, fold, and perhaps travel to, places we already know because, as suggested by many, they are inherently already a part of us.[1] At death all we take with us is light.

I have tried to show that the boundary of sleep is an ocean, our dreams the waves that interconnect, death the escarpment between different realms. The dream is a bird flying from one to another, ignorant of the illusion and boundary we keep during the waking state. This is how we keep the dead in our memory. This is how, near our own death, we become lucid, take flight, and are greeted in luminosity by the dead. And so we dream into the dream of matter and energy beyond our human dreaming until all mind and boundary are completely dissolved and transcended, and we dream ourselves into the infinite lifeblood of God.

The Family Dreams Research Project

Protocol for Participation

The Family Dreams Research Project is an ongoing national and cross-cultural study of the relationship between dreamlife and family processes that welcomes your participation. All reports are anonymous and, where necessary, other identifying references are changed or omitted prior to publication. Submission of individual and family dreams is understood to be a release and permission for the study to report and publish its findings to public, clinical, and scientific audiences.

Dream Reporting

Please include one or many of your own dreams and other family members' dreams with the following:

1. First name and last name initial of the people who dreamed or are in the dream itself.
2. Date(s) of dream/dream series.
3. Who was in the dream (e.g., what persons were involved).
4. What occurred (process) in the dream (e.g., events, conversations, actions in the dream process).

5. Feelings in the dream (e.g., happy, fearful, conflicted, or many feelings).

6. Story or outline of the dream (e.g., a family argument or meeting or powerful situation). This is open to all situations, regardless of how matter-of-fact or strange they seem. Include any "communication" that occurs.

7. Correspondence to any other events, symbolic or emotional, that occur in the dreamer's life.

8. It is helpful to know the relationships in the dream (e.g., mother-daughter, etc.).

Dream reports should be sent to:

Family Dreams Research Project
Edward Bruce Bynum, Ph.D.
P.O. Box 3121
Amherst, MA 01002

Kemetic* Imagery and Healing Assessment Protocol

Edward Bruce Bynum, Ph.D.

Tanya Anagnostopoulou, Ph.D.

Biographical/Treatment-Assessment Information

_____ Patient Name	Marital Status _____	
_____ Age	Height and Weight _____	
_____ Gender	Religion/ Philosophy _____	
_____ Race/Ethnicity	Disease Onset Dates _____	

---

*Kemetic comes from the ancient scientific tradition of drawing upon all experienced natural forces to aid in mobilizing the healing forces of the body-mind as they shift and transform themselves at all levels (e.g., psychological, somatic, psychospiritual, and psychoimmunological). This includes deep family and personal images along with transpersonal or noetic intuitions from the collective unconscious and from underlying diverse religious lineages.

Clinical Procedure

Explain to the subject/patient the need to gather information about his/her body's own natural healing potentials on several levels (e.g., immunological, somatic, and psychological). Create a therapeutic alliance. Do not rush this. Then explain, demonstrate, and teach the subject/patient *in sequence* the techniques of diaphragmatic breathing, alternate nostril breathing, and the focus of attention at the base of the nose where air from the two nostrils flows.* Emphasis is placed slightly on the *exhalation* phase of the breathing cycle. Take time to be sure this is done correctly and with some comfort. To do so with more competence usually requires several minutes on each practice sequence.

Then carry out a simple hypnotic induction or brief guided imagery and relaxation exercise with visualization and exhalation into the target areas. Ask the subject/patient to notice, without editing or resistance, whatever reaction or experience they have with their bodily sense, the symptoms of the disease process, and their subjective feelings. Do this for at least fifteen minutes. Bring the subject back to waking consciousness and gently elicit and then assess their experience with the following explorations:

I. Hypnotic/guided imagery responsivity of body-mind

A. *Bodily experience* of being somatically altered, disengaged, or changed in some noticeable way:

1	2	3	4	5
exceedingly clear	strong and clear	mildly clear	somewhat unclear	very unclear

---

*This technique will initiate conscious influence within the autonomic nervous system, coordinate higher cerebral cortical activity between both hemispheres, and stimulate a parasympathetic reaction throughout the organ systems, thereby opening the immune and other healing systems of the body-mind to conscious interaction.[1]

B. Type of hypnotic/guided imagery *perception* of body-mind and experience or event:

1	2	3	4	5
exceedingly clear	strong and clear	mildly clear	somewhat unclear	very unclear

C. Type of hypnotic/guided imagery experience in terms of being close to/identified with the experience or event:

1. Saw/relived event as though it *actually* occurred (revivification):

1	2	3	4	5
exceedingly clear	strong and clear	mildly clear	somewhat unclear	very unclear

or 2. Saw event from a distance, as if on a stage or in a movie:

1	2	3	4	5
exceedingly clear	strong and clear	mildly clear	somewhat unclear	very unclear

or 3. Saw in a mixed way; sometimes very real, sometimes like a movie removed from me:

1	2	3	4	5
exceedingly clear	strong and clear	mildly clear	somewhat unclear	very unclear

Assessing Relationship with and Feelings about the Body

A. Moving toward the body (liking it, taking good care of it, listening to its needs):

1	2	3	4	5
exceedingly clear	strong and clear	mildly clear	somewhat unclear	very unclear

B. Moving against the body (actively disliking it, rejecting it, punishing it):

1	2	3	4	5
exceedingly clear	strong and clear	mildly clear	somewhat unclear	very unclear

C. Moving away from the body (feeling embarrassed or indifferent):

1	2	3	4	5
exceedingly clear	strong and clear	mildly clear	somewhat unclear	very unclear

Total: _____

II. Disease cells and/or organs/systems of the body-mind

A. Clarity/vividness of the cells and organs/systems affected by the clinical problem:

1	2	3	4	5
exceedingly clear	strong and clear	mildly clear	somewhat unclear	very unclear

B. Activity/movement of the cells and organs/systems affected by the clinical problem:

1	2	3	4	5
exceedingly clear	strong and clear	mildly clear	somewhat unclear	very unclear

C. Strength/power of the cells and organs/systems affected by the clinical problem:

1	2	3	4	5
exceedingly clear	strong and clear	mildly clear	somewhat unclear	very unclear

D. Number/spread of the cells and organs/systems affected by the clinical problem:

1	2	3	4	5
exceedingly clear	strong and clear	mildly clear	somewhat unclear	very unclear

Total: _____

III. Immune system/body-mind capacity to struggle and transcend in imagery the clinical and deeply personal crisis

A. Vividness of imagery:

1	2	3	4	5
exceedingly clear	strong and clear	mildly clear	somewhat unclear	very unclear

B. Activity/movement of imagery:

1	2	3	4	5
exceedingly clear	strong and clear	mildly clear	somewhat unclear	very unclear

C. Number/vitality of imagery:

1	2	3	4	5
exceedingly clear	strong and clear	mildly clear	somewhat unclear	very unclear

D. Strength/power of imagery:

1	2	3	4	5
exceedingly clear	strong and clear	mildly clear	somewhat unclear	very unclear

Total: _____

IV. Clinical treatment process

A. Activity/movement of process:

1	2	3	4	5
exceedingly clear	strong and clear	mildly clear	somewhat unclear	very unclear

B. Power/strength of process:

1	2	3	4	5
exceedingly clear	strong and clear	mildly clear	somewhat unclear	very unclear

C. Family unconscious images and emotional associations with related or merely similar events and persons:

1. Positive or healthy memories/stories/legends/images/dreams in the family:

1	2	3	4	5
exceedingly clear	strong and clear	mildly clear	somewhat unclear	very unclear

A name or first names of significant others _____

2. Weaker or unhealthy memories/stories/legends/images/dreams in the family:

1	2	3	4	5
exceedingly clear	strong and clear	mildly clear	somewhat unclear	very unclear

A name or first names of significant others _____

D. Assessing family unconscious soma:

1. Patterns of disease (cardiovascular, cancer, GI, headaches, etc.):

_____

2. Deaths (ask for age at death): _____

_____

3. Family's attitude to health and disease/assessment of resiliency: I experienced _____ as a very confident person because they should overcome their disease emotionally and even physically. _____ complained all the time about their health. _____ got very depressed after the onset of their disease. In my family, health means:

_____

E. Collective unconscious images and emotional associations with related or merely similar events and persons:

  1. Positive or healthy memories/stories/legends/images/dreams in your collective unconscious:

1	2	3	4	5
exceedingly clear	strong and clear	mildly clear	somewhat unclear	very unclear

  2. Weaker or unhealthy memories/stories/legends/images/dreams in your collective unconscious:

1	2	3	4	5
exceedingly clear	strong and clear	mildly clear	somewhat unclear	very unclear

A name or first names of significant others _____

Total: _____

V. Sensation/perception/visualization of a current* or manifestation of energy moving through the body-mind associated with the clinical practice(s)

A. Visualization:

1	2	3	4	5
exceedingly clear	strong and clear	mildly clear	somewhat unclear	very unclear

_____

*The patient/subject may give this current or energy different names (e.g., ki, chi, prana, bioplasma, elima, wong, etc.). Focus on the current, not its label.

B. Somatic sensation kinesthetic movement:

1	2	3	4	5
exceedingly clear	strong and clear	mildly clear	somewhat unclear	very unclear

C. Perception/apperception of a current of light or living energy moving through the body-mind:

1	2	3	4	5
exceedingly clear	strong and clear	mildly clear	somewhat unclear	very unclear

Total: _____

VI. Finding a healing image

Good images and symbols are ego-syntonic. They must be kinesthetic and sensory as well as visual. Inanimate imagery is less powerful. Attempt to be as anatomically accurate and as clear as possible. With emotional arousal and focus, the conscious and unconscious processes are integrated along with the cortical and subcortical processes.

Clinical Balance and Magnification Training

A. Find a healing image. Ask the subject/patient which of the following images, if any, would make them feel better. Feel free to combine images or create your own.

Water

Swimming in water

Going up to a spring and drinking water, feeling refreshed

Applying magic fluid to the area of your symptom

Earth

Covering your body with mud that contains special healing ingredients

Covering yourself with warm sand

Sun/fire/light

Sunbathing, feeling the warmth of the sun inside your body, seeing light surrounding your body

Feeling a fire that warms up your body, brings life back

Becoming saturated with laser energy (note the color of the energy field: white, gold, rainbow, etc.)

Sounds and colors

Listening to certain sounds

Inhaling your favorite color

Symbolism

In your mind's eye seeing a wise old man or woman who gives you advice about what to do to get rid of your symptom

A saint showing up in your dream and telling you that you will be healed

A white knight/dragon/other animal helping you fight your disease

---

B. Now choose an image or object. Ask the subject/patient to steady their focus on the image/object slowly in conjunction with their breathing. Have them carry out the following changes/shifts in their perception of the image or object, focusing on the exhalation phase of the breathing cycle when visualization is most clear.

1. Visualize it as larger, then smaller.
2. Visualize it as heavier, then very light.
3. Visualize it as spreading out, then as concentrated and smaller.
4. Visualize it as actually imaginary, insubstantial, and fleeting.
5. Change or transmute it into something different.
6. Change or transmute it into something stronger, then weaker.
7. Change or transmute it into many parts, then one interconnected system.
8. Change or transmute it from something fearful to something friendly.
9. Visualize it as spreading out, then slowly disappearing.
10. Feel it as warm, then luminous and moving in the body-mind.
11. Visualize it as really empty, yet full of energy, bliss, and light.
12. Visualize it as moving, conducted through the body by the breath and the subtle metabolism of the body-mind.
13. See it in interaction with the disease process.

C. Thank the subject/patient for their cooperation in helping you to better understand and appreciate their inner life and its rich possibilities.

Films in Which Dreaming and/or Dreams Are Depicted

8 ½, 1963

Akira Kurosawa's Dreams, 1990

Altered States, 1980

American Beauty, 1999

American Werewolf in London, 1981

The Artist, 2011

Avatar, 2009

The Big Lebowski, 1998

Blade Runner, 1982

Brazil, 1985

Cabin in the Sky, 1943

Dreamscape, 1984

Dream Parlor, 1999

Dumb and Dumber, 1994

Dumbo, 1941

Eraserhead, 1977

Eternal Sunshine of the Spotless Mind, 2004

The Exterminating Angel, 1962

The Fly, 1986

Inception, 2010

Inside, 2007

Ivan's Childhood, 1962

Jacob's Ladder, 1990

Johnny Got His Gun, 1971

The Last Laugh, 1924

L'Atalante, 1934

Los Olvidados, 1950

Lucia, 2013

Manchurian Candidate, The, 1962

The Matrix, 1999

Minority Report, 2002

The Mirror, 1975

Mulholland Drive, 2001

Mysterious Skin, 2004

A Nightmare on Elm Street, 1984 (Series)

Office Space, 1999

One Hour Photo, 2002

The Phantom of Liberty, 1974

Razorback, 1984

Requiem, 2000

Rosemary's Baby, 1968

The Science of Sleep, 2006

Seconds, 1966

The Sea That Thinks, 2000

A Serious Man, 2004

Sherlock, Jr., 1924

Somewhere in Dreamland, 1936

Spellbound, 1945

Stalker, 1979

Star Trek: First Contact, 1996

Terminator: Judgment Day, 1991
Trainspotting, 1996
Twin Peaks: Fire Walk with Me, 1992
Vanilla Sky, 2001
Vertigo, 1958
Waking Life, 2001
Wild Strawberries, 1957

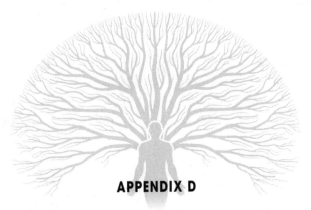

Recommended Reading

There is an abundance of literature focusing on dreams and dreaming. For the reader interested in exploring this vast field, I recommend the following titles, which have been divided into five categories.

I. ANALYTICAL-JUNGIAN PERSPECTIVES

Books relating to Freudian and Jungian dream analysis, including practical applications.

Bosnak, Robert A. *A Little Course in Dreams: A Basic Handbook of Jungian Dreamwork*. Boston: Shambhala, 1988.

Johnson, Robert A. *Inner Work: Using Dreams and Active Imagination for Personal Growth*. New York: Harper & Row, 1988.

Jung, Carl G. *Dreams*. Bolligen Series. Princeton: Princeton University Press, 1974.

Mindell, Arnold. *Dreambody: The Body's Role in Revealing the Self*. Boston: Sigo Press, 1982/London: Routledge and Kegan Paul, 1984.

———. *Working with the Dreambody*. London: Routledge and Kegan Paul, 1985, 1989.

Romanyshyn, Robert. *Technology as Symptom and Dream*. London: Routledge and Kegan Paul, 1989.

Von Franz, Marie-Louise. *On Dreams and Death*. Boston: Shambhala, 1987.

Whitmont, Edward C., and Sylvia Brinton Perera. *Dreams, A Portal to the Source*. London: Routledge and Kegan Paul, 1989.

II. EXPERIENTIAL-PRACTICE-DISCIPLINE

Experiential titles to expand your personal dream practice or discipline.

DeLaney, Gayle M. *Breakthrough Dreaming*. New York: Bantam Books, 1992.

———. *Living Your Dreams*. New York: Harper & Row, 1981.

Faraday, Ann. *The Dream Game*. New York: Perennial Library/Harper & Row, 1976.

Gackenbach, Jayne, and Jane Bosveld. *Control Your Dreams*. New York: Harper & Row, 1988.

Gackenbach, Jayne, and Stephen LaBerge, eds. *Conscious Mind, Sleeping Brain: Perspectives on Lucid Dreaming*. New York: Plenum Press, 1988.

Garfield, Patricia. *Creative Dreaming*. New York: Ballantine Books, 1974.

Koch-Sheras, Phyllis R., E. Ann Hollier, and Brooke Jones. *Dream On: A Dream Interpretation and Exploration Guide for Women*. Englewood Cliffs, N.J.: Prentice Hall (Spectrum Book), 1983.

Krippner, Stanley, ed. *Dreamtime and Dreamwork: Decoding the Language of the Night*. Los Angeles: Jeremy P. Tarcher, 1990.

LaBerge, Stephen. *Lucid Dreaming: The Power of Being Awake & Aware in Your Dreams*. Los Angeles: Jeremy P. Tarcher, 1985.

Parker, Derek, and Julia Parker. *Dreaming: Remembering, Interpreting, Benefiting*. Upper Saddle River, N.J.: Prentice Hall, 1989.

Rama, Swami. *Enlightenment without God: Mandukya Upanishad*. Honesdale, Pa.: Himalayan International Institute of Yoga Science and Philosophy, 1982.

Reed, Henry. *Getting Help from Your Dreams*. Virginia Beach, Va.: Inner Vision Publishing, 1985.

Saraswati, Swami Satyananda. *Yoga Nidra*. Bihar, India: Bihar School of Yoga, 1976.

Satyananda, P. *Yoga Nidra* (cassette). San Mateo, Calif.: Satyananda Ashrams of U.S.A., 1985.

Shohet, Robin. *Dream Sharing*. Wellingborough, England: Thorsons Press, 1985.

Ullman, Montague, and Nan Zimmerman. *Working with Dreams*. Los Angeles: Jeremy P. Tarcher, 1979.

III. CLINICAL-THEORETICAL
PERSPECTIVES

The clinical use of dreams in psychology.

Bonime, Walter. *The Clinical Use of Dreams*. New York: Basic Books, 1962.

Bosnak, Robert. *Dreaming with an AIDS Patient*. Boston: Shambhala, 1990.

Boss, Medard. *The Analysis of Dreams*. New York: Philosophical Library, 1958.

Foulkes, David. *Dreaming: A Cognitive-Psychological Analysis*. Hillsdale, N.J.: Lawrence Erlbaum Associates, 1985.

Freud, Sigmund. *The Interpretation of Dreams*. Translated by J. Strachey. London: Hogarth Press, 1953, 1988.

Fromm, Erich. *The Forgotten Language: An Introduction to the Understanding of Dreams, Fairy Tales, and Myths*. New York: Grove Press, 1957.

Garfield, Patricia. *Women's Bodies, Women's Dreams*. New York: Ballantine, 1988.

Gendlin, Eugene T. *Let Your Body Interpret Your Dreams*. Wilmette, Ill.: Chiron Publications, 1986.

Globus, Gordon G. *Dream Life, Wake Life: The Human Condition through Dreams*. Albany, N.Y.: SUNY, 1987.

Hall, Calvin. *The Meaning of Dreams*. New York: McGraw-Hill, 1966.

Hall, Calvin, and Robert Van de Castle. *The Content Analysis of Dreams*. Upper Saddle River, N.J.: Prentice Hall, 1966.

Hartmann, Ernest L. *The Functions of Sleep*. New Haven, Conn.: Yale University Press, 1973.

――――. *The Nightmare: The Psychology and Biology of Terrifying Dreams*. New York: Basic Books, 1984.

Hobson, J. Allan. *The Dreaming Brain*. New York: Basic Books, 1988.

Hunt, Harry T. *The Multiplicity of Dreams: Memory, Imagination, and Consciousness*. New Haven, Conn.: Yale University Books, 1989.

Jones, Richard M. *The New Psychology of Dreaming*. New York: Viking Press, 1970.

Maybruck, Patricia. *Pregnancy and Dreams*. Los Angeles: Jeremy P. Tarcher, 1989.

Ornstein, Robert, and David Sobel. *The Healing Brain: Breakthrough Medical Discoveries about How the Brain Keeps Us Healthy*. New York: Touchstone Books, 1988.

IV. CROSS-CULTURAL PERSPECTIVES

Perspectives on dreams and dreaming from various societies around the globe.

Ashanti, Kwabena Faheem. *Rootwork and Voodoo in Mental Health.* Durham, N.C.: Tone Books, 1990.

Brown, Carolyn T., ed. *Psycho-Sinology: The Universe of Dreams in Chinese Culture.* Washington, D.C.: Asia Program, Woodrow Wilson International Center for Scholars, 1987.

Cowan, James. *Mysteries of the Dream-Time: The Spiritual Life of Australian Aborigines.* Garden City, N.Y.: Avery Publishing Group, 1991.

Domhoff, G. William. *The Mystique of Dreams: A Search for Utopia through Senoi Dream Theory.* Berkeley: University of California Press, 1985.

Evans-Wentz, W. Y. *Tibetan Yoga and Secret Doctrines.* London: Oxford University Press, 1958.

Gupta, Krishna Das. *The Shadow World: A Study of Ancient and Modern Dream Theories.* Delhi: Atma Ram and Sons, 1971.

Hughes-Calero, Heath. *The Golden Dream.* Carmel, Calif.: Coastline Publishing, 1988.

Lee, S. G. "Social Influence in Zulu Dreaming." *Journal of Social Psychology* 47 (1958).

Métraux, Alfred. *Voodoo in Haiti.* New York: Schocken Books, 1972.

Parsifal-Charles, Nancy. *The Dream: 4000 Years of Theory and Practice; A Critical, Descriptive and Encyclopedic Bibliography.* West Cornwall, Conn.: Locust Hill, 1986.

Stewart, K. "Dream Exploration among the Senoi." In *Sources,* edited by Theodore Roszak. New York: Harper & Row, 1972.

Tart, C. "Altered States of Consciousness." In *Dream Theory in Malaya,* edited by Jon Hassell. New York: Doubleday, 1972.

Tedlock, Barbara, ed. *Dreaming: Anthropological and Psychological Interpretations.* Cambridge, Mass.: Cambridge University Press, 1987.

V. DREAMS AND PARAPSYCHOLOGY

Titles exploring the connections between parapsychology and dreaming.

Ehrenwald, Jan. *The ESP Experience: A Psychiatric Validation.* New York: Basic Books, 1978.

————. *Telepathy and Medical Psychology.* New York: W. W. Norton, 1948.

Rhine, Louisa E. *ESP in Life and Lab: Tracing Hidden Channels.* New York: Collier Books/Macmillan Publishers, 1967.

————. *Hidden Channels of the Mind.* New York: William Sloane, 1961.

Taub-Bynum, E. Bruce. *The Family Unconscious: An Invisible Bond.* Wheaton, Ill.: Theosophical Publishing House, 1984.

Ullman, Montague, and Stanley Krippner. *Dream Telepathy: Scientific Experiments in the Supernatural.* New York: Macmillan Publishers, 1973.

Van de Castle, Robert. *Our Dreaming Mind.* New York: Ballantine Books, 1990.

————. *Psychic Dreaming* (cassette). Audio Renaissance. Los Angeles: Jeremy P. Tarcher, 1989.

————. *The Psychology of Dreaming.* Morristown, N.J.: General Learning Press, 1971.

Wolman, Benjamin B., ed. *Handbook of Parapsychology.* New York: Van Nostrand Reinhold, 1977.

Notes

INTRODUCTION.
THE LABYRINTH OF DREAMS

1. Freud, "Dreams and the Occult," 108.
2. Freud, *New Introductory Lectures on Psycho-Analysis.*
3. Freud, "Psychoanalysis and Telepathy," 58–60.
4. Ellenberger, *Discovery of the Unconscious.*
5. Hornung, "Discovery of the Unconscious in Ancient Egypt"; King, *African Origin of Biological Psychiatry;* Morakinyo, "Yoruba Ayanmo Myth."

CHAPTER 1.
THE INNER LANDSCAPE OF DREAMS

1. Gurney, Myers, and Podmore, *Phantasms of the Living;* Sidgwick, "Phantasms of the Living."
2. Ullman, Krippner, and Vaughn, *Dream Telepathy.*
3. Ullman, "Mystery of Psychic Dreaming," 46.
4. Globus, *Dream Life, Wake Life.*
5. Freud, *Moses and Monotheism.*
6. Jung, *Psychological Reflections.*
7. Rhine, *ESP in Life and Lab.*
8. Taub-Bynum, *Family Unconscious;* Szondi, Moser, and Webb, *Szondi Test,* 98–103.

CHAPTER 2. THE ANCIENT WAY

1. Von Franz, *On Dreams and Death.*
2. Jackson, *Introduction to African Civilizations;* Diop, *Civilization or Barbarism;* Williams, *Destruction of Black Civilization;* Fairservis, *Ancient Kingdoms of the Nile.*
3. Bynum, *African Unconscious.*
4. Schwarz, *Psychic-Nexus.*
5. Krippner, *Dreamtime and Dreamwork.*
6. Wallace, "Dream in Mohave Life."
7. Spier, *Yuman Tribes of the Gila River,* 326.
8. Krippner, *Dreamtime and Dreamwork.*
9. Kilborne, "Ancient and Native Peoples' Dreams."
10. Perls, *Gestalt Therapy Verbatim.*
11. Cowan, *Mysteries of the Dream-Time.*
12. Duerr, *Dreamtime.*
13. Lawson, *Religions of Africa.*
14. Mbiti, *African Religions and Philosophy.*
15. Ashanti, *Rootwork and Voodoo in Mental Health.*
16. Métraux, *Voodoo in Haiti;* Bourguignon, "Dreams and Dream Interpretation."
17. Brown, *Psycho-Sinology.*
18. Krippner, *Dreamtime and Dreamwork.*
19. Simon, *Necronomicon.*
20. Garfield, *Creative Dreaming.*
21. Bernal, *Black Athena;* Olela, "The African Foundations of Greek Philosophy."
22. Ebbell, *Papyrus Ebers.*
23. King, *African Origin of Biological Psychiatry.*
24. Hornung, "Discovery of the Unconscious in Ancient Egypt"; King, *African Origin of Biological Psychiatry.*
25. Diop, *Civilization or Barbarism.*
26. Morakinyo, "Yoruba Ayanmo Myth."
27. Quoted in Garfield, *Creative Dreaming.*

CHAPTER 3. THE WEB OF DREAMLIFE IN FAMILY AND SELF

1. Magallón and Shor, "Shared Dreaming."
2. Taub-Bynum, *Family Unconscious.*

3. Hall and Van de Castle, *Content Analysis of Dreams.*

4. McGoldrick, Pearce, and Giordano, *Ethnicity & Family Therapy.*

5. Szondi, Moser, and Webb, *Szondi Test.*

CHAPTER 4. RESEARCH ON DREAMS:
THE CONTRIBUTION OF THE LABORATORY

1. Diop, *African Origin of Civilization;* Fairservis, *Ancient Kingdoms of the Nile.*

2. Darwin, *Descent of Man,* 158.

3. Aserinsky and Kleitman, "Two Types of Ocular Motility Occurring in Sleep" and "Regularly Occurring Periods of Eye Motility."

4. R. Jones, *New Psychology of Dreaming.*

5. Vogel, "Sleep-Onset Mentation."

6. Shapiro, "Comments on the 90-Minute Sleep-Dream Cycle," 23.

7. Hobson, *Dreaming Brain.*

8. Ibid.

9. Becker and Thoman, "Rapid Eye Movement Storms."

10. King, *African Origin of Biological Psychiatry;* Bynum, *Dark Light Consciousness.*

11. Maeda, "Infrared Spectrometry of Locus Coeruleus"; Moses, "Light and Electron Microscope Studies of Pigment"; Hiroswa, "Electron Microscope Studies on Pigment Granules."

12. Woodman, *Dreams;* Redgrove, *Black Goddess;* Walker, *Women's Encyclopedia of Myths and Secrets.*

13. Diop, *African Origin of Civilization.*

14. Gimbutas, *Gods and Goddesses.*

15. Diop, *Civilization or Barbarism;* Fairservis, *Ancient Kingdoms of the Nile.*

16. Woodman, *Dreams.*

17. Bynum, *Roots of Transcendence.*

18. Dean, "Plethysmograph as an Indicator of ESP."

19. Kardiner, "Bioanalysis of the Epileptic Reaction."

20. Levitan, "Traumatic Events in the Dreams of Psychosomatic Patients"; Warnes and Finkelstein, "Dreams that Precede a Psychosomatic Illness."

21. Ziegler, "Cardiac Infarction and a Dream"; Schneider, "Conversion of Massive Anxiety into Heart Attack."

22. Smith, "A Possible Biologic Role of Dreaming."

23. Delaney, "Personal and Professional Problem Solving in Dreams."

CHAPTER 5.
DEFINING NORMAL FAMILY DREAMS

1. Hartmann, *The Nightmare.*
2. Broughton, "Sleep Disorders."
3. Baranski, "Frequency Spectrum."
4. Dean, "Plethysmograph as an Indicator"; Dean and Nash, "Coincident Plethysmograph Results."
5. Jahn and Dunne, *Margins of Reality;* Targ and Puthoff, *Mind-Reach;* Hasted, *Metal-Benders.*

CHAPTER 6.
EXTRASENSORY FAMILY DREAMS

1. Rhine, *ESP in Life and Lab;* Hall and Van de Castle, *Content Analysis of Dreams.*
2. Rhine, *ESP in Life and Lab.*
3. Van de Castle, *Psychic Dreaming.*
4. Stanford, "Experimental Psychokinesis"; Roll, "Poltergeists."
5. Flammarion, *Death and Its Mystery,* 248, cited in Rogo, *Mind over Matter.*
6. Flammarion, *Death and Its Mystery,* 267.
7. Ibid., 273.
8. Robinson, *To Stretch a Plank.*
9. Rogo, *Mind over Matter.*
10. Hasted, *Metal-Benders.*
11. Jahn and Dunne, *Margins of Reality.*
12. Taub-Bynum, *Family Unconscious.*

CHAPTER 7.
FAMILY DREAMS OF ADULT CHILDREN OF ALCOHOLICS

1. Cermak, *Adult Children of Alcoholics.*
2. Laign, "Bards and Booze"; Benedict, "Alcohol and Writers"; Hayes, "Feeding the Muse."
3. Woititz, *Struggle for Intimacy.*
4. Black, *Never Happen to Me.*
5. Bowen, *Family Therapy.*

CHAPTER 8.
FAMILY DREAMS DURING PREGNANCY

1. Grof, *Beyond the Brain.*
2. Maybruck, *Pregnancy and Dreams.*
3. Stukane, *Dream Worlds of Pregnancy.*
4. Van de Castle and Kinder, "Dream Content during Pregnancy."
5. Hall and Van de Castle, *Content Analysis of Dreams.*
6. C. Jones, "An Exploratory Study of Women's Manifest Dreams during Pregnancy."
7. Gillman, "Dreams of Pregnant Women."
8. Deutsch, *Psychology of Women.*
9. Maybruck, *Pregnancy and Dreams.*
10. Kelly, "Effect of Fear upon Uterine Mobility."
11. Dick-Read, *Childbirth without Fear.*
12. Verny and Kelly, *Secret Life of the Unborn Child.*
13. Schwarz, *Psychic-Nexus.*
14. Ehrenwald, "Mother-Child Symbiosis."
15. Jung, *Synchronicity.*
16. Dean, "Plethysmograph as an Indicator."
17. Krippner, "Dreams and the Development of a Personal Mythology."
18. Massey, *Book of Beginnings.*
19. Freud, *Moses and Monotheism.*

CHAPTER 9.
FAMILY DREAMS IN THERAPEUTIC FORM

1. Jaynes, *Origin of Consciousness.*
2. Wilber, *Up from Eden.*
3. Shoumatoff, *Mountain of Names.*
4. Ader, *Psychoneuroimmunology;* Borysenko, *Minding the Body;* Achterberg and Lawlis, *Imagery and Disease.*
5. Tocqueville, *L'Ancien Régime et la Révolution,* vol. 2, chap. 2.
6. Naranjo, *Techniques of Gestalt Therapy.*
7. Hersh and Taub-Bynum, "Use of Dreams in Brief Therapy."
8. Jung, *Memories, Dreams, Reflections.*
9. Bynum, "Use of Dreams in Family Therapy."

10. Goldstein, "Clarification of Projective Identification."

11. Taub-Bynum, *Family Unconscious.*

12. Perlmutter and Babineau, "Use of Dreams in Couples Therapy," 66–72.

13. Hall and Van de Castle, *Content Analysis of Dreams.*

14. Andrews, Clark, and Zinker, "Accessing Transgenerational Themes."

15. Shohet, *Dream Sharing.*

16. Koch-Sheras, Hollier, and Jones, *Dream On.*

17. Ullman, "Access to Dreams."

18. Ibid, 539.

19. Zinker, "Dreamwork as Theater."

20. Gendlin, *Let Your Body Interpret Your Dreams.*

21. Ziegler, "Cardiac Infarction and a Dream."

22. Warnes and Finkelstein, "Dreams that Precede a Psychosomatic Illness."

23. Gendlin, *Let Your Body Interpret Your Dreams.*

24. Griaule and Dieterlen, *Pale Fox.*

25. Pribram, *Languages of the Brain.*

26. Luria, *Working Brain.*

CHAPTER 10. THE DREAM OF INFINITE LIFE: THE FURTHER REACHES OF THE DREAM IN FAMILY AND SELF

1. Luria, *Working Brain;* Pribram, *Languages of the Brain.*

2. Taub-Bynum, *Family Unconscious.*

3. Boylin, *Mom's Dead.*

4. Von Franz, *On Dreams and Death.*

5. Bohm, *Wholeness;* Bohm and Peat, *Science, Order and Creativity.*

6. Jung, *Letters.*

7. Evans-Wentz, *Tibetan Book of the Dead.*

8. Budge, *Book of the Dead.*

9. Asante, "The African American Mode of Transcendence."

10. Jackson, *Introduction to African Civilizations,* 232–63.

11. Smith, *Mediumship of Mrs. Leonard;* Podmore, *Mediums.*

12. Tyrrell, *Apparitions;* Gauld, "Discarnate Survival."

13. Eisenbud, "Paranormal Photography."

14. Krippner, *Human Possibilities.*

15. Moody, *Light Beyond;* Sabom, *Recollections of Death.*

16. Osis, *Deathbed Observations*.

17. Globus, *Dream Life, Wake Life*.

18. LaBerge, *Lucid Dreaming*.

19. Saraswati, *Yoga Nidra;* Rama, *Enlightenment without God*.

20. Sparrow, *Lucid Dreaming;* Evans-Wentz, *Tibetan Yoga,* 215–30.

21. Locke and Colligan, *Healer Within*.

22. Herbert, *Quantum Reality*.

EPILOGUE. FROM MATTER TO DREAM TO LIGHT

1. Bynum, *Dark Light Consciousness*.

APPENDIX B. KEMETIC IMAGERY AND HEALING ASSESSMENT PROTOCOL

1. Bynum, "Clinical Use of Bliss"; Werntz et al. "Alternating Cerebral Hemispheric Activity"; Klein and Armitage, "Rhythms in Human Performance"; Werntz, "Cerebral Hemispheric Activity"; Werntz et al. "Selective Cortical Activation."

Works Cited

Achterberg, Jeanne, and G. Frank Lawlis. *Imagery and Disease*. Champaign, Ill.: Institute for Personality and Ability Testing, 1984.

Ackerman, Nathan. *The Psychodynamics of Family Life*. New York: Basic Books, 1958.

Ader, Robert. *Psychoneuroimmunology*. New York: Academic Press, 1981.

Andrews, J., D. J. Clark, and J. C. Zinker. "Accessing Transgenerational Themes through Dreamwork." *Journal of Marital and Family Therapy* 14, no. 1 (1988): 15–27.

Asante, Molefi K. "The African American Mode of Transcendence." *Journal of Transpersonal Psychology* 16, no. 2 (1984): 167–68.

Aserinsky, Eugene, and Nathaniel Kleitman. "Two Types of Ocular Motility Occurring in Sleep." *Journal of Applied Psychology* 8 (1955): 1–10.

———. "Regularly Occurring Periods of Eye Motility and Concomitant Phenomena during Sleep." *Science* 118 (1953): 273–84.

Ashanti, Kwebene Faheem. *Rootwork and Voodoo in Mental Health*. Durham, N.C.: Tone Books, 1990.

Aurobindo, Sri. *Savitri: A Legend and a Symbol*. N.p.: Lotus Press, 1995. Originally published 1950–1951.

Baranski, L. G. "The Frequency Spectrum and the Principle of Resonance Absorption." *North American Aviation*, 1963.

Becker, P. T., and E. B. Thoman. "Rapid Eye Movement Storms in Infants: Rate of Occurrence at 6 Months Predicts Mental Development at 1 Year." *Science* 212 (1981): 1415–16.

Benedict, E. "Alcohol and Writers—A Long Day's Journey into Destruction." *Changes* (July–August 1989).

Bernal, Martin. *Black Athena: The Afroasiatic Roots of Classical Civilization.* New Brunswick, N.J.: Rutgers University Press, 1987.

Black, Claudia. *It Will Never Happen to Me: Adult Children of Alcoholics.* N.p: M. A. C. Publishing, 1982.

Bohm, David. *Wholeness and the Implicate Order.* London: Routledge and Kegan Paul, 1980.

Bohm, David, and F. David Peat. *Science, Order and Creativity: A Dramatic New Look at the Creative Roots of Science and Life.* New York: Bantam Books, 1987.

Borysenko, Joan. *Minding the Body, Mending the Mind.* New York: Bantam Books, 1987.

Bourguignon, Erika. "Dreams and Dream Interpretation in Haiti." *American Anthropologist* 56, no. 2, part 1 (1954): 262–68.

Bowen, Murray. *Family Therapy in Clinical Practice.* Lanham, Md.: Jason Aronson Publishers/Rowman Littlefield International, 1993.

Boylin, William. *Mom's Dead: A Guide to Mourning.* Unpublished manuscript.

Broughton, Roger. "Sleep Disorders: Disorders of Arousal?" *Science* 159 (1968): 1070–78.

Brown, Carolyn T., ed. *Psycho-Sinology: The Universe of Dreams in Chinese Culture.* Washington, D.C.: Asia Program, Woodrow Wilson International Center for Scholars, 1987.

Budge, E. A. Wallis. *The Book of the Dead: The Hieroglyphic Transcript of the Papyrus of ANI.* Secaucus, N.J.: University Books, 1960.

Bynum, Edward. "The Use of Dreams in Family Therapy." *Psychotherapy: Theory, Research, and Practice* 17, no. 2 (1980): 227–31.

———. "The Clinical Use of Bliss: Standardized Technique for Conscious Intervention into the Function of the Autonomic Nervous System (ANS)." In *Why Darkness Matters: The Power of Melanin in the Brain,* edited by Edward Bynum, 89–128. N.p.: Create Space Publishing, 2014.

———. *The African Unconscious: Roots of Ancient Mysticism and Modern Psychology.* New York: Cosimo Books (Columbia University Teachers College Press), 1999.

———. *The Roots of Transcendence.* New York: Cosimo Books, 2005. Previously published in 1999 by Haworth Press under the title *Transcending Psychoneurotic Disturbances.*

———. *Dark Light Consciousness: Melanin, Serpent Power, and the Luminous*

Matrix of Reality. Rochester, Vt.: Inner Traditions/Bear & Company, 2012.

Cermak, Timmen. *A Primer on Adult Children of Alcoholics.* Hollywood, Fla.: Health Communications, 1985.

Cowan, James. *Mysteries of the Dream-Time: The Spiritual Life of Australian Aborigines.* Garden City, N.Y.: Avery Publishing Group, 1991.

Darwin, Charles. *The Descent of Man.* London: Murray, 1871.

Dean, E. D. "The Plethysmograph as an Indicator of ESP." *Journal of the American Society for Psychical Research* 41 (1962): 351–53.

Dean, E. D., and C. B. Nash. "Coincident Plethysmograph Results Under Controlled Conditions." *Journal of the American Society for Psychical Research* 44 (1967): 1–13.

Delaney, Gayle. "Personal and Professional Problem Solving in Dreams." In *Dreamtime and Dreamwork,* edited by Stanley Krippner, 93–100. Los Angeles: Jeremy P. Tarcher, 1991.

Deutsch, Helene. *The Psychology of Women.* Vol. 2. New York: Bantam Books, 1973.

Dick-Read, Grantly. *Childbirth without Fear.* New York: Harper and Row, 1978.

Diop, Cheik Anta. *Civilization or Barbarism: An Authentic Anthropology.* Translated by Y. M. Ngemi. Brooklyn, New York: Lawrence Hill Books, 1991.

———. *The African Origin of Civilization.* Brooklyn, New York: Lawrence Hill, 1974.

Duerr, H. P. *Dreamtime: Concerning the Boundary between Wilderness and Civilization.* New York: Basil Blackwell, 1985.

Ebbell, B., trans. *The Papyrus Ebers: The Greatest Egyptian Medical Document.* Copenhagen: Levin and Munksgaard, 1937.

Ehrenwald, Jan. "Mother-Child Symbiosis: Cradle of ESP." *Psychoanalytic Review* 58 (1971): 455–66.

Eisenbud, Jule. "Paranormal Photography." In *Handbook of Parapsychology,* edited by Benjamin Wolman, 414–34. New York: Van Nostrand Reinhold, 1977.

Ellenberger, Henri. *The Discovery of the Unconscious: The History and Evolution of Dynamic Psychiatry.* New York: Basic Books, 1970.

Evans-Wentz, Walter Y. *The Tibetan Book of the Dead.* London: Oxford University Press, 1960.

———. *Tibetan Yoga and Secret Doctrines.* London: Oxford University Press, 1958.

Fairservis, Walter. *The Ancient Kingdoms of the Nile and the Doomed Monuments of Nubia.* New York: T. Y. Crowell, 1962.

Flammarion, Camille. *Death and Its Mystery.* Vol. 2, *At the Moment of Death.* New York: Century, 1922.

Freud, Sigmund. *New Introductory Lectures on Psycho-Analysis.* New York: W. W. Norton, 1950.

———. "Dreams and the Occult." In *Psychoanalysis and the Occult,* edited by G. Devereux. New York: International Universities Press, 1953.

———. "Psychoanalysis and Telepathy." In *Psychoanalysis and the Occult,* edited by G. Devereux, 58–60. New York: International Universities Press, 1953.

———. *The Interpretation of Dreams.* Translated by J. Strachey. London: Hogarth Press, 1953. First published in 1900.

———. *Moses and Monotheism.* New York: Alfred Knopf, 1939.

Garfield, Patricia. *Creative Dreaming.* New York: Ballantine Books, 1974.

Gauld, Alan. "Discarnate Survival." In *Handbook of Parapsychology,* edited by Benjamin Wolman, 577–630. New York: Van Nostrand Reinhold, 1977.

Gendlin, Eugene. *Let Your Body Interpret Your Dreams.* Wilmette, Ill.: Chiron Publications, 1986.

Gillman, Robert. "The Dreams of Pregnant Women and Maternal Adaptation." *American Journal of Orthopsychiatry* 38 (1968).

Gimbutas, Marija. *Gods and Goddesses of Old Europe, 7000–3500 B.C.: Myths, Legends, and Cult Images.* Berkeley: University of California Press, 1982.

Globus, Gordon. *Dream Life, Wake Life: The Human Condition through Dreams.* New York: SUNY, 1987.

Goldstein, W. N. "Clarification of Projective Identification." *American Journal of Psychiatry* 148, no. 2 (February 1991): 153–61.

Griaule, Marcel, and Germaine Dieterlen. *The Pale Fox.* Translated by S. C. Infantino. Chino Valley, Ariz.: Continuum Foundation, 1986.

Grof, Stanislav. *Beyond the Brain: Birth, Death, and Transcendence in Psychotherapy.* Albany, New York: SUNY, 1985.

Gurney, Edmund, Frederic Myers, and Frank Podmore. *Phantasms of the Living.* 2 vols. London: Trübner, 1886.

Hall, Calvin, and Robert Van de Castle. *The Content Analysis of Dreams.* Englewood Cliffs, N.J.: Prentice Hall, 1966.

Hartmann, Ernest. *The Functions of Sleep.* New Haven, Conn.: Yale University Press, 1973.

————. *The Nightmare: The Psychology and Biology of Terrifying Dreams.* New York: Basic Books, 1984.

Hasted, John. *The Metal-Benders.* London: Routledge and Kegan Paul, 1981.

Hayes, E. N. "Feeding the Muse." *Changes* (July–August 1989).

Herbert, Nick. *Quantum Reality: Beyond the New Physics.* Garden City, N.Y.: Anchor Press/Doubleday, 1987.

Hersh, Jeffery, and Edward Taub-Bynum. "The Use of Dreams in Brief Therapy." *Psychotherapy: Theory, Research, and Practice* 22, no. 2 (1985): 248–55.

Hiroswa, Kazushige. "Electron Microscopic Studies on Pigment Granules in the Substantia Nigra and Locus Coeruleus of the Japanese Monkey (Macaca Fusca Yuku)." *Zeitschift für Zellforschung* 88 (1968): 187–203.

Hobson, J. Allan. *The Dreaming Brain.* New York: Basic Books, 1988.

Hornung, Erik. "The Discovery of the Unconscious in Ancient Egypt." *Spring: An Annual of Archetypal Psychology and Jungian Thought* (1986): 16–28.

Jackson, John G. *Introduction to African Civilizations.* Secaucus, N.J.: Citadel Press, 1970.

Jahn, Robert, and Brenda Dunne. *Margins of Reality: The Role of Consciousness in the Physical World.* San Diego, Calif.: Harcourt Brace Jovanovich Publishers, 1987.

Jaynes, Julian. *The Origin of Consciousness in the Breakdown of the Bicameral Mind.* Boston: Houghton Mifflin, 1976.

Jones, Celia. "An Exploratory Study of Women's Manifest Dreams during Pregnancy." Ph.D. dissertation. Ann Arbor, Mich.: Microfilms Int., 1978.

Jones, Richard. *The New Psychology of Dreaming.* New York: Viking Press, 1970.

Jung, Carl. *Letters.* Vol. 2, *1951–1961.* Translated by R. F. C. Hull. Princeton, N.J.: Princeton University Press, 1975.

————. *Memories, Dreams, Reflections.* New York: Pantheon Books, 1961.

————. *Psychological Reflections.* Bollinger Series, vol. 31. New York: Pantheon Books, 1953.

————. *Synchronicity: An Acausal Connecting Principle.* New York: Bollinger Foundation, 1960.

Kardiner, Abram. "The Bioanalysis of the Epileptic Reaction." *Psychoanalytic Quarterly* 1 (1933): 375–483.

Kelly, J. V. "Effect of Fear upon Uterine Mobility." *American Journal of Obstetrics and Gynecology* 83, no. 5 (1962): 576–81.

Kilborne, Benjamin. "Ancient and Native Peoples' Dreams." In *Dreamtime and Dreamwork,* edited by Stanley Krippner. Los Angeles: Jeremy P. Tarcher, 1990.

King, Richard D. *African Origin of Biological Psychiatry.* Germantown, Tenn.: Seymour Smith, 1990.

Klein, R., and R. Armitage. "Rhythms in Human Performance: 1 1/2-Hour Oscillations in Cognitive Style." *Science* 204 (1979): 1326–28.

Koch-Sheras, Phyllis, E. Ann Hollier, and Brooke Jones. *Dream On: A Dream Interpretation and Exploration Guide for Women.* Englewood Cliffs, N.J.: Prentice Hall, 1983.

Krippner, Stanley. "Dreams and the Development of a Personal Mythology." In *Cognition and Dream Research,* edited by R. E. Haskell, 319–31. N.p.: Institute for Mind and Behavior, 1986.

———. *Dreamtime and Dreamwork: Decoding the Language of the Night.* Los Angeles: Jeremy P. Tarcher, 1990.

———. *Human Possibilities.* Garden City, N.Y.: Anchor Press/Doubleday, 1980.

Kuhn, Thomas. *The Structure of Scientific Revolutions.* Chicago, Ill.: University of Chicago Press, 1962.

LaBerge, Stephen. *Lucid Dreaming: The Power of Being Awake & Aware in Your Dreams.* Los Angeles: Jeremy P. Tarcher, 1985.

Laign, J. "Bards and Booze." *Changes* (July–August 1989).

Lawson, E. Thomas. *Religions of Africa: Traditions in Transformation.* San Francisco: Harper & Row, 1984.

Levitan, Harold. "Traumatic Events in the Dreams of Psychosomatic Patients." *Psychotherapy and Psychosomatics* 33 (1980): 226–32.

Locke, Steven, and Douglas Colligan. *The Healer Within: The New Medicine of Mind and Body.* New York: Mentor Books, 1986.

Luria, Aleksandr. *The Working Brain: An Introduction to Neuropsychology.* New York: Basic Books, 1973.

Maeda, T. "Infrared Spectrometry of Locus Coeruleus and Substantia Nigra Pigments in the Human Brain." *Brain Research Service.* Reference Bibliography 82 (1969): 1–30.

Magallón, Linda, and Barbara Shor. "Shared Dreaming: Joining Together in Dreamtime." In *Dreamtime and Dreamwork,* edited by Stanley Krippner, 252–60. Los Angeles: Jeremy P. Tarcher, 1990.

Marx, Melvin. "The General Nature of Theory Construction." In *Theories in Contemporary Psychology,* 4–46. London: Macmillan Publishers, 1963.

Massey, Gerald. *Book of Beginnings.* Vol. 2, 363–441. London: Williams and Norgate, 1881.

Maybruck, Patricia. *Pregnancy and Dreams.* Los Angeles: Jeremy P. Tarcher, 1989.

Mbiti, John. *African Religions and Philosophy*. Portsmouth, N.H.: Heinemann Educational Books, 1969.

McGoldrick, Monica, John Pearce, and Joe Giordano, eds. *Ethnicity & Family Therapy*. New York: Guilford Press, 1982.

Métraux, Alfred. *Voodoo in Haiti*. New York: Schocken Books, 1972.

Moody, Raymond. *Life after Life*. Covington, Ga.: Mockingbird Books, 1975.

————. *The Light Beyond*. New York: Bantam Books, 1988.

Morakinyo, Olufemi. "The Yoruba Ayanmo Myth and Mental Health Care in West Africa." *Journal of Cultural Ideas* 1, no. 1 (December 1983): 61–92.

Moses, Harold. "Light and Electron Microscopic Studies of Pigment in Human and Rhesus Monkey Substantia Nigra and Locus Coeruleus." *Anatomical Record* 155 (1966): 167–84.

Naranjo, Claudio. *The Techniques of Gestalt Therapy*. Berkeley, Calif.: SAT Press, 1973.

Olela, Henry. "The African Foundations of Greek Philosophy." In *African Philosophy,* edited by R. A. Wright. Washington, D.C.: University Press of America, 1979.

Osis, Karlis. *Deathbed Observations by Physicians and Nurses*. New York: Parapsychology Foundation, 1961.

Perlmutter, Richard, and Raymond Babineau. "The Use of Dreams in Couples Therapy." *Psychiatry* 46 (February 1983): 66–72.

Perls, Frederick. *Gestalt Therapy Verbatim*. New York: Bantam Books, 1971.

Podmore, Frank. *Mediums of the 19th Century*. Secaucus, N.J.: University Books, 1963. First published in 1902.

Pribram, Karl. *Languages of the Brain: Experimental Paradoxes and Principles in Neuropsychology*. New York: Brandon House, 1981.

Rama, Swami. *Enlightenment without God: Mandukya Upanishad*. Honesdale, Pa.: Himalayan International Institute of Yoga Science and Philosophy, 1982.

Redgrove, Peter. *The Black Goddess and the Unseen Real: Our Unconscious Senses and Their Uncommon Sense*. New York: Grove Press, 1987.

Rhine, Louisa E. *ESP in Life and Lab: Tracing Hidden Channels*. New York: Collier Books/Macmillan Publishers, 1967.

Robinson, Diana. *To Stretch a Plank: A Survey of Psychokinesis*. Chicago: Nelson-Hall, 1981.

Rogo, D. Scott. *Mind over Matter: The Case for Psychokinesis*. Wellingborough, England: Aquarian Press, 1986.

Roll, William. "Poltergeists." In *Handbook of Parapsychology,* edited by Benjamin Wolman, 382–413. New York: Van Nostrand Reinhold, 1977.

Sabom, Michael. *Recollections of Death: A Medical Investigation.* New York: Harper & Row, 1982.

Saraswati, Swami Satyananda. *Yoga Nidra.* Bihar, India: Bihar School of Yoga, 1976.

Schneider, D. "Conversion of Massive Anxiety into Heart Attack." *American Journal of Psychotherapy* 27 (1973): 360–78.

Schwarz, Berthold. *Psychic-Nexus: Psychic Phenomena in Psychiatry and Everyday Life.* New York: Van Nostrand Reinhold, 1980.

Shapiro, A. "Comments on the 90-Minute Sleep-Dream Cycle." In *Sleeping and Dreaming* by Ernest Hartmann, 23. Boston: Little, Brown and Company, 1970.

Shohet, Robin. *Dream Sharing.* Wellingborough, England: Thorsons Press, 1985.

Shoumatoff, Alex. *The Mountain of Names: A History of the Human Family.* New York: Simon and Schuster, 1985.

Sidgwick, Eleanor. "Phantasms of the Living." *Proceedings of the Society for Psychical Research* 33 (1923): 424–429.

Simon, trans. *Necronomicon.* New York: Avon Books, 1977.

Smith, Robert. "A Possible Biologic Role of Dreaming." *Psychotherapy and Psychosomatics* 41 (1984): 167–76.

Smith, Susy. *The Mediumship of Mrs. Leonard.* Secaucus, N.J.: University Books, 1964.

Sparrow, G. Scott. *Lucid Dreaming: Dawning of the Clear Light.* Virginia Beach, Va.: A.R.E. Press, 1976.

Spier, Leslie. *Yuman Tribes of the Gila River.* Chicago, Ill.: University of Chicago Press, 1933.

Stanford, Rex. "Experimental Psychokinesis: A Review from Diverse Perspectives." In *Handbook of Parapsychology,* edited by Benjamin Wolman, 324–81. New York: Van Nostrand Reinhold, 1977.

Stukane, Eileen. *The Dream Worlds of Pregnancy.* New York: Quill, 1985.

Szondi, Leopold, Ulrich Moser, and Marvin Webb. *The Szondi Test: In Diagnosis, Prognosis, and Treatment.* Philadelphia: J. B. Lippincott, 1959.

Targ, Russell, and Harold Puthoff. *Mind-Reach: Scientists Look at Psychic Abilities.* New York: Delta Books, 1977.

Taub-Bynum, Edward. *The Family Unconscious: An Invisible Bond.* Wheaton, Ill.: Theosophical Publishing House, 1984.

Teilhard de Chardin, Pierre. *The Phenomenon of Man*. New York: Harper Perennial Classic, 2008. First published in 1955.

Tocqueville, Alexis de. *L'Ancien Régime et la Révolution*. Paris: Michel Levy, 1856.

———. *Democracy in America*. New York: Harper & Row, 1966. First published 1835.

Tyrrell, George. *Apparitions*. New York: Macmillan Publishers, 1942.

Ullman, Montague. "Access to Dreams." In *Handbook of States of Consciousness*, edited by B. B. Wolman and M. Ullman. New York: Van Nostrand Reinhold, 1986.

———. "The Mystery of Psychic Dreaming." In "A Hitchhiker's Guide to Dreamland," by M. Barasch. *New Age Journal*, October 1983.

Ullman, Montague, Stanley Krippner, and Alan Vaughan. *Dream Telepathy: Scientific Experiments in the Supernatural*. New York: Macmillian, 1973.

Ullman, Montague, and Nan Zimmerman. *Working with Dreams*. Los Angeles: Jeremy P. Tarcher, 1979.

Van de Castle, Robert. *Psychic Dreaming* (cassette). Los Angeles: Audio Renaissance Tapes, 1989.

Van de Castle, Robert, and P. Kinder. "Dream Content during Pregnancy." *Psychophysiology* 4 (1968).

Verny, Thomas, and John Kelly. *The Secret Life of the Unborn Child*. New York: Summit Books, 1981.

Vogel, Gerald. "Sleep-Onset Mentation." In *The Mind in Sleep: Psychology and Psychophysiology*, edited by A. M. Arkin, John Antrobus, and Steven Ellman, 97–112. Hillsdale, New York: Laurence Erlbaum Associates, 1978.

Von Franz, Marie-Louise. *On Dreams and Death*. Boston: Shambhala, 1987.

Walker, Barbara. *The Woman's Encyclopedia of Myths and Secrets*. San Francisco: Harper & Row, 1983.

Wallace, W. J. "The Dream in Mohave Life." *Journal of American Folklore* 60 (1947): 252–58.

Warnes, H., and A. Finkelstein. "Dreams that Precede a Psychosomatic Illness." *Journal of Canadian Psychiatric Association* 16 (1971): 317–25.

Werntz, D. "Cerebral Hemispheric Activity and Autonomic Nervous Function." Doctoral dissertation, University of California, San Diego, 1981.

Werntz, D., R. Bickford, F. Bloom, and D. Shannahoff-Khalsa. "Selective Cortical Activation by Alternating Autonomic Function." Paper presented at the Western EEG Society Meeting, February 12, 1981, Reno, Nevada.

———. "Alternating Cerebral Hemispheric Activity and Lateralization of Autonomic Nervous Function." *Human Neurobiology* 2 (1983): 39–43.

Whitaker, Carl. *Midnight Musings of a Family Therapist.* New York: W. W. Norton, 1989.

Wiener, Leo. *Africa and the Discovery of America.* 3 vols. Philadelphia: Innes and Sons, 1920–1922.

Wilber, Ken. *Up from Eden: A Transpersonal View of Human Evolution.* Garden City, New York: Anchor Press/Doubleday, 1981.

Williams, Chancellor. *The Destruction of Black Civilization.* Chicago, Ill.: Third World Press, 1987.

Woititz, Janet. *Struggle for Intimacy.* Hollywood, Fla.: Health Communications, 1985.

Woodman, Marion. *Dreams: Language of the Soul* (cassette). Sounds True, 1990.

Ziegler, A. "A Cardiac Infarction and a Dream as Synchronous Events." *Journal of Analytic Psychology* 17 (1962): 141–48.

Zinker, J. C. "Dreamwork as Theater." *Voices: The Art and Science of Psychotherapy* 7 (1974): 18–21.

Author Index

Subject Index

About the Author

Edward Bruce Bynum, Ph.D., ABPP, is a diplomate in clinical psychology and a former director of the Behavioral Medicine Program at the University of Massachusetts Health Services. He is the author of several books in psychology and the arts, and a recipient of the Abraham Maslow Award from the American Psychological Association. He is currently in private practice at the Brain Analysis and Neurodevelopment (BAND) Center. His website is **www.obeliskfoundation.com**.

OTHER BOOKS BY THE AUTHOR

PSYCHOLOGY

Dark Light Consciousness: Melanin, Serpent Power and the Luminous Matrix of Reality

The African Unconscious: Roots of Ancient Mysticism and Modern Psychology

The Family Unconscious: An Invisible Bond

The Roots of Transcendence

Why Darkness Matters: The Power of Melanin in the Brain

POETRY

The Dreaming Skull

Godzillananda

Chronicles of the Pig & Other Delusions

BOOKS OF RELATED INTEREST

Dark Light Consciousness
Melanin, Serpent Power, and the Luminous Matrix of Reality
by Edward Bruce Bynum, Ph.D., ABPP

The Heart-Mind Matrix
How the Heart Can Teach the Mind New Ways to Think
by Joseph Chilton Pearce
Foreword by Robert Sardello

Ancestral Medicine
Rituals for Personal and Family Healing
by Daniel Foor, Ph.D.

Healing the Mind through the Power of Story
The Promise of Narrative Psychiatry
by Lewis Mehl-Madrona, M.D., Ph.D.

Remapping Your Mind
The Neuroscience of Self-Transformation through Story
by Lewis Mehl-Madrona, M.D., Ph.D.
with Barbara Mainguy, M.A.

Narrative Medicine
The Use of History and Story in the Healing Process
by Lewis Mehl-Madrona, M.D., Ph.D.

The DNA Field and the Law of Resonance
Creating Reality through Conscious Thought
by Pierre Franckh

The Book of Ho‘oponopono
The Hawaiian Practice of Forgiveness and Healing
by Luc Bodin, M.D., Nathalie Bodin Lamboy, and Jean Graciet

INNER TRADITIONS • BEAR & COMPANY
P.O. Box 388
Rochester, VT 05767
1-800-246-8648
www.InnerTraditions.com

Or contact your local bookseller